The New Competition

CPSIA information can be obtained
at www.ICGtesting.com
Printed in the USA
LVHW111543050419
613130LV00001B/220/P

THE NEW COMPETITION

Institutions of Industrial Restructuring

Michael H. Best

Harvard University Press
Cambridge, Massachusetts

First Harvard University Press paperback edition, 1993

Library of Congress Cataloging-in-Publication Data

Best, Michael H.
  The new competition: institutions of industrial
restructuring / Michael H. Best.
      p. cm.
  Includes bibliographical references.
  ISBN 0-674-60925-5 (cloth)
  ISBN 0-674-60926-3 (paper)
  1. Competition. 2. Organizational change.
3. Comparative organization.   4. Industrial
organization (Economic theory).
5. Managerial economics.   I. Title.
HD41.B38   1990
338.6—dc20   90-34371
                                             CIP

For my daughters: Melanie, Shavahn, Catherine, Chryssa, and Lydia

Contents

Preface and Acknowledgments

The genesis of this book is the crucible of experience. From 1983 until 1985 I was on leave from the University of Massachusetts working for the Greater London Enterprise Board. At the time, one-third of a million Londoners were unemployed and the Greater London area was arguably the site of the most rapid and extensive deindustrialization ever. This book is not about London or the London Industrial Strategy in particular; rather it is an analysis of the causes of industrial decline and the possibilities for industrial policy. The starting point is the presumption that industrial policy has no chance of success unless it is anchored by an understanding of the underlying principles of production and business organization, principles that cannot be found in either conventional economic analysis or the business press.

The task calls for an economic perspective that accounts for the business enterprise, strategic decision-making, and sector regulation. Armed with such a framework, we can proceed to examine the effects of industrial policy on the forces that influence the prosperity of a community or nation. Unfortunately, such concepts are alien to both micro-economic equilibrium theory and macro-economic stabilization theory. The focus of the quality management journals and business press on the firm is a welcome antidote to conventional economics but this attention is not on the interrelationships amongst production, interfirm regulation, and industrial policy. The task is to integrate a theoretical analysis of the business enterprise with extra-firm concepts of markets, competition, regulation, and planning that have been the preserve of economists. My aim in the following pages is to contribute to this task.

I hope that this book will partially redeem the many intellectual debts owed to the community of scholars in the academic and 'real' world concerned with similar matters. Most of the ideas have emerged from a working partnership with Robin Murray, of Sussex University, over the past seven years. Tea Petrin, of Ljubljana University in Yugoslavia, has scrutinized and offered valuable comments on every idea in the book from the perspective of a long-time champion of the dynamic possibilities of small firms.

Jane Humphries, of Cambridge University, has commented on most of the chapters and listened, too often, to the ideas in their formative stages. Two of my colleagues at the University of Massachusetts, Carol Heim and William Shepherd, have read most of the manuscript and provided valuable comments. Edith Penrose extensively commented on chapter 4. Toshio Aida pointed me to relevant Japanese government documents and professional research on industrial policy in Japan as well as reading and extensively commenting on several drafts of chapter 6. Two research assistants have left an imprint – Glen Hutloff on the arguments and content of chapter 1, and Richard Parkin, whose attention to detail has substantially improved every chapter.

Others with whom I have had conversations that altered or expanded the ideas in this book include Giacomo Beccatini, William Connolly, John Eatwell, Robert Forrant, Massimo Florio, Anthony Giddens, Ian Gibson, Dieter Haas, Roman Habtu, Robert Hopley, Michael Kane, Sir Arthur Knight, Samuel Leiken, Samuel Morris, Colin New, Martha Olney, Michael Piore, James Rafferty, William Robbins, Hannah Roditi, Dean Schroeder, Frank Wilkinson and Jonathan Zeitlin. I would also like to thank my many colleagues at the Greater London Enterprise Board, the Machine Action Project of Hampden County, Massachusetts, and the Massachusetts Product Development Corporation, and on the Cyprus Industrial Strategy mission. I owe special thanks to students in my graduate seminar at the University of Massachusetts who, besides sharing an enthusiasm for the associated literature, have offered criticism with notable tact and good humour, given fresh and thoughtful insights, and inspired me to be bold.

In the pages that follow my debt to three others will be evident: Sebastiano Brusco, William Lazonick, and Charles Sabel. In each case, I have benefited from numerous discussions over the matters examined in this book. The research on the Third Italy would not have been possible without my being able to draw upon the many associates and friends of Brusco, particularly Mario Pezzini and Adriana Zini. It will be obvious also that I have drawn heavily from the writings of four scholars of the modern business enterprise, namely Alfred Chandler, John Kenneth Galbraith, Edith Penrose, and Joseph Schumpeter. Finally, I wish to thank Sir Austin Robinson and John Thompson who urged me to write the book in the first place – Sir Austin because he supports any research that suggests a return to the business and industrial organization concerns that withered at Cambridge University with the Keynesian revolution and John because he thinks that the ideas were potentially an important contribution to political economy. I hope that the final product is worthy of their encouragement.

The author and publishers are grateful to the following for permission to reproduce figures:

Figure 1: Reprinted by permission of publisher from *The Financial Management Series*, No. 94:7, by T.C. Davis ©1950 AMACOM, a division of American Management Association, New York. All rights reserved.

Figure 5: Reprinted with permission of The Free Press, a Division of Macmillan, Inc. from *Triad Power* by Kenichi Ohmae. Copyright © 1985 by Kenichi Ohmae and McKinsey & Company, Inc.

1
Introduction

We will win and you will lose. You cannot do anything about it because your failure is an internal disease. Your companies are based on Taylor's principles. Worse, your heads are Taylorized too. You firmly believe that sound management means executives on the one side and workers on the other, on the one side men who think and on the other side men who can only work. For you, management is the art of smoothly transferring the executives' idea to the workers' hands.
We have passed the Taylor stage. We are aware that business has become terribly complex. Survival is very uncertain in an environment filled with risk, the unexpected, and competition . . .We know that the intelligence of a few technocrats – even very bright ones – has become totally inadequate to face these challenges. Only the intellects of all employees can permit a company to live with the ups and downs and the requirements of the new environment. Yes, we will win and you will lose. For you are not able to rid your minds of the obsolete Taylorisms that we never had. (Konosuke Matsushita, 1988)

Matsushita, founder of Matsushita Electric Industrial Company, may have identified the fundamental weakness of many Western economies. If so, it behooves us to understand his reasoning if his prophesy is to be negated. All too often, however, economic problems are defined in entirely different terms.

Industrial Decline and the New Competition

Deindustrialization has long been a topic of economic analysis; a number of explanations have been offered for both the historical decline of British industry and the contemporary "hollowing" of American industrial firms. But most explanations have been macro-economic in orientation: they have focused on government mismanagement of exchange rates, money supply, tax and tariff policies. Others have emphasized entrepreneurial failure: British capitalists were unwilling to invest long term in industry, putting their money into distributional and finance-related activities instead. Another line of inquiry has pointed to the power of organized labor to advance wages more rapidly than productivity gains, or to stifle technological advance.

Much of this literature has been valuable but it is all oriented to the spheres of circulation and finance. This book draws attention to the sphere of production and the key role of the internal organization of the firm. Unless analysts of the decline of American industry are prepared to follow me by going behind the factory gate, Matsushita will be proven right.

Debt buildup and the decline of savings in America became a public issue by the middle of the 1980s. Tax cuts, central to Reagan's supply-side economics, did not generate the hoped for increase in savings or tax revenues. But the deeper problem of deindustrialization has received scant public attention. The claim of this book is that the spending boom in the United States in recent years has masked a serious deterioration in industrial competitiveness which manifests itself in growing trade deficits and international debt. While attention is focused on international debt and a low savings rate, the deeper problem of deteriorating productive capability must also be addressed.[1]

The first cause of the deterioration is the emergence elsewhere of a "New Competiton" led by business enterprises based upon different production and organizational concepts. At the center of the New Competition is the entrepreneurial firm, an enterprise that is organized from top to bottom to pursue continuous improvement in methods, products and processes. The pursuit of continuous improvement is a production-based strategy that has redefined the meaning of entrepreneurial activity from its traditional individualist approach to a collectivist concept. The entrepreneurial firm seeks a competitive edge by superior product design, which may or may not lead to lower costs, but it

---

[1] Evidence that the debt buildup in 1980s America was used to finance a spending boom that was not matched by a parallel increase in domestic manufacturing capacity comes from statistics on the growth of United States manufacturing output. Between 1950 and 1973, manufacturing grew at an annual average rate of 4.0 percent but manufacturing growth slowed to 0.9 percent between 1973 and 1983. While controversy surrounds estimates of 1980s growth rates in American manufacturing productivity, one authoritative study estimates an average annual increase of 1.5 percent from 1972 to 1979 and 1.6 percent from 1979 to 1985. This would mean that manufacturing output as a share of gross national output dropped from about 22 percent in 1977 to between 18 and 19 percent ten years later, a fall of unprecedented proportions (Mishel, 1988).

demands organizational flexibility which in turn requires organizational commitments to problem solving, a persistence to detail, and an integration of thinking and doing in work activities.

The New Competition is manifest in a variety of inter-firm complexes which range from groups of small Italian firms linked by cooperative associations for joint marketing, technological advance, and financial underwriting, to giant Japanese organizational structures coordinating trading companies, banks, and manufacturing enterprises. While Japan, Germany, and Sweden have led the way in the development of new manufacturing methods and strategies geared to continuous improvement, examples can also be found in South Korea, Taiwan, Hong Kong, Singapore, and specific regions and enterprises within Europe and the United States.

True, the commitment to long-term industrial success is backed in these countries with high savings ratios, in some cases in excess of 20 percent of national income, and governmental interest and exchange rate policies that enhance the competitiveness of manufacturing firms. But we also find new strategically oriented industrial policy institutions which channel savings into productive investment. They are established in some cases at the central government level, and at other times at the local government level or by extra-firm agencies that are public and private hybrids.

Not surprisingly, the production philosophy of continuous improvement in product and process has taken widest hold in industrialized countries which were dependent on foreign oil, and where the challenge of the first oil shock of the early 1970s was most keenly felt. Faced with surging energy bills and fearing depreciating currencies, enterprise managers and economic policymakers concentrated their attention on strategies for advancing export revenues from manufacturing.

The second cause of American industrial decline is the widespread failure in America to pose the problem in organizational terms. The deterioration is defined in productivity terms instead. The reason is that defining America's industrial decline in terms of slow rates of productivity growth is consistent with an image of an organizationally sound economy in need of minor adjustments. It implies that industry can be revived by a set of government and managerial policies that do not require deep-seated organizational changes.

If the claim of the emergence of a New Competition is right, we will soon look back to see the Reagan years as a time when massive foreign borrowings were used to finance consumption as opposed to productive investment, precisely when American industry was in need of an overhaul; likewise we will see the British monetarist experiment as a time when the vast British oil revenues were used to finance a spending boom instead of rebuilding the productive base of the country. For in 1980s Britain, like America, the trade balance went sharply into the red.[2] Both the America and the Britain of the 1990s will be forced to look to new sources for financing manufactured import levels that consumers enjoyed in the previous decade. Both countries are likely to endure the delayed effects of a declining industrial base built on obsolete principles. One of those effects will be a return of inflationary pressures as exchange rates decline with the inevitable drop-off in foreign borrowing by the United States and North Sea oil sales by the United Kingdom. But the two countries share more than a rapidly rising trade deficit. Both define the economy in terms that are responsive to demand management instruments of the central government. In this they share a collective capacity to deny the reality that a deeper production-rooted problem exists. Britain's denial began in an earlier day.

A Historical Analogy: the United Kingdom and the United States

At the turn of the century, optimists argued that the statistics of poor production performance by the United Kingdom's industry merely reflected increased specialization in the world economy as other countries followed along the industrialization path. But from another perspective the troubling appearances reflected less the difficulties of redeploying productive resources and more those of organizing industry on the basis of new principles of production. Most of British industry has never succeeded in re-establishing itself on the basis of the leading organizational principles of the day. As a result, British per capita income dropped from the highest in the world in 1870 to half that of the leading industrial nations a hundred years later. Just as Britain has been the first industrialized nation, it became the first to face the double-pronged challenge of restructuring: adapting to the methods embodied in the new products and processes, and withdrawing from the old.

Twentieth century industrial practice represents a history of resistance to such restructuring. Between 1899 and 1929 Britain's share of exports of manufacturers from amongst the eleven main industrial countries dropped from 33.2 to 22.9 percent (House of Lords, 1985, p. 23). By the interwar period the issue of productive rationalization had become a major political issue. It was diffused in the mid-1930s by economic

---

[2] The British trade balance declined virtually without interruption from a surplus of nearly £4 billion in 1980 to a deficit of £10 billion in 1987. Manufacturing output in 1987 Britain was below its 1973 peak (*OECD Economic Survey*, various years).

growth generated by protectionism, government reflationary measures, and (eventually) war spending. But it was growth without restructing in the old industries, and even where growth did occur, particularly in the new industries, management was slow to adapt to organizational innovation (Elbaum and Lazonick, 1986; Heim, 1983).

The postwar period witnessed enterprise reorganization in Britain involving both private and public sectors. Numerous corporations were reorganized along American multidivisional lines, and several Labour Party governments followed a series of industrial policies aimed at reducing the fragmentation of productive ownership, which led to the nationalization of the coal, shipbuilding, steel, and eventually car industries.

But the slide in world share of exports of manufactures continued from 25.4 percent in 1950 to 7.6 percent in 1984 (House of Lord, 1985, p. 23). Value added in manufacturing as a percentage of gross domestic product in the United Kingdom dropped from 32.1 percent in 1960 to 21.0 percent in 1983, and exports of manufactured goods as a percentage of imports dropped from 225 percent in 1963 to around 60 percent in 1984. As a result a surplus in the balance of trade of manufactured goods of £12 billion in 1963 had turned into the growing deficits of the 1980s.

The reforms of business organization and the adoption of demand management governmental policies in the 1960s and 1970s did not arrest the decline of British industry because competition emerged from two new sources: the spread of mass production methods to low wage countries, and the development of new production systems in high wage countries that competed on the basis of product quality and innovation as well as price.

Britain was not alone in feeling the sting of increased international competition. The US share of world manufacturing exports has also declined over the postwar period from around a quarter in the early 1950s, to a fifth in the 1960s, to under a sixth in the late 1970s (Williams et al., 1983, pp. 116–7).

Through rose-colored spectacles, the long-term decline in share of manufactured exports and the lower productivity gains could be viewed simply as other countries catching up with America by emulation: reconstructing their industrial systems on the same production and organizational principles established in the United States. For example, it is written in the *The Economic Report of the President (1983)* that

> [t]he U.S. has not experienced a persistent loss of ability to sell its products on international markets . . .[even though] . . .changes in the relationship to the world economy . . .have made the U.S. look less competitive by some traditional measures.

The Council of Economic Advisors' diagnosis has an ominous similarity to the optimism voiced by British economic policy-makers in the 1920s. Each derives from a reliance upon economic concepts which obscure organizational deficiencies in business enterprises.

However, a look at individual sectors suggests a more sobering view. US manufacturers are under competitive pressure to maintain market share within the United States across a broad range of products. Imports as a percentage of sales in the United States in 1981 were 26 percent in cars (and projected to reach 50 percent in 1990), 25 percent in steel, 60 percent in consumer electronic products made up of televisions, radios, tape recorders and phonographs, and 43 percent in calculators. Even more alarming was the upsurge in import shares of machine tools to 27 percent in metal forming tools, 35 percent in textile machinery, and 53 percent of numerically controlled machine tools. It would appear from the import penetration figures that slow US productivity growth was not simply a reflection of catch-up by foreign firms to American levels of productivity.

Production-Oriented Perspectives on the Causes of Industrial Decline

How is relative decline explained? Many facile explanations in terms of government regulation, unit labor costs, and size of the public sector persist: Japanese firms are more highly regulated than their US counterparts, unit labor costs are higher in Germany and Japan in 1987 (Hickok et al., 1988, p. 11), and Sweden enjoys higher productivity levels and a considerably larger public sector.

Production-oriented explanations receive less attention. In a widely referenced article two Harvard Business School professors, Robert Hayes and William Abernathy, blamed an American "managerial gospel":

> Our experience suggest that, to an unprecedented degree, success in most industries today requires an organizational commitment to compete in the marketplace on technological grounds – that is, to compete over the long run by offering *superior products*. Yet, guided by what they took to be the newest and best principles of management, American managers have increasingly directed their attention elsewhere. These new principles, despite their sophistication and widespread usefulness, encourage a preference for (1) analytic detachment rather than the insight that comes from "hands on" experience and (2) short-term cost reduction rather than long-term development of technological competitiveness. It is this new *managerial gospel*, we feel, that has played a major role in undermining

the vigor of American industry. (Hayes and Abernathy, 1983, p. 523, emphasis added)

But blaming the entrepreneur is also reminiscent of an earlier debate on the decline of British industry. What Hayes and Abernathy do not explain is why American managers have not directed their attention to "superior products" and, thereby, have "abdicated their strategic responsibilities" (p. 527).

The argument of this book is that American Big Business suffers from rigid command and control production organizations – a rigidity made apparent by the emergence of an alternative production paradigm termed the "New Competition". The "management gospel" blamed by Hayes and Abernathy is a symptom of a challenge facing American industry that is similar to that faced by Britain's at the turn of the century: the need to restructure according to the organizational principles of a new production paradigm in the face of social inertia resulting from the legacy of a past industrial order.

Bernard Elbaum and William Lazonick (1986), building on Alfred Chandler's (1977) analysis of the modern corporation, contend that the decline of the twentieth century British economy was due to a failure of business enterprises to adapt to the new organizational principles that accompanied the emergence of mass production in America. In this respect, the New Competition at that time was American Big Business and the Old Competition was market-coordinated vertically specialized industrial enterprises. Chandler argues that the visible hand of hierarchical coordination outcompeted the invisible hand of market coordination. The reason? Administrative coordination was required to realize the quantum leaps in speed and volume of throughput made possible by mass production technologies and market-expanding infrastructural developments in transportation and communication. British enterprises, coordinated by prices in the market, were ill equipped to compete with American enterprises, administratively coordinated by managerial hierarchy. They simply could not drive costs down as could the management teams utilizing the organizational innovations that constituted American Big Business.

Chandler's analysis, as applied to Britain by Elbaum and Lazonick, does provide a compelling account of the decline of British industry, but it does not explain the decline of American industry, the rise of Japanese industry, or the international success of groups of small firms in Germany, Italy, and elsewhere that have never been dominated by hierarchical organization.

Michael Piore and Charles Sabel (1984) also present a comparative institutional analysis anchored in distinctive organizational principles of production. The rise of American industrial power can be explained in terms of the adoption of mass production as a "system of markets, technologies, and institutions" (Piore and Sabel, 1984, p. 14). The corporation, for Piore and Sabel, was a means of administratively balancing supply with demand in mass production industries. With the emergence of high fixed costs the days of spontaneous market coordination were over. So far, Piore and Sabel do not diverge far from Chandler. But the similarity stops here.

For Piore and Sabel, mass production with corporate hierarchy is not the only path to industrial modernization: an alternative, "flexible specialization", path based on craft principles of production was (and is) also available. The flexible specialization alternative path is

> a strategy of permanent innovation: accommodation to ceaseless change, rather than an effort to control it. This strategy is based on flexible – multi-use – equipment; skilled workers; and the creation, through politics, of an industrial community that restricts the forms of competition to those favoring innovation. (Piore and Sabel, 1984, p. 17)

The industrial districts of modern Europe provide the institutional context for Piore and Sabel. The German machine tool industry, for example, is populated by numerous small, technologically advanced, and internationally competitive firms. In a flexibly specialized system individual firms are not spontaneously coordinated, as in the neoclassical economic model of atomistic firms producing identical products and driven by the invisible hand.

Piore and Sabel's analysis makes two major contributions. First, it accounts for the success of regions dominated by groups of small firms which, from the Chandlerian perspective, are simply cases of pre-modern industrial organization waiting for mass production technology and a managerial hierarchy to bring them into the modern world. Along with Italian researchers such as Beccatini (1978) and Brusco (1982), Piore and Sabel provide an antidote of institutionalist pluralism to the perception of business history as driven by an immanent logic of organizational advance from small to large enterprise.

Second, Piore and Sabel explain the stability of capitalism populated by Big Business without depending upon the assumption of market clearing, the equilibrating mechanism of neoclassical economic theory. Influenced by regulation theory as an alternative conceptual framework, they describe various ways in which mass consumption became linked to mass production in different countries.[3] In the United States collective

---

[3] The regulation school rejects the presuppositions that market clearing is the only regulatory mechanism of capitalism and that price must be the central organizing concept

bargaining played a central, if inadvertent, role in stabilizing corporate capitalism (Piore and Sabel, 1984, chapter 4).[4] Here Piore and Sabel contribute to a reconceptualization of the integration of macro- and micro-economics which is consistent with real world institutions. They suggest a dialectical relation between macro- and micro-stabilization, which would imply that the Japanese corporation is articulated with industrial policy in Japan, Big Business with demand management in the United Kingdom and the United States, and small enterprises in the Third Italy with dynamic industrial districts.

The weaknesses of Piore and Sabel's analysis are related to its strengths. First, instead of extending their critique of a single organizational imperative to allow for a variety of possible organizational forms they stop short by distinguishing between only two possible types of production systems: mass production or flexible specialization. The result is a narrowing of production organizations to one of only two possible types and a historical perspective of recurring industrial divides between one and the other; Piore and Sabel risk replacing one immanent logic with another and losing the contingent dimension to economics and economic policymaking institutions. In the process they seriously underplay the revolutionary advance in low cost production capability created by mass production methods.

From the New Competition perspective of this book, flexible specialization is not the single alternative to mass production. Instead, it is a dynamic version of Alfred Marshall's industrial district: a particular strategy for competitive success that is open to groups of small firms. But success will depend upon being able to distinguish between the Japanese corporation and dynamic industrial districts as competitive models and to allow for a comparative assessment of the strengths and weaknesses of each. This may mean that the target of flexibly specialized firms is either market niches or markets that have never been conquered

---

of micro-economic theory. John Kenneth Galbraith's concept of countervailing power (examined in chapter 3) is an example of a non-market-clearing regulatory mechanism. But in Galbraith's words: "The notion that there might be another regulatory mechanism in the economy has been almost completely excluded from economic thought" (1952, chapter 9). Examples of French regulation school research (to which the term commonly refers) are the publications of Michel Aglietta (1979) and Robert Boyer (1979); a survey can be found in Michel De Vroey (1984).

[4] The aim of collective bargaining is to remove individual adjustments from the process of wage settlements, just as the aim of the establishment of Big Business is to remove price flexibility from product markets. Market-clearing mechanisms based on atomistic individual actions in labor, capital, intermediate input, and final product markets will likely be destabilizing. The claim is not that markets do not exist but that price and quantity adjustments are constrained by rules or guided by market leaders.

by the *kaisha*, the Japanese term for company. Competitive success may lead to challenging the kaisha, but never head on, for the strengths of flexible specialization would then be negated.

Second, Piore and Sabel describe "four faces of flexible specialization", namely, regional conglomerations or industrial districts, federated enterprises such as the "prewar Japanese *zaibatsu*", solar firms, exemplified by Boeing which maintains long-term consultative relations with satellite component suppliers which themselves maintain independent design capabilities, and workshop factories (Piore and Sabel, 1984, pp. 265–8). But they fail to account for either strategic choices amongst organizational forms or the mutual dependence between strategy and structure. Structure includes both the "organizational shells" and the inner organization of production units. Consequently, the dynamic industrial districts of the Third Italy (regional conglomerations) and the market-share-dominating corporations of Japan (federated enterprises) are simply different faces of flexible specialization.

To conclude, by allowing for the possibility of a dynamic industrial district, Piore and Sabel make sense of real world institutions that are obscured by Chandler's dichotomy between the market and hierarchy. But the failure of Piore and Sabel to integrate mass production with a concept of hierarchy leads them to ignore distinctions in "organizational shells" that are critical to understanding organizational variants between the Old and the New Competition and within the New Competition. Allowing for such distinctions creates space for strategic choices amongst organizational forms, choices which are both crucial to long-term economic performance and ignored in conventional theory. The cost is high, for Piore and Sabel are weakest where Chandler is strong: the theory of flexible specialization is not grounded in a conceptual analysis of the firm as a strategic entity.

While a full treatment of these issues has yet to be accomplished, the claim of this book is that any such analysis must be grounded in an analysis of the firm as the driving force in an economy. I seek to give conceptual substance to the entrepreneurial firm by building on the Schumpeterian concepts of entrepreneurship and competition, and the Penrosian concepts of experience, teamwork, and growth of the firm. But while the idea of the entrepreneurial firm points toward certain distinctions, the specific features can only be understood by institutional examination.

Four Dimensions of the New Competition

The New Competition can be distinguished from the old in four dimensions: organization of the firm, types of coordination across phases in the production chain, organization of the sector, and patterns of industrial policy. The New Competition is about strategic actions within each dimension. The term "strategic" refers to market-shaping activities in contrast with market-reacting responses. The arguments are briefly summarized in this section; more complete examples are provided by the case studies in later chapters.

The Firm: The Collective Entrepreneur

Whereas Adam Smith is the theorist of the market and John Maynard Keynes the theorist of demand management, Joseph Schumpeter is the theorist of the firm. What distinguished Schumpeter from both Smith and Keynes, and their disciples, was his critique of market and price competition as the starting points for economic analysis. For Schumpeter, it is not the market but the firm that demands center stage, and not price competition but the ". . .competition from the new commodity, the new technology, the new source of supply, the new type of organization. . ." which governs the wealth of a nation (Schumpeter, 1942, p. 84).

The entrepreneurial firm, as distinct from the hierarchical firm of Chandler and Oliver Williamson, builds on the idea of Schumpeterian competition. The first feature of the entrepreneurial firm is a strategic orientation: a strategically oriented firm chooses the terrain on which to compete; a hierarchical firm takes the terrain as given.[5] Thus the entrepreneurial firm does not seek to maximize profits simply by minimizing costs but seeks strategic advantage on the basis of Schumpeterian innovation in product, process, or organization.

The second distinction between the entrepreneurial and the hierarchical firm is that the goal of the entrepreneurial firm is to gain strategic

---

[5] The distinction between entrepreneurial and the hierarchical firm is analytical. Clearly, in the real world hierarchical firms that pursue Schumpeterian competition do exist, but I argue that the strategic possibilities are fewer than for the entrepreneurial firm. Strategic behavior for Williamson is defined as opportunistic behavior, or where an agent's word is not as good his bond. An opportunistic agent is one who seeks to extract advantages "between contract renewal intervals" (Williamson, 1985, p. 31). Chandler works with two strategies, namely vertical integration and diversification; I argue that the New Competition is about establishing productive organizations that can pursue a range of strategies. While Schumpeterian competition allows for strategy implicitly, there is more to the entrepreneurial firm.

advantage by continuous improvement in process and product; the goal of the hierarchical firm is to gain minimum production costs by continuity in production operations, product runs, and product design. Organizing production according to the principle of continuity does not deny the importance of innovation. Innovation is important to the hierarchical firm; after all Henry Ford and Frederick Taylor, the two major architects of production continuity, were great innovators. But the notion of innovation for the hierarchical firm is one of radical structural change: a brilliant engineer envisages a revolutionary way to drive down costs and new production facilities are built around it. Once the new idea is implemented and operating costs are driven down any further change is anathema. Working practices are routinized and discontinuity is abhorred as disruptive.

Innovation has a different connotation for the entrepreneurial firm. It is not about abrupt changes but the accretion of marginal adjustments in product, process, and organization. In the words of Guiliana Benetton: "You'll never discover a new design, you merely make small changes in the old one" (Labich, 1983, p. 115). As such the source of innovation is not restricted to the insight of the specialist engineer but is an ongoing social process in which problems are solved and new problems are identified.

The third distinction between the entrepreneurial and the hierarchical firm is in the organization of production. Success, in an age of Schumpeterian competition, depends upon maintaining the organizational flexibility required to be able to adjust a firm's competitive strategy depending upon the strengths and weakness of its competitors at any point in time. But strategic adjustment is impossible without organizational flexibility at the micro production level.[6]

Organizational flexibility demands a radically different organization of work from that in the hierarchical firm. The reason is that the philosophy of continuity fosters the imposition of a minute subdivision of labor and the elimination of thinking within production: all that is needed is to repeat the same operation endlessly. The pursuit of

---

[6] The micro production level, or work organization, includes the work and management tasks for a single operational activity. The definition of a single operational activity is technologically dependent: for example, it can be as small as a lathe operation or as large as an assembly operation that links a series of machines. At the same time, the technical and social aspects of production are interdependent. Piore and Sabel postulate two types of micro production unit: mass production, which combines unskilled labor and specialist machines to produce general or standard products and craft, which combines skilled labor and general machines to produce specialist products. I argue that this classification is too simple and closed to capture the interactions between work organization and higher organizational levels.

continuous improvement, in contrast, seeks competitive advantage from superior product performance and demands perpetual problem solving. In this the entrepreneurial firm depends upon learning to maintain competitive advantage.

For a learning firm, improvement is always possible and ideas for improvement can come from everyone, including consumers, workers, suppliers, staff, and managers. As a social process, innovation involves the interaction of people engaged in functionally distinct activities. It demands persistent and comprehensive re-examination of productive practices.[7]

The emphasis on problem solving and learning suggests a distinction between two types of hierarchical firm and an entrepreneurial firm. A hierarchical firm, in the real world, may or may not pursue Schumpeterian competition. Henry Ford, as noted, developed a new product and created a mass market. More, he gave meaning to the concept of mass production. Andrew Carnegie pursued a strategy of continuous innovation in pursuit of dominant market share, much like the kaisha of today. While Carnegie's strategy was more akin to that of the new competitor than Ford's, neither enterprise was organized into an entrepreneurial firm: both were Taylorist. A Taylorist organization can pursue a strategy of innovation, but it is not well suited to pursue a strategy of continuous improvement.

A strategy of innovation can be pursued by an organization with a large research and development budget and a staff of product and process engineers that specialize in the design of new products and processes. A strategy of continuous improvement, however, demands an organization in which a persistence to detail operates at every activity level. The persistence to detail is about incorporating learning from doing into improved ways of doing. It requires an organizational culture that is alien to Taylorism. The industrial enterprises of Ford and Carnegie were not organized to promote learning throughout the organization, to integrate thinking and doing within production, or to promote teamwork across functional activities for the purposes of design refinement or new product development. Instead, work practices at Ford's factories were governed by the principles of Taylorism. One index of the rigidity of work organization at the Ford Motor Company is the growth in the number of pages in a wage contract from four in 1940 to hundreds in

---

[7] Learning suggests that a distinction be made between information, a core concept for the conventional theory of the firm, and knowledge and its refinement. Creating production knowledge by problem solving involves more than the flow of information: information is already existing knowledge; problem solving is the creation of knowledge. The latter is the secret weapon of the entrepreneurial firm.

the 1980s. The regulation of work had become highly bureaucratized. The pressures to design productive organizations with the capacity to integrate thinking and doing and promote teamwork are increasing. The reason is that Schumpeterian competition is turning into time competition. Mass production is about one form of time competition: economies of time in throughput. Time competition has entered into two dimensions beyond the reach of the hierarchical firm. The first is about process time, or the time that materials take to be processed within a plant. Japanese firms have organized plants that reduce the time that products are in process from a magnitude of days to hours without increasing the speed of work or machines (Stalk, 1988). The second is an extension of Schumpeterian competition: economies of time in the implementation of new product designs. Firms can succeed by being the first to identify and respond to an emerging market, a segmenting market, or a change in consumer requirements in a previously stable market. Responding to changing market demands means being able to supply consumers with a newly designed product; it will involve refinements in production methods and technologies. In each of these cases success depends not upon being the lowest cost (or highest throughput) producer, but upon the minimization of product development and product changeover times. The neoclassical presumption, that eventually the firm with the lowest cost production methods will dominate in the marketplace, does not account for the increased relevance of the capacity to compete on the basis of product, process, and response times.

The Production Chain: Consultative Coordination

The second level of organization links micro production units into a production chain extending from the first to the last operational phase in turning raw material and labor into a final product.[8] Conventional economic theory, and the real world counterpart firms of the Old Competition, presuppose the market–plan dichotomy: consecutive micro-unit production phases are coordinated either by price in the market or by administration in a managerial hierarchy. The transactions cost framework of conventional economic theory provides criteria for determining whether hierarchical or market coordination will prevail. In this book, four forms of coordination across the production chain are distinguished: hierarchical–bureaucratic and hierarchical–clan within vertically integrated enterprises, market amongst autonomous and

---

[8] Examples of consecutive operations in the production of a wooden cabinet from chipboard could include sawing, veneering, drilling, sanding, polishing, assembling, and packaging.

independent firms, and consultative–cooperative amongst mutually interdependent firms.[9]

Inter-firm coordination in the New Competition cannot be explained in terms of the traditional hierarchy or market dichotomy; allowance must be made for consultative coordination or cooperation amongst mutually interdependent firms each of which specializes in distinct phases of the same production chain. The pressure for inter-firm cooperation comes, in part, from the competitive lead that accompanies problem solving at a time of rapid technological change. For suppliers and buyers can be a source of ideas as well as sellers of inputs and purchasers of outputs. Hierarchical coordination is less risky given stable technologies because a multiple production phase investment over an entire production chain will not be as vulnerable to obsolescence in the event of the development of a superior design for any single phase by a competitor.

Market coordination of consecutive phases does not solve the problem of rapid technological change. The problem with a pure market relationship is that it also depends upon standardized components and processes for each phase in the production chain. But a technological change in any single phase may demand a modification in the design of all related production stages. This will be especially difficult in the cases of product-led competitive strategies. In such cases a problem-solving capability is required which can be best met by a long-term consultative or networked relation as distinct from either an impersonal market relationship or hierarchical coordination. The following example illustrates the difference between market and consultative inter-firm coordination. For Ford, read "the Old Competition" in its heyday and for Nissan read "the New Competition".

Ford's external supplier relations were market driven. Ford engineers prepared the specifications for component products and sent them out to a list of subcontractors who bid on the basis of price. The components' design characteristics were "in the specifications". Ford's innumerable suppliers made it impossible for Ford engineers to interact consultatively with suppliers on production and design refinement. Legal contracts were drawn up to ensure that suppliers met the specifications promised in their bid.

Nissan's external supplier relations are design driven. Nissan engineers do not prepare the specifications for the part and send them to a list of

---

[9] This second level of organization is what Piore and Sabel call the organizational shell. If the analysis of this book is right, the organizational shell has effects upon the elements within, and the organization of, the micro production unit: for instance, the skills and activities of workers, the tasks of management, and the types of machines.

subcontractors. Instead, they describe the function of the product and ask a familiar supplier to design it. The supplier offers a prototype that is then examined by Nissan engineers who may suggest alterations. A process of dialogue on the performance, quality, and production characteristics ensues until eventually the desired product is agreed upon.

At full capacity a Nissan assembly plant will work with only 120 suppliers. To go beyond 120 would be to risk undermining the intimate knowledge and mutual responsibility required for high quality supplier relations. It is crucial that the production engineers at Nissan and the suppliers know one another and can directly and personally discuss problems and explore new possibilities. This requires the nurturing of personal relationships and a common production language. Neither can be accomplished without cooperation, which takes time.

At Ford customer–supplier relations were permeated by gamesmanship. Price bargaining was conducted strategically with both sides offering initial bids geared to moving the eventual settlement price in their direction, but neither was expected to offer unbiased information on production costs: it was a market relation. At Nissan the customer–supplier relations are more consultative and an unusual degree of information disclosure is exhibited.

However, the existence of consultative supplier relations does not mean that price competition no longer exits. Small firms in Japan face continuous pressures from lead manufacturers to lower prices and costs. The difference is that the struggle over prices goes on within the context of a long-term relationship based upon established norms of mutual responsibility. "Shared network norms" (see chapter 5) enable the interfirm flow of ideas as well as material orders, money, and products. They also facilitate long-term investment in highly specialized activities and components with less fear of being exploited after the investment has been made and the supplier is dependent upon the lead manufacturer.

The idea that the benefits of joint action can depend upon the establishment of norms that guide individual actions is not new to economic theory. What is new is the application to topics such as intrafirm organization and inter-firm relations, both in practice and theory.[10] Norms, however, are always subject to erosion unless potential violators can be successfully punished. Clearly, the means by which individual responsibility is ensured to sustain the benefits of joint action will

---

[10] The parable of the prisoner's dilemma illustrates that achieving an individual's interests can depend upon the supply of trust. Recently, game theory applications to industrial organization have confirmed that, since people learn over time, repeated games will lead to cooperation (Axelrod, 1984).

depend upon specific social arrangements which can best be examined empirically.

The Sector: Competition and Cooperation

The representation of an industrial sector found in neoclassical economics is one of organizationally carbon copy firms producing indistinguishable products and competing by price. The Old Competition, compared with the New Competition, is consistent with this model. But conventional economics, which sharply divides micro-economic from macro-economic topics, obscures a third level of organization crucial to explaining the competitiveness of firms, namely, sector institutions, or what Piore and Sabel label "extra-firm infrastructure".

A sector can include a variety of inter-firm practices and extra-firm agencies such as trade associations, apprenticeship programs, labor education facilities, joint marketing arrangements, and regulatory commissions, each of which facilitates inter-firm cooperation. We are left with images of a sector as more than a collection of autonomous firms, and of inter-firm relations as involving more than price competition. Sector institutions, then, can impact back upon the organization of individual firms, their strategies, and their collective competitiveness relative to sectors located elsewhere. From this viewpoint, firms not only compete, but they can also cooperate to provide common services, to shape "the rules of the market game", and to shape complementary investment strategies.

The one form of cooperation suggested by neoclassical theory is the formation of cartels. Neoclassical theory and American antitrust law hold that imperfect competition and inter-firm cooperation, including cartels, limit output, increase prices, and reduce innovation. How, then, can the coexistence in Japan of imperfect competition and widespread cartels and quasi-cartels with a growing, innovating, and non-inflationary economy be explained?

The coexistence of imperfect competition and growth is not a paradox for Schumpeterian theory which presumes that price competition can be both an incentive to short-term allocative efficiency and a disincentive to long-term productive efficiency. John Kenneth Galbraith appeals to a Schumpeterian link between market power and investment in an enterprises future:

> The power that enables the firm to have some influence on price insures that the resulting gains will not be passed on to the public by imitators (who have stood none of the costs of development) before the outlay for development can be recouped. In this way market power protects the incentive to technical development. (Galbraith, 1952)

The argument is an illustration of the private rationality bias of market provision and conventional theory. The benefits of investment in research and development are not exclusive to those who pay the market price. As a result private action in the market will lead to an undersupply: any one firm will be hesitant to invest in product design staff, for example, knowing that other firms can free ride on their results. Patent law is one way to counter the free-rider: he becomes an outlaw.

A second means of enforcing individual responsibility to the common interest is to establish institutions of inter-firm cooperation. Cooperation can be implemented by extra-firm institutions including quasi-government agencies, trade associations, and professional bodies. Examples in ensuing chapters include German cartels which have promoted technological advance and component standardization, the financial consortia of the Third Italy, which created a credit market, and the postwar Japanese Union of Scientists and Engineers which applied statistical quality control methods across much of Japanese industry. In each case a common interest is identified and collectively pursued by inter-firm cooperation as opposed to government imposition.

Beneath the apparent paradox of cooperation and growth is a real paradox of competition. Intense local price competition can reduce global competitiveness, particularly in high fixed costs industries, by limiting the capacity of the sector to invest in its future; the result is a diminished capacity to compete against rival sectors located elsewhere.

From this perspective, sector development can be fostered by restricting price competition during periods of excess supply or substantial new investment, or in industries characterized by high fixed costs. Firms can cooperate over prices in order to compete over, for example, product quality, innovation, or technological leadership. Here, inter-corporate regulation of the market is predicated upon the common interest of all firms in precluding privately rational actions which undermine collective rationality.

At the same time the proposition that inter-firm cooperation can stifle economic performance is also true. The challenge is to establish means of cooperation that generate common benefits to the firms involved and the local economy, without the stifling effects presupposed by the conventional view. One prerequisite for inter-firm cooperation to enhance competitiveness is the negotiation of a well-defined purpose for cooperation. Establishing a purpose is to develop and implement a sector strategy which builds from, and acts back upon, the individual enterprise strategies within a sector. A second prerequisite for successful inter-firm cooperation is a means of monitoring and enforcing enterprise actions to counter the free-rider tendency.

Thus the implementation of a sector strategy is a partial means of realizing the joint benefits of Schumpeterian non-price forms of competition. Strategically managed inter-firm associations can promote the long-term development and competitiveness of a sector; non-strategically managed inter-firm association will likely have the opposite effect. What distinguishes the New Competition from the Old Competition is not an awareness of the paradox of competition, but the institutional capacity to turn the paradox to advantage.

The creation of a sector strategy can emerge from private action by firms within a sector. If, for example, members of different firms cooperate in labor training, export marketing, or financing research, they may also develop the capacity to adjust mutually to new challenges and respond collectively to new opportunities. In these debates and discussions strategies are compared, investments are considered, and specialization by production phase is promoted. The concept of a sector strategy can also be a feature of industrial policy.

The Government: Strategic Industrial Policy

The theme that a healthy industrial sector depends upon combining competition with cooperation has far-reaching implications for public policy. It suggests that the task of industrial (including antitrust) policy is not to establish an ideal as defined by the neoclassical theory of perfect competition but to administer a paradox: cooperation alone can ensure that commitments are made to the long-term infrastructural development of a sector; competition alone can ensure that business enterprises remain innovative and responsive to new challenges and opportunities.

From this perspective American antitrust policy has been expected to accomplish the impossible, namely, to reshape the real world according to an abstract theory that presumes the norm of a market-clearing equilibrium but does not even account for the existence of supplier organizations or the possibility of product, as opposed to price, competition. Industrial policy, which has never been integrated with antitrust policy in either theory or practice in American and Britain, has often been based on the inverse of the free market ideal: state planning can achieve allocative efficiency where the market fails.

Given the misguided ideal that has informed public policy toward industry, it is little wonder that industrial policy has a bad name both in economic circles and public opinion in America and Britain. It is associated with an infirmary for bailing out sick firms in dying industries or it evokes visions of special interest politics seeking to subsidize bad management and powerful unions against the less organized common interest. Elsewhere, however, industrial policy does not carry the same connotations of hindering economic adjustment. Indeed, the industrial policies of the Japanese government are often credited with enhancing the competitiveness of Japanese firms. Both views are partially right. Industrial policy can enhance or inhibit economic adjustment. While industrial policy is examined more thoroughly in succeeding chapters, three elements of successful industrial policy activities in Japan and the Third Italy stand out.

The first element in a successful industrial policy is a creative use and shaping of the market. Industrial policy fails when it overrides or ignores the market and is based upon the presumption that plans and markets are alternative means of economic coordination. The purpose is not to substitute the plan for the market but to shape and use markets. The market, it has been said, is a good servant, but a bad master. A central theme of the book is that effective policy toward industry depends upon breaking with the plan or market dichotomy that informs conventional economic theory and is taken for granted by policymakers guided by that theory.

Second, successful industrial policy has a production as opposed to a distributional focus. The primary goal of industrial policy in Japan is to promote the New Competition: the entrepreneurial firm, consultative buyer–vendor relations, and inter-firm associations and extra-firm agencies which facilitate continuous improvement in production. As an employment or distributional instrument industrial policy is inherently flawed. Together, industrial policy and demand management can promote employment, but the task of industrial policy is to relieve the balance of payments constraint so that labor-intensive sectors such as construction, education, and health can be expanded without generating a trade deficit.[11] The sorry record of industrial policy in both American and British experiences has been a failure to target industrial policy to production advancement.

Third, Japanese industrial policy *has* been strategically focused. It is about the targeting of strategic sectors to maximize industrial growth. It means moving into new sectors a step ahead of the competition. The idea of moving into a sector does not mean simply producing a new product but developing an organizational and strategic superiority amongst a group of firms. The goal is to increase the value added to resources steadily as Japan establishes competitive predominance in more organizationally complex and knowledge-intensive processes.

Strategic sectors are those where an international competitive advantage can be secured by gaining organizational superiority. But the target is

---

[11] For a discussion on the related theme of "deindustrialization" see Ajit Singh (1977).

moving. It started with labor-intensive goods, moved to skilled-labor medium-capital and skilled-labor raw-materials intensive sectors, and eventually on to knowledge-intensive sectors. Today, Japanese firms are increasingly concentrating on products and product designs that demand organizationally complex and skilled-labor-intensive processes.

The absence of a concept of industrial policy in conventional economics and in political discourse has contributed to a very different set of economic policies in America and Britain. While government economic policy in these two countries was preoccupied with fighting inflation by high interest rates and overvalued currencies, Japan was strategically marching through sectors picking off the competition where it had become lethargic and incapable of responding to the New Competition.

Finally, the focus on sectors helps to make sense of distinctions that inform industrial policy. For example, the idea of a sector strategy suggests distinctions between types of sectors, forms of sector coordination, and the possibility of groups of firms within one locality sharing a common strategy against competitor groups located elsewhere. The claim is that without such distinctions we will continue to misunderstand the relations between government and firms common to the New Competition and, as a consequence, the forces that are reducing the competitiveness of business enterprises organized according to the Old Competition.

Competing Production Systems and Social Inertia

The emergence of the New Competition has put pressure on firms everywhere to reorganize according to the new principles of production. The task is difficult because, as we have seen, the New Competition is not simply about transformed principles and practices within enterprises, but extends to buyer–vendor relations, inter-firm associations, and industrial policies. Efforts by a single firm to break out of the extra-firm institutional matrix of the old competition require a Herculean effort compared with establishing a firm within an already existing New Competition institutional configuration. Without the extra-firm infrastructure, enterprises seeking to become entrepreneurial firms will likely pursue a "go it alone" strategy and be at a competitive disadvantage in the international arena.

A second reason, which is less obvious but equally important, will be explored here because it is germane to the central issue of the role of ideas in economics and, particularly, in the potential for industrial renewal. It addresses the concept of the firm itself. If business enterprises were merely "factors of production", namely land, labor, and capital, combined in a firm to economize on coordination costs the task would be a straightforward technical exercise.[12] The problem is that firms are social institutions with unique cultures. A company's culture is not a commodity that can be bought and sold in the market like "factors of production"; it is more like an individual person's identity. This suggests that firms, as collectivities of people, have sophisticated means of resisting change, one of which is to deny the need for it.

Conceptual debates, then, play a role in promoting, sustaining, and undermining economic institutions. For example, the failure to develop or even consider concepts for explaining the source of industrial decline in terms of competing paradigms of production is itself a barrier to change. For only with such concepts can responses that address the organizational root of the problem be negotiated. Instead, the problem is often defined in terms appropriate to the Old Competition, namely declining productivity.[13] The temptation is to define it in these terms because then it can be managed *within the existing institutional setup*. If the claims of this book are on the right track, such a response is a failure of economic discourse which limits political imagination and, ultimately, economic performance.

In fact, efforts to increase competitiveness on the basis of increasing productivity can, at times of production paradigm transition, intensify the problem. The reason is that the sources of competitive disadvantage are neither distributional (high wages or profits causing high prices) nor restrictive practices by powerful unions but organizational: production is organized according to outdated principles which results in an incapacity to respond strategically to the New Competition.

The dearth of production-related concepts in economics is not a consequence of the triumph of mathematical economics alone. The Keynesian revolution meant, in effect, the denial of the issue of production or supply as an independent variable. Production, for Keynesian theory, was dependent upon expenditures; economics became the study of the determinants of aggregate demand. Questions about the price level replaced those about relative prices. The rise of Keynesian economics was accompanied by the decline of the Marshallian applied micro-economics tradition represented by Dennis Robertson (1923) and Austin Robinson (1931). When micro-economics reappeared in the

[12] Oliver Williamson's "transaction costs" theory of the firm, which has organizational as well as technical implications, is examined in chapter 4.
[13] Wickham Skinner (1986) uses the expression "the paradox of productivity" to capture the self-defeating aspect of increasing competitiveness by the pursuit of increased productivity when the problem is not the intensity of resource use but the way in which resources are organized.

postwar period it was in the form of Walrasian general equilibrium theory which, like its Keynesian rival (an awkward partner in the neoclassical synthesis) and unlike its Marshallian predecessor, did not address production.[14]

Outline of the Book

To understand America's industrial decline, I start with a historical examination of the sources of American industry's success. The British labelled the new competition of the mid-nineteenth century the "American System of Manufactures" or the "American System". The "American System" revolutionized industrial production with the development of interchangeable parts and specialist machines. According to Chandler (1977, p. 75), "[m]odern factory management. . .had its genesis in the United States in the Springfield Armory" where interchangeability was first established.

In chapter 1, the Springfield Armory is examined as the first site of the "American System of Manufactures". Two claims are made: first, the Springfield Armory was the hub of an industrial district along the Connecticut River Valley populated by small firms which had many features in common with the highly successful and flexibly specialized industrial districts of today examined in later chapters; second, the Springfield Armory was an inadvertent industrial policy agency. The Armory not only supplied collective services to a large group of private firms, but it also created entrepreneurial resources by training skilled craftsmen in the new methods. Many of these men established their own firms to apply the new principles to other products. The Connecticut River Valley metalworking district is contrasted with the small arms industrial district of Birmingham, England. The basis of success of the American System was not differences in factor costs or culture but advanced principles of production.[15]

---

[14] The claim that ideas as well as interests are fundamental to economic explanation is not original. Keynes's closing words from the last paragraph of *The General Theory of Employment, Interest, and Money* (1936) are elegant testimony: ". . . the ideas of economists and political philosophers, both when they are right and when they are wrong, are more powerful than is commonly understood. Indeed the world is ruled by little else. Practical men, who believe themselves to be quite exempt from any intellectual influences, are usually the slaves of some defunct economist. Madmen in authority, who hear voices in the air, are distilling their frenzy from some academic scribbler of a few years back. I am sure that the power of vested interests is vastly exaggerated compared with the gradual encroachment of ideas."

[15] Throughout the book I follow the practice of capitalizing the title of specific productive

While the Springfield Armory embodied new principles of both production and organization the American System was not Big Business. In chapter 2, the key components of American Big Business, namely mass production and managerial hierarchy, are examined. Two perspectives are contrasted on why Big Business emerged when it did, and in the form it did. The Chandlerian perspective implies an organizational imperative in response to technological change and expanding markets; a second perspective advances the claim that Big Business was created in response to a class conflict over the control of work organization which had far-reaching implications for the particular form that Big Business came to assume and, ultimately, its organizational weaknesses in the era of the New Competition. The second perspective implies that business and industrial organizations are not explained by efficiency alone.

The debate has explanatory implications for business and industrial organization. For example, was the metalworking industrial district of the Connecticut River Valley an inherently backward form of business and industrial organization as implied by the Chandlerian perspective, or was it an alternative form of organization based upon networked groups of small firms that could have, as implied by the flexible specialization perspective, led America along an entirely different but equally successful industrial trajectory? I return to this issue in the context of the New Competition in chapters 7 and 8, for it bears on the efficacy of industrial policy in today's world, particularly at the local and state, or regional, level.

In any case, the self-regulating properties of the market and the dynamics of the capitalist economy were permanently altered with the rise of Big Business. Two key aspects of the new dynamics were the tendency to overproduction and the counter-tendency to develop regulatory institutions to coordinate supply decisions and administer prices. Chapter 3 includes a description of a range of inter-firm regulatory institutions – formal and informal, public and private – that emerged with Big Business. The claim is that production and regulation are interactive: mass production led to new forms of inter-firm coordination (regulation), just as the particular form of regulation that was negotiated amongst firms and between firms and government in each sector reacted back on the development of firms in the sector.

The forms of regulatory system that dominated in the United States are contrasted with those of Germany and Britain to suggest links

---

paradigms or systems, for example the American System, Big Business, the New Competition. When the new competition is not capitalized it refers not to a specific production paradigm but to an organizational innovation that has altered the terms of competition.

between sector regulation and enterprise development and, in turn, international competitiveness. This lesson has not gone unnoticed by Japan, which adopted German regulatory forms and converted them into the powerful instrument of industrial policy described in chapter 6.

Chapter 4 juxtaposes competing economic theories of the firm, starting with Marshall's dilemma: the incompatibility between allocative efficiency, required for the neoclassical theory of price, and productive efficiency, required for a theory of the firm. Post-Marshallian theories of the firm diverged, either moving along the neoclassical path that defines the firm in terms that are compatible with the restrictive assumptions of equilibrium price theory and yielding allocative efficiency, or along the Schumpeterian path that constructs a dynamic theory of the firm with an open-ended theory of price. As already noted, Schumpeterian theory converts the constraints upon the neoclassical theory of the firm into strategic variables for gaining competitive advantage; technology, organization, product, and process, for example, all become part of the competitive process and targets for entrepreneurial activity.

It is Edith Penrose's theory of the growth of the firm that, combined with Schumpeter, offers most to the concept of the entrepreneurial firm. Penrose's framework gives integrity to the firm as an organization in which experience and teamwork play explanatory roles. Most importantly, Penrose provides an analysis of the internal pressures for growth and the limits to growth that confront business enterprises. In this Penrose points towards the limits of the processes of industrial concentration as well as the potentially self-destructive forces within a flexibly specialized industrial district. Furthermore, her development of the paradox of competition is crucial to the idea of the entrepreneurial firm.

In chapters 5–8, two case studies of the New Competition are presented: Japanese production and regulatory institutions in chapters 5 and 6, and the production and regulatory institutions of the Third Italy in chapters 7 and 8. Despite wildly dissimilar instititional and cultural settings, they share the common organizational principles of the New Competition. Japanese economic success is based upon an institutional complex of large firms, hierarchical and captive value-adding networks with large firms at the apex and vertical tiers of ever smaller firms, and industrial policy agencies of the central government; the institutional complex of the Third Italy is composed of networked groups of small firms, inter-firm collective service associations, and industrial policy agencies of local government.

In the last section of chapter 8, I return to Japan and examine the role of government industrial policy towards organized groups of small firms. The similarities between the active governmental support of inter-firm networks and production-type associational activities in Japan and the Third Italy are emphasized.

In chapter 9, two other interpretations of a new competition are contrasted with the interpretation developed in this book. All three share the emphasis on organizational innovations in business enterprises that undermine earlier forms of business organization and spearhead economic restructuring. First, David Birch's perspective on the role of the small firm in economic restructuring is contrasted with the dynamic industrial district perspective; second, Kenichi Ohmae's analysis of the global corporation and international networking, within the "triad" of Europe, Japan, and the United States, focuses on the same issues from the perspective of the giant firm. This leads into a summary of the opportunities for, and challenges to, strategic industrial policy in the New Competition. I turn then to a brief consideration of a series of challenges that the powerful disruptive forces of the New Competition present to firms, labor, communities, and government.

The four case studies in the book can be read independently but in each case, except that of chapter 1 on the American System of manufacture, a chapter on the concepts of production is followed by one on the associated regulatory principles – hence chapters 2 and 3 on American Big Business, chapters 5 and 6 on Japan, and chapters 7 and 8 on the Third Italy. The first section of chapter 4 focuses on debates within economic theory and may not be pertinent to the general reader; it situates the Schumpeterian and Penrosian dynamic theories of the growth of the firm that are drawn upon throughout the book.

PART I

The Old Competition

1

The American System of Manufacture

It was that which gratified me so much at Colonel Colt's, to see the spirit that pervaded the machines; they really had a very decided and peculiar character of judicious contrivance. (English inventor and engineer, James Nasmyth, Parliamentary testimony, 1854; cited in Wallace and Whitworth, 1969, p. 45)

Over the first three-quarters of the nineteenth century output per capita in America grew at 0.3 percent annually. Over the last quarter it leapt to an annual rate of 2.0 percent. Between 1839 and 1899 the share of output in manufacturing rose from 17 to 53 percent (Gallman, 1960, p. 26). In these years America emerged as an industrial power with business enterprises that were setting the world standard for competitiveness in sector after sector. To understand the transition we have to go beyond the marketplace and into the world of production, for America's economic success was propelled by the establishment of productive enterprises based on new principles.

The American System, as it was described by the British, was the new competition of the middle decades of the nineteenth century. In this chapter the production and organizational principles of the American System are examined in the context of the Connecticut River Valley metalworking industrial district and its early center, the Springfield Armory. I argue that the Springfield Armory was an inadvertent industrial policy agent. But whatever the role of the Armory as a catalyst, the American System established a new standard of international competitiveness that could not be matched by one major but earlier pacesetter, the small arms industrial district of Birmingham, England. The implication is that the slow decline of Birmingham as a small arms manufacturing area was not caused by restrictive working practices, high or low wages,[1] or managerial failure. Rather, it was the failure to adapt to the principles of production and organization of the new competition of the day.

The Crystal Palace Exhibition

The Crystal Palace Exhibition of 1851 was an opportunity for American manufacturers to show off their products. Leading English engineers and military men were startled by what they observed because of the revolutionary production methods that were implied. The response was so positive that some entrepreneurs stayed on or returned to England to set up production facilities. Samuel Colt was one.

With the commencement of production in early 1853, Colonel Colt's London revolver factory became a demonstration site for the new production system. In 1854, the English machine tool maker James Nasmyth described his visit to the Colt factory before a Parliamentary Select Committee on Small Arms as follows:

> The first impression was to humble me very considerably. I was in a manner introduced to such a masterly extension of what I knew to be correct principles, but extended in so masterly and wholesale a manner, as made me feel that we were very far behind in carrying out what we know to be good principles. (Wallace and Whitworth, 1969, p. 44)

The Colt factory was a representative of a new system of production that used specialist machines to produce interchangeable parts tested by precision gauges at a time when Britain still practised handicraft methods. Because of the undeveloped state of English machine making, Colt took both machines and men to London (Haven and Belden, 1940, p. 86).

Interchangeability was of special interest to military authorities. It meant that an army could go to battle with spare parts instead of skilled fitters. Before interchangeability an armament with a broken part was

---

[1] Perhaps the leading explanation for the emergence of America as an industrial power was the pressure of high wages on the development of machinery. English manufacturers, enjoying lower wage costs, did not substitute capital for labor and fell behind in technological development (Habakkuk, 1962). The implicit counter-argument in this chapter is that it was not factor prices reflecting labor scarcity that explains the emergence of the American System but rather the development of new principles of production and organization which established a superior product, virtually independent of relative factor scarcities.

useless without a fitter to handcraft a new part. With interchangeable parts, equipment could be returned to service by replacing the defective part with a prefit substitute.

Thus the British military was quick to respond to what they observed at Crystal Palace. The revelation of the new methods led to a Department of Ordnance proposal to ". . .erect a Government establishment capable of producing muskets in large numbers, and at a moderate price, by the introduction of machinery into every part of the manufacture where it was applicable" (Wallace and Whitworth, 1969, p. 91). The proposal meant transcending the traditional British craft-organized arms production system based on private procurement with government assembly and inspection.

In preparation the British government sent a team of officers to the United States ". . .with the power of buying such machinery as they might consider would be more productive than that used in England. . ." (Wallace and Whitworth, 1969, p. 91). The machinery they bought formed the basis for the first English government armory, established at Enfield in North London. One team member, John Anderson, the Ordnance Inspector of Machinery and a leading English mechanical inventor, understood the challenge of the American Manufacturing System to British industrial leadership and saw a twofold purpose in constructing the Enfield Armory: to produce a large supply of cheap arms and to educate the British on the advanced production methods of the Americans. In his words:

> The American machinery is so different to our own, and so rich in suggestions, that when fully organized it should be thrown open to the study of the machine makers of the kingdom. . .A few hours at Enfield will show that we shall soon have to contend with no mean competitors in the Americans, who display an originality and common sense. . .which are not to be despised, but on the contrary are either to be copied or improved upon. (Wallace and Whitworth, 1969, p. 66).

The Springfield Armory

The new production methods were first established at the US government armory in Springfield, Massachusetts. Not by coincidence the Springfield Armory is famous as a site of managerial innovation as well. In Alfred Chandler's words, "Modern factory management (but not it must be stressed the management of large modern multi-unit enterprises) had its genesis in the United States in the Springfield Armory" (Chandler, 1977, p. 75). Production at the Springfield Armory involved innovations in technology, management methods, and work practices. In Chandler's words, "[T]he systems and controls developed at the armory were as critical to the development of what became known as the 'American System of Manufacturing' as the new metalworking machinery and machine tools" (Chandler, 1977, p. 75). Nevertheless the technical features of the new production system were the most striking, particularly the concept of interchangeability.

Interchangeable Parts

In the words of J.W. Roe, "By interchangeable manufacturing we mean the production of complete machines or mechanisms, the corresponding parts of which are so nearly alike that they will fit into any of the given mechanisms" (Roe, 1937, p. 755). The American System was based on the principle of interchangeable parts, but only in rare cases were whole factories organized according to interchangeability. In fact the first example, and certainly one of the few, was the Colt Armory of Hartford, Connecticut, organized by Elisha Root and completed in 1855, in which "[n]o handwork at all was allowed" (Roe, 1937, p. 757).[2] But by the mid-nineteenth century many American factories could be found in which interchangeable methods were in use.

The idea of interchangeability required breaking down products into their simplest parts, designing a specialist machine capable of producing each piece, and inspecting each part with a custom-designed set of gauges. As distinct from European practice, where a fitter tailor-made each part, interchangeability meant that parts could be machine processed and assembled by workers who had not been apprenticed in the craft tradition. At the same time, considerable skill was required for the design and making of the ubiquitous specialist machines, fixtures, and gauges.

Many American factories used specialist machines but did not achieve interchangeability particularly as the precision standards were rapidly and incessantly upgraded. One historian, David Hounshell, distinguishes "armory practice" where interchangeability was systematically pursued and achieved from the American System which signifies specialist machines but which continued to rely upon craftsmen to handfit parts (Hounshell, 1984). Nevertheless, interchangeability was an ideal that gave direction to the American System.

---

[2] Roe (1937, p. 757) calls the finishing of the Colt Armory at Hartford in 1855 a "date that marks an epoch in American manufacturing". He describes the Colt Armory as the "most influential shop in the country". What distinguished it from all earlier examples of the American System was the commitment to organize every operation according to the principle of interchangeability.

Influenced by Colt, an English delegation of machine makers and military men visited New England and conducted a famous test of the the interchangeability claim at the Springfield Armory. They dismantled ten Springfield muskets, each produced in a different year between 1844 and 1853, and put the same parts from each rifle in a separate box. The muskets were then haphazardly reassembled. To the surprise of some of the visitors but none of the Americans, the performance of the muskets was unaffected.[3] The English team set about purchasing the full range of machines and gauges, as well as hiring American machinists, to set up at the new Enfield Armory in North London (Smiles, pp. 362–3, cited in Roe, 1937).[4]

Specialist Machines and Precision Gauges

The American System required the design of a special machine for each individual operation. The first special machine deployed by the Springfield Armory was a woodworking lathe invented by Thomas Blanchard and exhibited in 1819. By 1826 Blanchard had built 14 different machines at the Springfield Armory, each of which performed a single operation in the making of a gun stock (Smith, 1977, p. 135).

A number of shops emerged that specialized in the building of machine tools for interchangeable manufacture. Robbins and Lawrence, located up the Connecticut River at Windsor, Vermont, mounted an impressive exhibition at Crystal Palace and along with the American Manufacturing Company, the Ames Manufacturing Company, and Pratt and Whitney received orders from the visiting British delegation (Roe, 1937, p. 758). All supplied the Springfield Armory with specialist machines.

To ensure that the machining operations were meeting the tolerances so that the machined part could move on to the next machine without the requirement of handfitting, a system of specialized gauges was

---

[3] The Americans were not surprised because such experiments had been going on since about 1800 when Eli Whitney amazed a group of Army officials with such a test using ten guns (Roe, 1937, p. 755). Thomas Jefferson, in a letter to James Monroe, wrote: "He has invented molds and machines for making all the pieces of his locks so exactly equal, that take 100 locks to pieces and mingle their parts and the hundred locks may be put together as well by taking the pieces which come to hand" (Ford, 1926, cited in Roe, 1937). Jefferson had become an interchangeability enthusiast after meeting a French workman named LeBlanc while minister to France over a decade before (Roe, 1937). French manufacturers, however, are not known to have pursued the idea.
[4] A machine made at the Ames Manufacturing Company and shipped to the Enfield Armory in the 1850s was returned to the newly opened Springfield Armory Museum over a hundred years later. According to Enfield officials it had been in operation for most of that time.

developed. One was for the operator, a second for a supervisor, and a third master gauge was used to check the first two periodically. Shops also emerged that specialized in the making of gauges and fixtures.

Production without Fitters

The British team that visited the Springfield Armory saw interchangeable parts and a system of specialist machines, but it also saw an unfamiliar organization of work.

The British were familiar with production methods that depended upon the feel of the craftsman to ensure a proper fit, but not the formal measurement methods of the American System. The traditional craftsman working with his file was no longer the prominent figure. Interchangeability meant that departments within factories could assemble pieces produced in preceding stages without fitters. As Henry Ford observed in the next century: "In mass production there are no fitters" (Ford, 1926, p. 822). Instead of a craftsman producing each part to a noncodifiable standard, the American System designed specified tolerances into the machines. A failure to meet the specifications was indicated by gauges which could be read by an operator.

The extent to which the new methods deskilled craft labor is disputed by historians. John Hall, the inventor–machine maker who was probably the first to propose that an entire factory be organized according to the principle of interchangeability, was given a government contract to do so on a small scale at Harpers Ferry Armory (Smith, 1977). He bragged that "[O]ne boy by the aid of these machines can perform more work than 10 men with files, in the same time, and with greater accuracy" (Smith, 1977, p. 240). The operation of Blanchard's lathes is reputed to have had similar, if less dramatic, effects in the gunstock division of the Springfield Armory. By 1926, Blanchard's battery of 14 specialist machines had, in the words of Merritt Roe Smith, ". . .completely mechanized the process of stocking and eliminated the need for skilled labor in one of the three major divisions of armory production" (Smith, 1977, p. 135).

The widespread substitution of detail labor for craft labor is also implied by Colonel Roswell Lee who wrote in reply to an Ordnance Officer seeking employment for his son in 1925:

> . . .I think some other trade would be more beneficial to him, as there are but very few in the Armory that work at all branches. . .and although it might afford him a living yet it would not be a trade that he could set up and carry on for himself under ordinary circumstances. . .A carpenter and joiner, cabinetmaker or Black or White Smith, would be preferable in my opinion. . . (Uselding, 1973, p. 76)

But Charles Fitch, writing a century ago, argued that the demands of precision work limited the use of unskilled labor:

> Machinery may contract the province of certain skilled trades. . .but the fact remains that the increased fineness and accuracy required in the manufacture of firearms demands the most skillful and experienced oversight, and unskilled labor can only be employed with the best results upon limited portions of the work. (Fitch, 1883, p. 6)[5]

Felicia Deyrup observed that increased mechanization divided the workers into two groups with marked wage differences. She refers to one study of the Springfield Armory in the 1840s that "noted a decided diminution in the skill of the average arms worker after 1820" but "arms making remained. . .among the most highly skilled occupations in American industry" (Deyrup, 1948, p. 100).

Available evidence, then, does not warrant an unambiguous conclusion that interchangeability and specialist machines as deployed at the Springfield Armory systematically deskilled the labor force. However, it certainly altered its composition.

Management Control by Information Systems

For Colonel Lee, the barrier to quality and reliability in armaments production was the control that fitters exercised over the shopfloor. Thus Lee was receptive to the new methods of production because they provided a means of shifting control of the factory from the craftsman to the manager, a process he had initiated in 1815 when assuming command of the Springfield Armory. But the power of managerial supervisors was limited by the personal methods of control. Lee sought impersonal methods of control. His task was to establish production control by devising methods of forcing worker accountability to production schedules and for material usage that did not depend upon the personal relationship between supervisors and workers. In Lee's view, workers would always establish the standards of output and quality under such a system.

The claim that the Springfield Armory was the original site of modern factory management is based on Lee's creation of impersonal or bureaucratic management control methods which entailed new managerial tasks. First, Lee created middle management posts of assistant master armorer for each "principle branch of work" to advance quality control by a verifiable inspection system (Uselding, 1973, p. 72). Both the worker and the assistant master armorer cum inspector put a signatory

---

[5] Glen Hutloff (1988) makes this point.

mark on each piece made. In this way any malfunction in the field could be traced to an individual worker and inspector. Second, Lee put clerks under the supervision of the master armorer to control material wastage and monitor the performance of both workers and management. The clerk's job was to maintain a day book with records of all of the materials and tools received by the department. These amounts were transcribed monthly into a ledger book which kept track of monthly totals of materials received, on the debit side, and products produced, work in progress, inventories, and scrap on the credit side. In addition, each foreman kept a similar ledger for each worker. Any excess waste or unaccountable materials were deducted from the workers' pay. These accounts were consolidated by the master armorer for the factory as a whole. The result was that Lee could monitor the performance of each worker, foreman, shop, and branch. The 1819 report to the War Department's Ordnance Department proclaimed: "Complete accountability is established and enforced throughout; and if there is any error committed, it will be discovered on a comparison with the books and it can be traced to its source" (Chandler, 1977, p. 74).

The innovations in organization and production at the Springfield Armory were mutually reinforcing. Together they represented the first steps toward the mass production paradigm that provided a vision for achieving advances in production efficiency in every sector of industry. Colonel Lee did not use the information he demanded of subordinates to develop product costings or estimate rates of return on capital.

Claims for the productivity potential of the new system were made at the time. Blanchard bragged that his recessing machine for carving out a space for locks in gun stocks could ". . .make a closer joint in one minute than a Stocker can in one *hour*" (Smith, 1977, p. 134, emphasis in original). The visiting English team noted that, whereas in the United Kingdom a worker would make eight to ten stocks in a week, the Blanchard turning lathe could provide a stock in 22 minutes.

Nevertheless, the Springfield Armory did not exploit the potential for driving throughput up and prices down. As shown in table 1, Deyrup estimated that the cost of the Springfield musket dropped slightly between 1821 and 1831 but then rose erratically over ensuing decades. In Deyrup's words, "Mechanization, however great its value in improving the quality of arms, failed. . .to bring a marked reduction in costs" (Deyrup, 1948, p. 132). Springfield Armory guns were expensive, as were the products of private firms that established interchangeability in other sectors such as Singer sewing machines, McCormick reapers and Columbia bicycles (Hounshell, 1984, p. 9). Colonel Lee used interchangeability to create a new system of factory governance that could ensure a safe and reliable supply of quality armaments to the

Table 1 Costs or prices of Springfield musket and breech-loading rifle, 1798–1858

	Contract price ($)	Ordnance Department estimate of cost ($)	Deyrup's estimate of cost ($)
1798	13.40		16.28
1803			6.70
1810	10.75	12.06	13.16
1811			10.07
1815	14.00	12.06	18.81
1821	12.25	12.51	13.41
	14.00		
1825	12.25	12.23	12.01
1831	12.25	11.26	11.80
1839	12.25		14.38
1840	12.25	17.44	27.47
1849		13.00	14.41
1858		13.22	23.13

Source: Deyrup, 1948, pp. 229–31.

military; it was not used to drive down prices.

Nor did Lee pursue the time and motion measures of "scientific management". But the impersonal system of management that originated at the Armory did portend a definition of management in America as "the art or science, concerned with *planning, directing, and controlling* the work of human beings. . ." (Burbidge, 1968, p. 3) just as the establishment of specialist machines anticipated the rise of mass production. The vision of an entirely new order of production was coming into focus. Was the American System of Manufactures as practised at the Armory but a stage in a technologically determined trajectory to mass production and Big Business? While this topic reappears in the next chapter another dimension of the Springfield Armory suggests space for institutional alternatives.[6]

[6] Sabel and Zeitlin (1985) examine a large number of historical cases that suggest an alternative flexible specialization path to mass production. Flexible specialization as a strategy for industrial growth is explored in chapters 7 and 8.

The Springfield Armory as Inadvertent Industrial Policy

The small arms that shocked the British at the Crystal Palace Exhibition had not been organized by vertically integrated Big Business enterprises. Nor had the industry emerged spontaneously by entrepreneurs responding to, and coordinated by, prices in the free market. In the first place arms manufacturing was protected by tariffs (Deyrup, 1948, p. 41). Secondly, the consumer was the government. Thirdly, in the words of Deyrup, "the early [arms] industry acquired a spirit of cooperation and mutual helpfulness which was one of its most conspicuous features" (Deyrup, 1948, p. 55). The spirit of cooperation did not emerge spontaneously: it was part of the social fabric of an industrial district with the Springfield Armory at the center. In fact, the Springfield Armory was more than the center of an industrial district; it performed a number of economic functions that merit its consideration as America's first active industrial policy.[7]

Coordinator of Activities

In the early decades of the nineteenth century, the Armory played the coordinator role attributed to the invisible hand of the market in economic theory or the plan in the vertically integrated business enterprise. The Armory was the center of a supplier network of private firms all along the Connecticut River Valley. While many produced their own products, others specialized in stocks, barrels, bayonets, lockwork, mountings, and other components (Deyrup, 1948, p. 44). This supplier network combined elements of cooperation and competition and operated as an industrial district.

An industrial district is a means of coordination that combines elements of market and plan. It suggests a system of firms producing complementary as well as substitutable products and linked by associative institutions; the conventional presupposition of a sector is of a group of indistinguishable firms producing substitute products and integrated only by prices in the market.

The small firms within the industrial district were like departments within a single firm in that they produced complementary products and services but they were not captives of a single hierarchy and they could develop independent design and proprietary product capabilities with the active support of the central "office", in this case the Armory. The small firms were also like independent units coordinated by the market,

---

[7] An example of a passive industrial policy, by contrast, would be protective tariffs.

but cooperation allowed individual firms to develop specialities which, in turn, insulated them from the market pressures of "commodity" producers. At the same time no firm was exempt from competition; even the Armory, like private firms, often had to bid for contracts.

As a coordinator of diverse economic activities the Armory played a role that would later be played by middle management in a vertically integrated managerial hierarchy. But it also performed two other roles: provider of collective services and promoter of new methods. In pursuing these roles the Armory can be described as an industrial policy.

Provider of Collective Services

Deyrup (1948, p. 66) writes that the contract system between the Department of Ordnance and the Springfield Armory literally brought the industry into existence. The constitutive "spirit of mutual helpfulness" manifested itself in a number of non-market exchanges of mutual benefit and the delivery of collective services by the Springfield Armory to the nascent manufacturing firms.

1 Exchange of advice and information: knowledge flowed freely with respect to "interchangeability, gun design, manufacturing processes and machine tools" (Deyrup, 1948, p. 66). Expert Armory mechanics visited supplier factories and offered advice, and workers from other plants "freely examined the Armory's tools and machinery, and in return the Armory occasionally took castings of valuable machines developed by the contractors" (Deyrup, 1948, p. 119). Furthermore the Armory "openly aided contractors by advising them of strategic times for applying for contracts" (Deyrup, 1948, p. 66).
2 Exchange of raw materials: on occasion the Armory bought and inspected materials for its suppliers "for which return was made in money or parts" (Deyrup, 1948, pp. 66, 119). Deyrup (1948, p. 66) adds that raw materials were often exchanged and paid for with "other stocks which because of requirements as to size, shape, or extent of seasoning were usable by one party only". Thus neither the Armory nor the contractors used market power to leverage parts prices against the other. Had they done so the efficiency of raw material usage would have suffered.
3 Sharing of tools and machine patterns: "Tools which were difficult for a contractor to acquire or limited in their uses were loaned by the Springfield Armory" (Deyrup, 1948, p. 66). In addition, "[p]atterns for machines were frequently exchanged" (Deyrup, 1948, p. 66).
4 Sharing of specialist services: "Specialized services, such as difficult forging or grinding, were also exchanged. A very common service

with which the Armory favored contractors was rolling the bar iron. . .into the various sizes required for making the different parts of the gun (Deyrup, 1948, p. 67). According to Deyrup the Armory only charged a "nominal fee" for using its rolling mill to roll the iron of suppliers to specified sizes.

5 Sharing of skilled labor: the Armory loaned skilled labor to the suppliers. In exchange, writes Deyrup, "[c]ontractors paid the transportation expenses and the regular Springfield Armory rate of wages to the workers they borrowed. Afterwards workers might return and continue in their positions. . .unless the Armory was willing that they should leave its service". Thus the contractors were able to acquire the services of highly skilled pattern makers and tool makers, useful for a short period only. In this connection in 1818 Lee informed the New England contractors that "[s]hould you be in want of any workmen in your establishment such as first rate barrel welders – triphammers men-forgers, filers, stockers or finishers, you can probably be supplied from this place, by giving me information, mentioning the number and description you may want" (Deyrup, 1948, p. 67).

6 Agreement on wages: Superintendent Lee entered into agreements with private firms not to "outbid one another in the labor market" (Deyrup, 1948, p. 67). The idea was not to create a perfect labor market, but to regulate the allocation of labor as done by middle management in Big Business.

Thus the Armory was both a coordinator of economic activities and a supplier of collective services. But the developmental role of the Armory stretched to a third activity: as the promoter of interchangeability, it was the purveyor of new principles of production. The pressure for interchangeability emanated from outside the Armory and was crucial in the shaping of the Armory itself.

Promoter of Production Rationalization

The unique features of the Springfield Armory began with the key idea of the American System: interchangeability. The development of interchangeability of parts in the Springfield Armory was the culmination of a long and expensive effort financed by the Ordnance Department of the Department of War dating from the War of 1812. Following that war, the Ordnance Department was created and given jurisdiction over the federal armories at Harpers Ferry and Springfield, as well as over government contracts to private armories. The early Chiefs of Ordnance were determined to upgrade the safety and durability of armaments. As already noted, a faulty weapon was dangerous to its user, and a weapon with a single faulty part was useless without the availability of a skilled fitter. Referring to the first two Chiefs of Ordnance, Merritt Roe Smith writes, "both men became zealous advocates of the 'uniformity system' and relentlessly pursued the idea of introducing it at the national armories" (Smith, 1977, p. 107).

The impact of the government's drive to establish uniformity was not limited to the publicly owned armories or primary contractors to the Department of Ordnance. The Armory came to monitor the performance of subcontractors in terms of meeting the test of interchangeability, for every firm that wanted to supply the Armory had to meet the new standards of precision which could be tested by gauges. But, as noted above, it played a developmental role in assisting firms to meet the standards.

Thus the Springfield Armory was not simply a coordinator of a network of firms, but a setter of standards and a purveyor of new methods. The gauge-tested system created new standards of performance that were required of suppliers as well. In this the Springfield Armory was a force not only for technological convergence but also for production method convergence (Hutloff, 1988).

The availability in one geographical area of a complete range of specialist metalworking services made the region attractive to entrepreneurs who were developing any of a wide variety of new products. In other cases craftsmen in machine making, trained at the Armory on the principles of interchangeability and cognizant of the need for specific machines, set up private firms or were employed by machine tool makers to sell to the Armory. Thus the Ordnance Department fostered the development of an industrial district of networked machine tool makers and metal and wood fabricators that would come to produce machines, components, and parts for virtually every manufacturing sector.

The inter-industry ripple effects of interchangeability on American industry were not lost on John Anderson:

> . . .this system of special tools is extending into almost every branch of industry where articles have to be repeated. This applies to furniture, hardware, clocks, watches, small arms, ammunition, and to an endless variety of other things. (Rosenberg, 1972, p. 97)

In this sense the government's promotion of interchangeability was a catalyst for the spread of the American System. By exerting pressure for the adoption of best-practice manufacturing principles the government, however unintentionally, was pursuing an industrial policy. It might not have been a deliberate policy based on a long-term strategy for building America's industrial base but, at least for a time, it worked as if it had been.

The Birmingham Small Arms Manufacturers

In the mid-nineteenth century, Birmingham, England, was also a regional center for small arms manufacturing. The inability of the industry to supply firearms made with interchangeable parts led the British government to restructure it. The first step was to establish the Enfield Armory which was owned and operated by the government. Previously, British armories had only inspected arms that had been produced elsewhere, primarily in Birmingham. The Enfield Armory, as noted above, was supplied with American-made machines and utilized the American System of production. Thus began the slow decline of the Birmingham small arms manufacturing industry.

While a definitive story of the decline awaits a careful historical analysis, a production-oriented comparison with the Connecticut River Valley metalworking industrial district suggests first that the Birmingham small arms industry was based upon different principles of production and organization and second that it did not prove capable of adapting to the new methods and organization. The following evidence is supportive of the claim.

Birmingham arms manufacturers were organized by handicraft methods utilizing highly skilled labor. Firms could produce hundreds of product types and could shift product lines altogether. Catalogues with 500 different types and sizes of steam engines, for example, were common (citations in Rosenberg's introduction to Wallis and Whitworth, 1969, p. 72). When the demand for guns declined, such firms could shift to shoe buckles or brass buttons. Thus these firms were extremely flexible, but within the limits of handicraft manufacturing methods. In the words of Rosenberg:

> The apparent adaptiveness of the Birmingham metal trades was deceiving, however, for it was adaptive only within the limits of a sharply circumscribed technology. The Birmingham metal trades were capable of producing any of a wide range of articles which could be produced by highly skilled and ingenious craftsmen working only with tools and the simplest machinery. . .(Wallace and Whitworth, 1969, p. 78)

Large size and the lack of specialization amongst firms made many Birmingham general engineering workshops inflexible in a second way: length of run. J.R. Richardson, an English engineering shop owner, explained his reluctance to buy American machines in the following terms:

It was not that the English engineers did not understand American methods, but that Americans did not as a rule understand the conditions which obtained in large engineering works in England having a big general practice. There must be a large run of work. Even the most enthusiastic Americans had told him that a large quantity was not needed, that it could be done perfectly well with a dozen, but very often a dozen was a large quantity. (Orcutt, 1902, pp. 72–3)

From this quote it would appear that the Birmingham gunmaking industry was less like an industrial district of specialist firms and more like an economics textbook sector of homogeneous firms all producing and competing over the same product.[8]

Finally, the Birmingham gunmaking industry did not enjoy three services supplied by the Springfield Armory: administrative coordinator of activities, particularly between machine tool makers and gunmakers, supplier of collective services, and promoter of new production methods. The success of the Connecticut River Valley arms makers was based upon the development of the new methods associated with interchangeability and with the protean capacity of the district to subdivide and spread the new methods to other branches of industry.

Market Failure Rationale for a Sector Development Agency

The Armory's activities can be explained in terms of the economic theory of market failure. The Armory provided three services undersupplied by the market: information, labor education, and technology transfer. The Armory invested in information that benefited the community but for which private firms could not establish property rights. The very concept of interchangeability is an example. The Armory also financed labor training for which the benefits were realized by private firms that could hire away skilled workers without paying the price for their training costs. In addition, the Armory served as an alternative to the patent system as a promoter of technological innovation but one which did not entail restricting the benefits to licensed firms. Thus by developing new machines that could be readily copied the Armory stimulated the spread of new production methods.

Finally, the Armory was a catalyst for a technological transformation which depended upon joint action amongst a group of firms. While it was not in the interests of any single firm acting alone to specialize in one phase of the new production system, it was in the interest of each

---

[8] Clearly, more research has to be done on the actual degree of specialization and inter-firm networking before this claim can be demonstrated with confidence.

of a group of firms, each specializing in complementary phases of production, to make the transition. Thus success for each individual firm depended upon other firms making parallel moves in the complementary processes. While the real world did not fit this model precisely, the Armory was in a position to coordinate such moves across a group of firms. The private interests of firms could then be met only through joint action because no single firm could risk specializing unless it was part of a coordinated effort.

Conclusion: The Springfield Armory as Industrial Policy without a Concept

The industrial district is an alternative means of mobilizing and coordinating a cluster of vertically related production activities to either a managerial hierarchy within a single firm or by prices in the market. The autonomy of individual producing units allows each unit the opportunity to supply a range of buying firms and to design and even supply proprietary products independently. In the case of the Connecticut River Valley arms manufacturing district, the fact that the firms were not connected by market alone allowed a flow of information and skilled labor across firms as well as products and money. Furthermore, operating within the umbrella supplied by the Springfield Armory, as a government agency, provided a degree of relief from the day-to-day pressures of the market so that firms could think long term.

The Springfield Armory's role as a development agent was powerful but short lived. The shift occured abruptly in 1841 when the War Department prohibited the Armory from rolling iron to specified sizes for Armory contractors because of inconvenience to the Armory. This prohibition, writes Deyrup (1948, p. 119), "was symbolic of the end of cooperation between the Springfield Armory and the contractors". Worse, the "spirit of cooperation and mutual helpfulness. . .among the arms makers. . .disappeared when the industry became independent of government aid" (Deyrup, 1948, p. 55).

The Connecticut Valley metalworking district did not continue to

---

[9] The evolution of the concept of an industrial district is explored in chapter 8, as is the interaction between the refinement of the concept and institution making in the Third Italy. The claim with respect to the Springfield Armory is that Colonel Lee and his associates lacked a conceptual analysis of the mutual dependence of firms which was required if the district was to continue to evolve. In this, the participants were role bearers of the hidden structures, and not self-conscious agents concerned about how to maintain or refine such structures.

develop into a learning district that could carry on adapting as challenges and opportunities unfolded. One reason was that the idea of an industrial district was missing.[9] The idea of an industrial district would have made evident the roles that the Armory had played as coordinator of independent business units, as provider of collective services such as labor training programs, and as a catalyst for technological upgrading. But since the industrial district functions of the Armory were not appreciated the local government was not under pressure to assume an industrial policy role as the federal government withdrew. Nor were individual firms that had benefited from joint action, implicit in the idea of an industrial district, put under pressure to assume individual responsibility or obligation to the maintenance of the district.

The conventional wisdom is that modernization meant the transcendence of small firms by large firms. From this perspective, continued technological advance demanded that the industrial district surrounding the Springfield Armory be replaced by vertically integrated corporations. But recently a competing perspective has re-emerged to challenge the dominant view. The competing perspective holds that the Connecticut River Valley metalworking industrial faced a historical, if unrealized, choice. One direction was to build systematically on the elements of the existing industrial district and develop it into a system of flexibly specialized firms (Piore and Sabel, 1984; Sabel and Zeitlin, 1985). Another led towards the development of a single giant firm in which each productive unit was but a department. In fact, neither path was chosen and the region declined as an industrial center. Whatever chance the industrial district model had was overwhelmed, at least in the public eye, by the emergence of the vertically integrated managerial enterprise to which we turn next. But we will return to the idea of an industrial district as an alternative to mass production in chapters 7 and 8, where the Third Italy is examined as an illustration of the New Competition.

2
Big Business: Mass Production and Managerial Hierarchy

A Transformed Economic Landscape

If the Springfield Armory was an organizational catalyst of the American System of manufacturing, the railroad companies were the same for mass production. Only two to three decades separated the first "modern factory management" (Chandler, 1977, p. 75) at the Springfield Armory and the professional managerial hierarchies which governed the railroads. No railroad better symbolized the new organizational form than that run by the Pennsylvania Railroad Company. In the 1850s, when even the largest American textile firms had considerably under 1,000 employees, the Pennsylvania had 4,000. But in the ensuing years railroads created a new scale and mode of economic organization. By 1865, the Pennsylvania had 30,000 employees. It was the largest business enterprise in the world in terms of revenues, assets, and employees (Livesay, 1975, p. 35). The Pennsylvania, in league with half a dozen other railroads, spearheaded an expansion of railroad receipts from $40 million in 1851 to $130 million in 1860 and $334 million in 1867 (Livesay, 1975, p. 31).

The corporate enterprises that were created to run the railroads were emulated in leading sectors of late nineteenth century American industry, including steel, petroleum, chemicals, electrical equipment, standardized machinery makers, and processed food. By 1917, the 278 firms in America with over $20 million in assets produced about a quarter of all manufacturing output (Navin, 1970, cited in Chandler, 1977, p. 346). The new administrative giants combined, under a single managerial hierarchy, a geographically scattered and diverse range of business and production activities. Coordination by managerial hierarchy replaced coordination by market.

The financial requirements of the corporate enterprises were of a new magnitude: whereas the largest pre-Civil War industrial firms were capitalized at around $1 million, US Steel was incorporated in 1901 with a capital value of $1 billion (Porter, 1973, p. 9). In the 1890s, investment bankers created and managed industrial securities markets to mobilize the finance required by the newly emerging corporate giants (Davis, 1966; Best and Humphries, 1986). As ownership became increasingly dispersed, a managerial class took charge of production and distribution in many enterprises. In others, majority share owners or investment bankers used their control over finance to wield influence over corporate executives. Big Business had arrived.

Two Perspectives on the Rise of Big Business

That the economic landscape was transformed is beyond dispute; the reason why is contested. Contemporaneously, classical economic theory was giving way to neoclassical economics. The focus of the classical economists on class relations amongst landlords, capitalists, and workers and the implications for distribution and growth gave way to concerns about individual choices in the market and the implications for the optimal resource allocation. Neoclassical theory sought to demonstrate how, given certain assumptions, a decentralized market economy of atomistic individuals could be both self-regulating and utility maximizing. Issues of production, technological change, and business organization were shunted aside by the ascendancy of neoclassical economics.

Classical economic theory had two other offshoots. Marx used the classical labor theory of value to predict increasing concentration of production and immiseration of the working class. The facts that real wages increased and that the wage share of income stayed roughly constant with the establishment of Big Business is not consistent with Marx's prediction of proletarian impoverishment, whether absolute or relative.

The Cambridge, England, school of economics, as a holdout of classic economic concerns, does not explain prices and distribution by either neoclassical utility theory or Marxian labor time. The Cambridge tradition maintains that distribution cannot be explained independently of relations of property and power but offers no explanation of distribution. Like neoclassical economic theory, the Cambridge classical tradition is primarily a theory of exchange, but one that explains prices without reference to utility. Production, like distribution, is left unexplained.

Consequently, economic theory in both its neoclassical and classical variants suffers from severe limitations in attempting to explain the rise of Big Business. In such theories the market is treated ahistorically. It is as if the market was a natural object rather than a social institution shaped, in part, by social conventions and power relations. For a historical account of markets we must turn to the institutionalist tradition.

The leading institutional account of the rise of Big Business is that of Alfred Chandler. For Chandler, the emergence of Big Business was a means for driving down costs by increasing throughput: the speed and volume of material flow in production. Size was not a cause but a consequence of throughput. In Chandler's words:

> Increases in productivity and decreases in unit costs (often identified with economies of scale) resulted far more from the increases in the volume and velocity of throughput than from a growth in the size of the factory or plant. (Chandler, 1977, p. 281).

Furthermore, Big Business was the only way to increase throughput and thereby reduce costs. Again in Chandler's words:

> To maintain and continue a high volume of flow demanded organizational innovation. It could be achieved only by creating an administrative hierarchy operated by many full-time salaried managers. (Chandler, 1977, p. 236)

The managerial hierarchy of the larger enterprises did not stop with production: "[T]hey administered the flow from the suppliers of the raw materials through all the processes of production and distribution to the retailer or ultimate consumer" (Chandler, 1977, p. 283).

For Chandler, the railroad was a prerequisite for the spread of the managerial enterprise for three reasons. First, the railroads enhanced the volume and velocity of transport flow from raw material to factory, and from factory to consumer. Second, the railroads were great organizational innovators that created the management systems required to execute mass production. Third, the railroads supplied the right of way used by the telegraph industry which, in turn, established the communications system to coordinate the flow of materials and goods across widely scattered branches.

Once the railroads were established, Big Business emerged rapidly in those industries in which high throughput technologies could be deployed. Driving costs down by administrative coordination created profits in the form of quasi-rents to the early birds in a sector.[1]

---

[1] Rent is a return to a factor that is fixed in supply above the return required to coax it to market. The first firm to drive costs down would be receiving a form of rent in that the price would be determined by higher cost competitors. A quasi-rent, unlike a rent from natural monopolies, can be competed away by the introduction of the same

Followers, however, had to struggle for a market share against a firm already achieving throughput economies.

Chandler's account is consistent with orthodox economic theory in that the winners and losers in the competitive struggle are determined by efficiency; at the same time, Big Business contradicts the assumption of perfect competition upon which the properties of allocative efficiency and economic self-regulation depend. The omnipresence, in Chandler's perspective, of a divergence between productive and allocative efficiency suggests that monopolistic, not atomistic, competition is the norm in the American economy. Furthermore, violation of the allocative efficiency criterion suggests a permanent and pervasive role for regulatory agencies, a subject not taken up by Chandler.

A competing historical explanation for the rise of Big Business focuses on the predatory drive to monopolize exemplified by US Steel's control of iron ore deposits, or Standard Oil's control of oil pipelines. The predator seeks to dominate rivals by gaining control over a critical link in the vertical production and distribution chain between raw material and final consumer.

The predatory story cannot readily account for why some market control schemes work and others fail, for late nineteenth and early twentieth century America was littered with unsuccessful attempts to control markets by horizontal merger activity (Livermore, cited in Chandler, 1977, pp. 337ff). The elements of productive efficiency must be integrated with the drive for market control to explain why some efforts to create Big Business failed and others succeeded.

More sophisticated versions of the market control explanation go some distance towards such integration. James Livingston (1987, p. 72), writes that ". . .the innovation we know as the modern corporate system was an economic solution to a stubborn social impasse, not merely an administrative response to market integration or technological imperatives". For Livingston, the social impasse was a consequence of, on the one hand, the combined existence of competitive prices in product markets and administered prices in labor markets and, on the other, an increasing tendency to overproduction. Overproduction in competitive markets generated lower prices. But, because workers were organized, wages did not drop. The consequence was a rise in real wages, a squeeze on profits, and a slowing of growth.

"Ruinous competition" is a tendency associated with industries in

---

production methods in other firms. But to the extent that the lower costs are due to organizational features, such as experience and teamwork, they may depend on elements that are not easily reproduced or purchased in the market. These issues are developed in chapter 4.

which firms have high fixed costs. Faced with declining gross revenues, companies attempt to recover profits by dropping prices and selling more at lower margins. While it would be collectively rational for the companies to reduce output and increase margins, it is privately rational to chase each other down a declining demand curve.[2] The problem is analogous to the free-rider problem of public goods. In both cases the private and collective rationality split requires cooperation if private interests are to be met. The problem of ruinous or cutthroat competition is associated with high fixed cost industries because prices can drop much further in these industries and still cover variable costs. This means that companies can be hemorrhaging in cash flow but still operating.

The response of capitalists to the risk of ruinous competition took two forms: first, to seek control of product markets to coordinate supply and demand at profit-making price levels; second, to seek control of work organization to establish mass production. According to this account, Big Business emerged, not for reasons of efficiency, but to organize markets to counter the tendency to ruinous competition and reduce the collective power of workers.

Livingston's market control perspective depends upon three historically specific developments: first, the tendency to overproduction based on high fixed costs leading to "ruinous competition"; second, the capacity of workers to resist money wage decreases by collective action; third, the capacity of capitalists to replace the invisible with the visible hand in the product market and to introduce new production methods in the factory.

Were workers capable of resisting wage cuts by collective action in the 1870s and 1880s? Livingston cites the research of a number of leading labor historians suggesting that they were. Herbert Gutman, David Montgomery, and Lawrence Goodwyn describe the formal and informal means of collective action which shaped the development of the American working class in this period. The intensity of the class struggle at the Homestead Strike in 1892 lends credibility to the theses of both worker collective action and Carnegie's commitment to break it.

That prices dropped is beyond dispute. The wholesale price index collapsed from 193 in 1864 to 68 in 1896. While all such indicators are subject to qualification (for example, 1864 was a war year), a series of economic studies have documented the drop in commodity prices, the

---

[2] An assumption required for these results is that demand be inelastic for the lower prices. Mancur Olson (1965) develops this example more fully.

rise in real wages, and the squeeze on profits (Livingston, 1987, p. 76). Today, a broad consensus supports the claim of a profit squeeze along with higher real wages between the early 1870s and the mid-1890s. However, Livingston does not explain why overproduction and cutthroat competition emerged when and where they did. Market control analysis, by itself, cannot provide an explanation of the ascendancy of Big Business in America because it ignores precisely those sources of overproduction that are central to Chandler's account of mass production and managerial hierarchy. But at the same time, Livingston's account relaxes the immanent organizational logic of Chandler, and his notion of a social impasse resulting from a tension between the external dynamics of inter-firm competition and the intra-firm dynamics of the class struggle is worth pursuing. It suggests that the specific resolution of that impasse was important to understanding the ensuing evolution of industrial, business, and work organizations.

In this chapter, I examine developments in production and business organization that spawned the tendency to overproduction and cutthroat competition, which, in turn, induced innovations in productive organization. I start with the principles of mass production and hierarchy, the organizational building blocks of Big Business. I conclude that the American corporation was created to establish market control but control turned out to be a moving target. In chapter 3, I argue that the logic of the rise of Big Business, based upon the principles of flow, scientific management, and managerial hierarchy, led to the pursuit of inter-firm cooperation and government regulation for the same reason: pursuit of market control.

Mass Production

". . .[T]he basic axiom of mass production", writes Chandler (1977, p. 257), is that "economies and lower unit costs resulted from an intensification of the speed of materials through an establishment rather than from enlarging its size." For Chandler, and mass production, the focus is on economies of time. The principle of flow and "scientific management" are both about economies of time; they became guiding principles for designing production facilities in America.

The Principle of Flow

The American System was not mass production. Interchangeability of parts, specialist machines, and precision gauges were used for the purpose of producing a standardized product. Each is also an element in mass production. But the American System did not include another element which is fundamental to mass production – organizing production to exploit economies of time or, in Chandler's concept, to increase the speed and volume of throughput. The same idea is captured by the principle of flow, a production engineering concept. In the words of Burbidge:

> If there is such a thing as a master principle of production, one which governs or over-rules all other principles, then it is probably the principle of flow. (Burbidge, 1968, p. 38)

Mass production is the American System plus the principle of flow.[3] But organizing production facilities according to the principle of flow had far-reaching implications. This can be seen by comparing a functional with a flow-based organization.

Machines in early American factories, as in factories elsewhere, were laid out according to function. The lathes would be grouped in one location, the grinders in another, and the drills in yet another. Production involved moving materials and semi-finished products around the factory in batches. Thus a batch might start in the milling area before proceeding to the grinding shop after which it might return for additional milling before moving to the boring department before proceeding to a subassembly department.

Every product in a batch would complete each machining operation before the batch proceeded to the next operation. The number of machines in each functional group would depend upon the cycle time of the respective machines. If machining operation A took three times

---

[3] It is somewhat arbitrary to distinguish between the American System, based on the principle of interchangeability, and mass production as interchangeability plus the principle of flow. We can say that "Armory practice", as distinct from the American System, did not then involve the principle of flow. But the earliest examples of mass production overlapped with the American System. J.W. Roe (1937) cites a number of examples of factories in which interchangeability was used to drive down costs and increase volume. The first was in the wooden clock industry as early as 1820. About that time Eli Terry reduced the price of wooden clocks from $25 to $5 and was sharply increasing the volume of production (Roe, 1937, pp. 756–7). Perhaps the leading example of early mass production was that of rolled brass clocks made by Chauncey Jerome, who had learned machine methods from Terry. The cost of Jerome's brass clock was driven down to 50 cents by 1840, a price that led to exports to England and, by 1855, a volume of 400,000 clocks per year (Roe, 1937, p. 757). In the next decades the same story can be told for watches.

Such examples, which are largely confined to the clock and watch industry, illustrate that the American System and mass production cannot be divided into two periods by a single date. My emphasis is on the analytical difference between the two principles.

as much time as operation B, then three A machines would be necessary for each B machine to ensure that production could proceed without bottlenecks. The machining operations would then be in balance (Robinson, 1931, p. 25). Increasing the efficient scale of output in a batch production system involved adding another round of the balanced mix of machines. But adding more machines did not increase the rate of throughput, only the scale of output. In fact, increasing traffic congestion and work-in-progress inventories created diseconomies and increased the complexity of scheduling as ever more batches crisscrossed one another.

Establishing a balance of processes could generate economies of large scale and thus scale efficiency. But this was countered by the throughput inefficiency of batch production (as measured by the ratio of the time that a product is being machined to the time the product is in the production system). One way to increase throughput efficiency was to replace functional machine layout with a flowline sequential layout.

The idea of a flowline is to lay out the machines in the order of the machining operations. Thus, instead of transporting batches from department to department, the machining operations would be laid out in a series that corresponded to the sequence required for production. A flowline held out the promise of less transport and handling time as goods could be moved directly from machine to machine rather than from department to department. Furthermore, intermediate inventories declined as the operations were streamlined.

Different time cycles for each machine created a challenge to arrange the machines in the order of the production sequence, much as batch production created pressures to expand production capacity until a balance of processes was achieved. Flowline arrangements made it obvious that each stage had a different time cycle; consequently, bottlenecks would occur at the machines with longer cycles. Developing a flowline for products that embodied a series of components or that used a variety of machines was a formidable challenge to mechanical engineers. The advance of time economies on any one machine would immediately create excess capacity for that machine or lead to bottlenecks at the next machine along the line.

The vision of a flowline concentrated the attention of mechanical engineers on bottlenecks as barriers to throughput. By shortening the time cycle of the machine requiring the longest time cycle, engineers could speed up the whole line. But each time the bottleneck was relieved at one machine station, it reappeared elsewhere. The layout engineers were again stuck with one of three options: run a machine below its potential, add machines at the bottleneck station, or reduce the time cycle required by the slower machines (Burbidge, 1968, p. 37).

By the 1880s the pursuit of flowline methods had led from flowline to continuous flow processes. Whereas under flowline products continue to be machined in batches even though the plant is laid out in the order of the machining operations, under continuous flow products move individually through the sequence of machines: no two products are ever at the same stage of production. The idea was to link functionally distinct specialist machines into a single complex machine that took material in one end and pushed the processed product out the other.

Continuous process technologies came first to the refining and distilling industries because these industries utilized gas and liquid materials. But another example from Chandler is the Bonsack machine which revolutionized cigarette making. Whereas previously a highly skilled laborer could produce 3,000 cigarettes per day, the endless tape of a Bonsack machine took in tobacco at one end, compressed it, wrapped it with paper, pasted the paper, and deposited cigarettes at the other end. Fifteen Bonsack machines, each producing 120,000 cigarettes per day, could have saturated the demand for cigarettes in 1880 America. The cost dropped from 60 pence to 10 pence per 1,000. The result?

> Not surprisingly, the first two firms to adopt the Bonsack machine – those of James B. Duke in the United States and Wills in Britain – dominated the cigarette industry . . . in their own countries. Within a decade they were joined in battle for the world market. (Chandler, 1977, p. 250)

Designing complex integrated machines capable of exploiting economies of time became a challenge for mechanical engineers in all industries. Where it was possible, it created an opportunity to establish market dominance.

Henry Ford's genius was to apply the principle of flow to a metalworking industry that required a large number of complex components. The Model T, more than any other application before or after, captured the public imagination.

In the spring of 1913, Ford engineers broke the production process of the magneto coil down into 29 complementary operations performed by 29 different workers (Hounshell, 1984, p. 248). In the process each operation was mechanized and material flow was speeded up. The time taken to make a magneto dropped from 20 to 13 minutes. The magneto was produced on an assembly line, but not a moving assembly line. Workers stood in a row along a sliding surface performing the same operation on each product and then hand pushed it two or three feet along to the next worker for the next task.

The magneto line suggests a positive relation between rate of throughput, process complexity, and minimum efficient size of plant.

Whereas under the old workbench method a one-person shop could assemble magnetos, maximizing throughput on the flow line meant 29 linked operations and 29 workers standing side by side. In this case, increasing throughput led to increased size; maximizing throughput dictated placing the machines side by side. Thus it was not always "big" machines such as steel blast furnaces or chemical processing plants that created economies of scale; rather, it was the logic of combining machines to maximize throughput. This meant large investments in machines and transfer mechanisms.

Within a year Ford engineers had applied and extended the flowline principle to the assembly of motors and transmissions and to final assembly itself. In the summer of 1913, in an experiment, a Model T chassis was pulled slowly across 250 feet of factory floor and the time required for assembly was decreased from 13 hours to five hours and 50 minutes. In January 1914, Ford installed the first automatic conveyor belt, modelled after the overhead trolley deployed by meatpackers, and within two months cars were being assembled in an hour and a half (Hounshell, 1984, pp. 254–6).

The first firm in an industry to use mass production methods to set a new low cost floor could be assured of dominant market share and margins to afford self-financing. Other mass production firsts in a sector included Carnegie, Rockefeller, du Pont, Eastman, Diamond Match, Procter and Gamble, Campbell, and Heinz (Chandler, 1977). In each of these cases productivity leaped as a consequence of establishing flowline principles of production. However, furniture, leather products, and textiles are industries that were not restructured according to the dictates of the flowline. In each of the latter cases, and for whatever reason, production engineers were not successful in creating flowlines that substantially increased the rate of throughput. In these cases, efforts to create Big Business floundered in debt.

Scientific Management

The systematic application of science to production and the development of flowline principles created new challenges for scientists and engineers. But new challenges were also created for the organization of people, in this case workers. Driving down costs by pushing up the velocity and volume of throughput depended upon synchronizing work activities with the new technological opportunities. Workers, unlike machines, could consciously resist the new system and, unlike managers, they could not be motivated by a managerial career ladder. The redefinition of work activities to separate planning, the prerogative of managers, from doing, the activity of workers, became the defining characteristic of "scientific management".

At the time of Frederick W. Taylor, existing management control systems were dependent upon foremen. Carnegie Company, as an example of a leading company of the 1880s, used a factory management system based upon routing slips that accompanied each order through the production stages and upon which foremen were responsible for recording the costs in terms of labor, materials, asnd machine usage. But the informational control systems were often opposed or inadequately filled in by the foremen. The hiring of clerks for recording purposes went some distance towards improving the quality of information but the clerks lacked the authority to confront the foremen and workers who controlled operations. In the words of Chandler (1977, p. 266): "[e]ffective coordination of throughput required the placing of vigorous management controls over these despots". The term "despots" here refers to the foremen, labor subcontractors, and craft laborers who governed the flow of materials and products.

Taylor pursued numerous avenues to increase throughput. He sought alloys to make machines to increase cutting speeds, and devised mathematial formulae to design optimal machining systems. But he is most famous for redesigning the methods of work according to principles established in his "time and motion" experiments. For Taylor the design of the machine and of work were reducible to the same logic. Just as the principle of interchangeable parts had led to the decomposition of production into a series of precisely measured and endlessly repetitive movements, each of which could be done by a specialized machine, Taylor sought to decompose worker tasks into a series of precisely measured and endlessly repetitive movements.

Taylor's experiment with an immigrant pig-iron handler illustrates his meticulous rearrangement of the method and timing of work activities. Each pig weighed 92 pounds and the handler had to pick it up and carry it a few yards to a pile. The average handler hauled 12.5 tons per day, but Taylor was able to increase worker productivity nearly fourfold by applying his time and motion methods. In Taylor's words:

> Schmidt started to work, and all day long, and at regular intervals, was told by the man who stood over him with a watch, "now pick up a pig and walk. Now sit down and rest. Now work – Now rest," etc. He worked when he was told to work and rested when he was told to rest, and half past five in the afternoon had his 47 1/2 tons loaded on the car. . .One man after another was picked out and trained to handle pig iron at the rate of 47 1/2 tons per day until all the pig iron was handled at this rate and the men were receiving 60 percent more wages than the workmen around them. (Taylor, 1967, p. 47)

For Taylor, effective supervision depended upon time and motion studies. Only then do supervisors have an "objective" measure for comparison with actual worker effort and only then are workers' activities dictated by the economies of time. Scientific management required that workers' movements be synchronized with the flow of the materials through the machinery. Craftsmen, who historically controlled the definition and pace of work, were to be replaced by acquiescent employees whose every motion was proscribed by scientific plan. The new principles radically redefined the tasks of lower management as well as labor. Taylor underscored the increased responsibilities of management:

> The managers assume new burdens, new duties and responsibilities never dreamed of in the past. . .for instance, the burden of gathering together all of the traditional knowledge which in the past has been possessed by the workmen and then of classifying, tabulating, and reducing this knowlege to rules, laws and formulae which are immensely helpful to the workers in doing their daily work. (Taylor, 1967, p. 36)

It became lower management's function to plan and organize the activities of every worker. The minute specialization required intricate coordination and planning. Neither the definition of work nor the flow of production would any longer be dependent upon the skill or pace imposed by workers. As usual, Taylor's language was unambiguous on this point:

> The work of every workman is fully planned out by the management at least one day in advance, and each man receives in most cases complete written instructions. . .This task specifies not only what is to be done but how it is to be done and the exact time allowed for doing it. (Taylor, 1967, p. 39)

Taylor's mission was not to establish despotic managerial methods but "scientific" methods. In fact, his system called for an end to the foreman as general manager and the substitution of a planning department to administer the factory. Workers would report to and be assisted by a staff of eight clerks in the planning department. Individual clerks would specialize in time and motion studies for job analysis, in speed for setting standards of output, in routing for scheduling the flow of orders, in instructions for setting daily work plans, in inspection for refining controls and keeping constant check on all costs, and in personnel for recruiting and firing workers and on repair for maintenance. The task of the planning department was not to motivate workers, at least not directly. That was the function of an incentive wage system based upon detailed job analysis. Each worker would be paid a differential piece rate: lower rates for less than standard output, and higher rates for greater than standard output. Taylor impelled managers to observe the link between work effort and pay as fundamental to the operation of scientific management.

Although Taylor's ideal work and management organizational recommendations were probably never carried out in a single factory, work organization was reconstituted in the American factory with the arrival of mass production. The management quest for high rates of throughput was translated to the shopfloor as the need for a pliable labor force willing to operate the machines to full capacity. Labor responded by building trade unions that organized most of the mass production industries. Eventually a compromise was achieved that gave management its most fundamental demand – control over the processes and operations of work. Managers and staff alone would have responsibility for planning work along the lines of the Taylorist system. Workers' responsibilities were to obey instructions. The company had no responsibilities for upgrading worker skills and could freely lay workers off during business downturns. Management's fear of dependence on skilled workers led to the design of jobs so that little training was required and workers, like parts, could be rendered interchangeable.

Workers gained the rights to organize, seniority, a grievance procedure, and high wages. Pay was determined by evaluation and job classification systems and not by the skills that a worker possessed. Any disagreement could be aired and much of unions' activities involved grievances. The resulting system is described as follows by Michael Piore and Charles Sabel:

> The logic of the system of job classifications and seniority rights, and the judicial process by which they are supervised, operates to ensnare ever more of factory life in a net of rules with an ever finer mesh. (Piore and Sabel, 1984, p. 114)

I will argue in chapter 5 that the limitations of the American system of shopfloor control have become apparent with the emergence of an alternative production paradigm. A New Competition has exposed the system of shopfloor control as the Achilles heel of American capitalism. Flexible production systems geared to high quality have set standards that the American mass producer cannot meet without jettisoning the organization of work upon which it has been based. But this is jumping ahead of the story.

Hierarchical Organization

Mass production is not equivalent to Big Business. The principles of mass production can be employed for a single phase of production. Big Business, however, involves the creation of a managerial hierarchy to coordinate, monitor, and plan over multiple phases along the production chain.

The rationale for mass production is to achieve economies of time by organizing production according to the principle of flow. The rationale for vertical integration is not so obvious. For Chandler, Big Business emerged purely for reasons of production efficiency. In this section, I will examine the principles of organization that emerged with Big Business in America. My account draws heavily on Chandler's work.

Centralized Administration and Decentralized Operations

Establishing flowline production systems required the reorganization of management as well as work. The Pennsylvania Railroad Company was not the first three-tiered managerial hierarchy. That accomplishment belongs to the Western Railroad, and was prompted for reasons of safety following a head-on collision in 1841. The Western, which operated over 150 miles between Worcester and Albany, established three divisions and three layers of salaried management.

The Western did not use the military model of hierarchy in which authority and information flowed directly from top to bottom along a single chain of command. Instead, management at the Western was organized into three specialist chains and one general chain of command emanating from the head office. Each of three chief specialists in the head office had authority over their professional subordinates in the divisions who, as a consequence were responsible not to the line or divisional superintendent but to their professional counterpart in the head office. Thus, for example, the senior mechanic in each division had authority over mechanics in his division and reported directly to the master mechanic in headquarters.

Parallel chains of command meant that lower management specialists could exercise authority over higher management in the general management chain of command. For example, the authority for starting and stopping trains and sticking to schedules did not flow from the president to the general superintendent to the division superintendent and on down to the conductor. Instead, in order to facilitate coordination amongst trains such authority was delegated to the conductors. Every conductor was given a timetable established by a committee of middle and lower line management. But no one, from the president on down, could direct the movement of a train except the conductor. The conductor was responsible for adhering to the time schedule; without assigning authority to the conductor, responsibility would be dissipated.

The Western's overlapping command form of organization was a substantial modification of the military hierarchy in which authority and information travel uninterruptedly from top to bottom along the same channel. It was successful in improving the safety of the railroads. As a multiple branch system it also offered opportunities for increasing the throughput of traffic compared with market coordination across independent business units: transshipments could be minimized, uniform equipment could be installed, common operating standards could be enforced, schedules could be coordinated, finance could be arranged, and overhead expenditures could be shared over greater output. Internalization of such activities within a single firm may not have been the only way to achieve the benefits of multi-unit cooperation, but low cost transportation required some form of cooperation across operating units.

However, overlapping chains of command created two management control problems. The first problem was that performance was impaired by the blurring of responsibility for divisional performance. Neither specialist managers, who were only responsible for their respective functions, nor the division superintendents, who did not have authority over the specialist personnel in their branches, could be held responsible for poor operating performance of the branches. Organizational performance is enhanced by first pinpointing responsibility and second linking authority with responsibility. At the Western Railroad good efforts could go unnoticed and responsibility for bad efforts could be displaced along the hierarchy. A second problem was that staff positions, such as the committee in charge of setting the timetable, were also line, or authority, positions for other activities. This meant that staff or interdivisional activities such as establishing common procedures, coordinating material flows or providing collective services were being performed by men who also had line responsibility. Individuals held dual roles of middle management and staff.

To overcome the tension between specialist and general management chains of command, J. Edgar Thomson of the Pennsylvania Railroad devised, and in 1857 set up, the first decentralized divisional structure based on the "line and staff" distinction (Chandler, 1977, p. 106). His goal was to imitate the motivational and entrepreneurial advantages of small business with the economies of scale of specialist staff in railroading. He sought to combine the advantages of centralization and decentralization by locating responsibility and authority at the divisional level.

The new line and staff form of organization cleanly separated staff (or professional) from line (or managerial) authority positions. While a single line of authority from top to bottom of the organization was the backbone of the managerial hierarchy it was not the only channel of information nor did it establish a single-dimensional conduit for relations of authority. In fact, information flowed along specialist occupational channels and the authority channel had break points that delegated authority for specific purposes along the way.

The critical break in the authority channel was at the divisional headquarters. Divisional managers were given authority to run their divisions just as the conductors on the Western were given authority to direct the movement of the trains. But authority was more substantial for the divisional managers: it meant the power to hire and fire staff personnel, maintain a separate set of books, coordinate functional activities across the division, and even, in some cases, to set prices, propose investment strategies, and implement rationalization programs.

At the same time, the divisions enjoyed access to a wide range of centralized services. The Pennsylvania had a staff in the head office with specialists in finance, engineering, legal matters, and personnel policy as well as general staff managers who coordinated, monitored, and planned across divisions. Staff personnel in the head office had no authority or responsibility except over their immediate offices. They did not issue orders to functional subordinates in the branches of the enterprise and were not responsible for their performances.

The decentralized structure solved problems that had always limited the sustained success of business enterprises over time. First, it freed top management from being caught on the treadmill of day-to-day operational decisionmaking. Once the decentralized divisional structure was in place, Thomson and his advisors could concentrate their energies on long-run considerations including external finance, interdivisional resource allocation, and evaluating middle and lower management.

Second, the decentralized structure eased succession problems by creating experienced managerial decisionmakers who could step into top positions. Decisionmaking by general managers in the field encouraged initiative and independent thought. As Charles E. Perkins, President of the Chicago, Burlington & Quincy Railroad, put it: "Men's minds and abilities grow and expand with use and responsibility" (Chandler, 1977, p. 181). Many who learned the new management methods on the railroads, such as Andrew Carnegie, took their skills to new industries. The virtues of decentralization in developing "minds and abilities" did not extend below managers to workers who, instead, came under the dictates of scientific management.

Management Accounts: Supervising without Supervisors

We have seen that obtaining the benefits of scale led the top management of the railroads to create a decentralized administrative hierarchy. Decentralization, however, created potential for inefficiency unless a surrogate for market discipline could be created. The problem was not how managers could control hourly workers but how top management could control lower management within an operationally decentralized hierarchy. Personal systems of supervision were labor intensive, cost inefficient, and highly subjective. The challenge was to create objective measures of performance.

Financial statements measure the financial condition of a company for purposes of stockholders and creditors. But balance sheets and income statements are not management tools; they do not provide performance criteria, reveal sources of operating inefficiency, or offer means of evaluating subordinate management performance. This is the terrain of management accounts.

The development of management accounting was as integral to the rise of Big Business in America as was the development of scientific management. But a single name such as that of Frederick Taylor is not synonymous with its creation. Instead, management accounting evolved through a series of stages set in motion by the early railroad executives. In the early 1850s railroad executives began monitoring the performance of subunits with operating ratios: direct costs, labor, materials, energy, and other costs that vary with output, divided by the sales attributed to the operating unit. The greater was the gross margin (the percentage difference between direct costs and sales), the greater was the contribution of the unit to overhead or collective expenses of the entire enterprise. But an objective measure of direct costs was not simple. Expenses came in a variety of seemingly incomparable units. How could the costs of maintenance, running a station, and coordinating schedules, for example, be summed up and compared across railroad districts for measuring performance?

The railroad men responded to the challenge. In the late 1860s Albert Fink, a civil engineer, redesigned all the statistical data of the Louisville and Nashville Railroad according to common categories of cost rather than department or function. Every expense was recorded within one of four categories and converted by formula into the common unit of costs per ton-mile. Thereafter costs per ton-mile became the statistical basis for pricesetting, monitoring performance, and controlling subordinates within the managerial hierarchy (Chandler, 1977, p. 116). Top management used these statistics to drive down costs relentlessly. The best means was increasing the utilization of capacity. Systems were set up to keep track of every car owned by a railroad company and its contribution to reducing ton-mile costs. Rates were set at the maximum consistent with full utilization.

The use of direct cost measures was applied mercilessly in the emerging mass production industries. Carnegie, who was trained at the

Pennsylvania Railroad, named his first plant the Edgar Thomson Works after his partner and teacher of organizational principles. Carnegie's cost sheets were meticulous. As reported by James Bridge:

> The minutest details of cost of materials and labor in every department appeared from day to day and week to week in the accounts; and soon every man about the place was made to realize it. The men felt and often remarked that the eyes of the company were always on them through the books. (Bridge, 1903, p. 85, cited in Chandler, 1977, p. 268)

But, remarkably, Carnegie's justification for incessant updating of plant and equipment on the basis of establishing a competitive edge in product costs paid little attention to overhead and capital costs. The costs in Carnegie's expression "Watch the costs and the profits will take care of themselves" (Livesay, 1975, p. 101) referred to the direct costs of labor and material detailed on his cost sheets. H. Thomas Johnson writes:

> Carnegie's operating strategy was to push his own direct cost below those of all competitors so that he could charge prices that would always ensure enough demand to keep his plant running at full capacity . . . Secure in his knowledge that his costs were the lowest in the industry, Carnegie then engaged in merciless price-cutting during economic recessions. While competing firms went under, he still made profits. (Johnson, 1981, p. 515)

Led by Carnegie's relentless pursuit of technological modernization, steel production quadrupled between 1870 and 1900. Between 1880 and 1900, Carnegie increased the rate of investment by a factor of ten. Like the railroad top management, Carnegie evaluated performance in terms of operating ratios. Operating ratios worked for Carnegie. But financial indicators, particularly for monitoring and planning multiple product enterprises, depended upon measurements that accounted for capital structure as well as operating ratios.

Management accounts were converted into a powerful planning instrument with the development of a formula for combining cost and capital accounts by Donaldson Brown at Du Pont in 1915. Brown's formula states that R (return on investment) equals P (ratio of net profit to sales) times T (capital turnover, or ratio of sales to investment). P was not new. Measuring earnings as a percentage of sales was as old as bookkeeping. It is the information that constitutes the income or profit and loss account of a business enterprise. Likewise, T was not new in that it uses the data found in the balance sheet. But defining turnover as the ratio of output to investment, breaking it down by department, and linking it to the cost accounts was new.

The beauty of Brown's formula was its simplicity and comprehensiveness. Figure 1 breaks T and P down into their component parts. Every manager could understand it and respond to goals defined in terms of

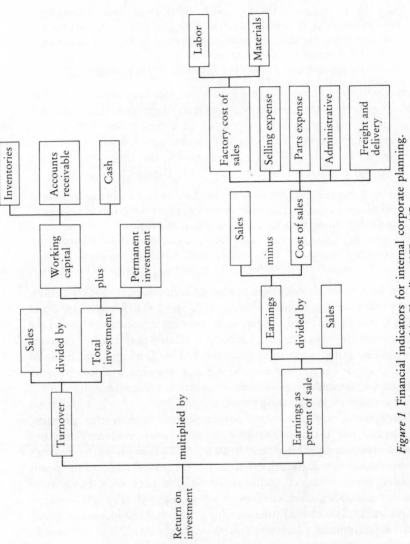

Figure 1 Financial indicators for internal corporate planning.
Source: Davis, 1950; cited in Chandler, 1977, p. 447.

it; at the same time it accounted for virtually everything that could be measured in every department. For top management it was like an X-ray cutting through to the bones beneath the surface flesh: the source of any divergence from plans or company norms could be pinpointed. Thus, if a division's returns were down, top management could quickly scan the components of both capital productivity and profit margins and isolate the source. Each division prepared reports monthly, and sometimes daily, so that top management could immediately identify unexpected variations and seek corrections.

The opportunity to apply and extend Donaldson Brown's accounting framework at General Motors soon arose. In 1919, General Motors was nearly bankrupt following a severe inventory crisis. The major stockholders, Du Pont and J.P. Morgan, installed a new management team which included Brown to gain control over a disorganized and uncoordinated group of divisions. Little information, let alone financial control instruments, existed. Within two years, General Motors was drastically reorganized and converted into an enormously successful business enterprise by a series of organizational innovations that allowed "coordinated control of decentralized operations" (Sloan, 1965, p. 139). The positive effects were indicated by the increase in average annual turnover of total inventories from 1.5 in 1921 to 6.3 in 1925. It is likely that similar productivity increases occurred in other working capital items such as cash and accounts receivable and in fixed capital (Johnson, 1978, p. 510).

Standard Volume Pricing

Carnegie's costs sheets were inadequate for a second reason: they did not account for phases of the business cycle. Managers would look good during upswings in the business cycle and bad during downswings independently of their actual performance. But worse, Carnegie's cost sheets were not designed to anticipate the business cycle, which could have had disastrous consequences. If, for example, Carnegie invested heavily in output-increasing capacity which came on line during the early stages of a prolonged slump, the company would be at a competitive disadvantage compared with non-investing rivals that did not have to cover the costs of the new plant and equipment.

The system of financial controls developed at General Motors addressed this problem. In the process a pricing system was created that accounted for the existence of the business cycle. Alfred P. Sloan Jr, chief executive officer of General Motors, was acutely aware that basing prices on costs would intensify the already highly cyclical nature of the automobile market. Volume production with high fixed costs meant that costs per unit of output would increase in economic downturns and decrease in upturns. General Motors had no intention of reinforcing such swings because of the potentially devastating organizational effects. To solve this pricing problem Brown developed the idea of "standard pricing".

General Motors was not guided by the policy of maximizing profits: as stated by Donaldson Brown, ". . .the object of management is not necessarily the highest attainable *rate of return* on capital, but rather the highest return consistent with attainable volume. . ."(emphasis in Sloan, 1965, p. 141). Profits, Brown argued, could not be pursued at the "sacrifice of wholesome expansion".

The financial goal of General Motors was to make a long-run return on investment of 20 percent when output equalled 80 percent of capacity, the "standard volume". "Long run" meant over the business cycle. The resulting "standard price" took account of the inadvisability of adjusting prices to costs independently of the business cycle. If General Motors increased prices in times of downturns to cover higher fixed costs per unit output and reduced prices in business upturns, the impact of the business cycle would have been intensified. The existence of high fixed costs and constant prices meant that profits adjusted dramatically. Thus the problem for top management was to devise a standard for evaluating performance that was detached from the variations of profits over the business cycle. Otherwise divisional managers would be faulted for downswings in the business cycle, a factor over which they had no control.

To distinguish between planned variations in profits caused by swings in the business cycle and controllable variations caused by operating inefficiencies, General Motors devised a "flexible budget" to compare actual profits with the planned profits over a range of actual output levels. Thus a standard price was calculated at standard volume for a 20 percent rate of return. The forecast established "standard" values for each of the major factors affecting return on investment such as fixed and variable costs and capital turnover rates. The purpose was to establish norms for comparing the performance of operating units and as performance targets for operating units.[4]

In addition, General Motors' system of financial controls increased its capacity to respond rapidly to market changes and less vulnerable to cashflow and inventory crises that plagued the automobile industry. Whereas the economic downturn of 1918–19 put General Motors in the

---

[4] Using the flexible budget to adjust accounts for the uncontrollable variations in fixed costs per unit output, the comptroller's office could measure the norm for each of the key turnover and operating ratios and make comparisons with the actual results.

control of its creditors, the same company survived a decline in sales from a peak of 1.90 million total units worldwide in 1929 to 0.53 million units in 1932 and from a new peak of 1.93 million units in 1937 to only 1.11 million units in 1938 (Sloan, 1965, p. 214). No other firm had such capability.

The system of financial controls at General Motors was a far cry from Carnegie's cost sheets. Not only were overhead and fixed costs included in the calculation, but divisional managers were not held responsible for items that they could not control. At the same time General Motors was a decentralized system in that responsibility and authority for operations were lodged with the divisional managers. Thus "the coordinated control of decentralized operations" underlay an organizational form that could expand without loss in efficiency beyond anything imagined before. It also allowed for planned contraction in output in ways that were unintelligible to managers trained on Carnegie's cost sheets. Chandler summarizes:

> With these innovations, modern managers had completed the essential tools by which the visible hand of management was able to replace the invisible hand of market forces in coordinating and monitoring economic activities. (Chandler, 1977, p. 448)

A Firm's Concept, Strategic Planning and Product Diversification

In one lengthy sentence, Alfred Sloan identifies the "concept" or unique idea that guided General Motors' competitive strategy. Sloan sets the scene by dividing the history of the automobile industry into three periods:

> There was the period before 1908, which with its expensive cars was entirely that of a *class* market; then the period from 1908 to the mid-twenties, which was dominantly that of a *mass* market, ruled by Ford and his concept of basic transportation at a low dollar price; and after that, the period of the mass market served by better and better cars, or what might be thought of as the *mass–class* market, with increasing diversity. This last I think I may correctly identify as the General Motors concept. (Sloan, 1965, p. 150, his emphasis)

Crucial to the success of General Motors during Alfred Sloan's 45 year reign, 23 years as chief executive officer, was that every new corporate diversification opportunity was tested for consistency with the General Motors "concept". General Motors became involved in numerous industries but always returned to cars because no product better fitted the organizational capabilities founded on the mass–class concept. I will illustrate the mass–class concept with three examples of product diversification as described by Sloan, and then comment briefly on the idea of a firm's "concept". It is a recurring idea, particularly in the latter chapters of the book.

General Motors established the diesel locomotive industry in America. Within a decade of entering the locomotive industry in the early 1930s, it outsold all of the other locomotive manufacturers combined. Why? First General Motors initiated the concept of a standard locomotive when all other manufacturers produced customized vehicles, and second General Motors developed the diesel engine, a German invention, while the rest of the industry retained steam power (Sloan, 1965, p. 352).

Similarly, General Motors led the revolution in the refrigerator industry. Concerned that the car business would be declared non-essential during the First World War, in 1918 the then head of General Motors, William C. Durant, purchased Guardian Frigerator Company, a company that had sold 34 refrigerators in its three-year history. General Motors followed the diesel locomotive model: it offered a standardized product based on a new technology, in this case freon gas that was developed by General Motors chemists. In 1921, the first full year of mass production operation, General Motors sold 2,100 refrigerators which increased to 63,500 in 1925 as Frigidaire's market share climbed to over 50 percent. Prices were driven down from $714 in 1922 for a wood refrigerator with brine tank and water-cooled compressors to $468 for a steel cabinet refrigerator with an air-cooled compressor and direct-cooling coils weighing about 40 percent of the earlier model.[5]

General Motors entered the aircraft industry in 1919 with the acquisition of the Dayton Wright Airplane Company. In the 1920s and early 1930s General Motors bought major interests in Fokker, Bendix, and North American, and played a major role in building managerial organizations in each. The reason behind the acquisitions is given by Sloan:

> Our original motive for investing in the aviation industry. . .[was]. . .the feeling that the industry might somehow produce a flivver plane which could compete with the automobile. . .(Sloan, 1965, p. 368)

Bendix and North American became Big Business during the Second World War. Whereas each had sales of $40 million in 1940, each was in the $700–$800 million mark by 1944. Nevertheless, General Motors withdrew from the aircraft industry following the War. Why? In 1942 Sloan reasoned that the General Motors concept was inconsistent with any of the three aircraft markets that he foresaw. The military market,

---

[5] All data in this paragraph are from Sloan (1965, pp. 355–8).

in the words of Sloan, "would involve a large amount of engineering and development work with *continuous modification* of low-volume models" (Sloan, 1965, p. 372).[6] In the commercial field Sloan foresaw a rapidly expanding market but "sales volume to a manufacturer would be limited". Finally, the market for small private planes "would not become a serious competitor of the motorcar in the foreseeable future" unless there was some revolutionary breakthrough in safety (Sloan, 1965, p. 372). Consequently General Motors maintained North American as an accessessories supplier but otherwise withdrew from the aircraft industry.

General Motors' locomotive and refrigerator divisions were also sold. The reason was that inadequate market size precluded employing General Motors' mass production techniques successfully. Both locomotives and planes were sold to companies with smaller production capacities and less rigid production methods. Neither these products nor refrigerators fitted the second feature in the General Motors concept – a class good. Furthermore, class had a double meaning. It meant income level, but also lifestyle. Class in the General Motors notion of mass–class encompassed the idea of annual model changes. A class product denoted recent vintage as well as model. Each of these notions was one of the criteria by which General Motors determined whether a product could achieve the volume that was consistent with their distinctive organizational capabilities and overhead structure.

However, as we shall see in the next chapter, top management at General Motors did not always take market size as a given. Strategic planning involved shaping the market for transportation to fit General Motors' organizational and production capabilities.

For Sloan, strategic planning and a corporation's concept were not the same thing. A firm's concept defines its distinctive competence – the one activity or purpose that gives a firm a unique and inimitable position in the market and with which any specific strategy must be compatible. A firm's concept is like a compass — it gives direction to an organization by shaping its priorities. Without a clear concept, a firm risks losing cohesiveness by spreading its resources into disparate activities. Every firm with a sustained record of success has a concept that distinguishes it in the market, but to thrive a firm must continue to refine, develop, and act upon its concept in a world in which change

---

[6] Continuous modification is my emphasis. Ironically, continuous improvement is what distinguishes the New Competition from the Old which General Motors represents. However, General Motors 1987 supplier's manual describes General Motors' new management philosophy of "continuous improvement".

is ever present. A firm can reshape its concept but it is like a person altering his or her personality: it does not happen often or easily.[7]

Conclusion: Production Efficiency and Market Control

Not only does Chandler describe the transformation of the American economy to one dominated by Big Business, but he also describes the emergence of an industrial managerial class that does not fit into the capitalist–worker dichotomy. The managerial class did not derive economic power from ownership. Their ascendancy was a quiet revolution which coincided with a radical transformation of the economy. The owning class maintained legal power over firms and sat on the boards of directors, but the power to make production decisions was relinquished to the managerial class, who had become the real directors of production.

Certainly, many of the pathbreakers to the new order based on mass production were not simply managers. But being a manager as well as a capitalist created men who fitted uneasily in the capitalist class. Owner–managers of mass production enterprises, such as Carnegie, du Pont, and Ford, saw themselves as technocratic leaders of a new productive order. Carnegie maintained emotional allegiances, however loose and contradictory, to the Chartist movement that inspired his father in Scotland, du Pont was more an organizer of the managerial class than the working class, and Ford shattered the going wage with his $5 day in 1913, a move that was resented by other owners.

Furthermore, whatever the intention of the organizers of mass production enterprises, the new system had an internal logic that democratized consumption in two ways. First, it improved the consumption capacities of the working class. Mass production depended upon and created the first mass consumption society. Incomes increased partly through higher nominal wages, but more by the increased efficiency of production which meant lower prices and a vastly improved standard of living to the worker and his or her family. But mass production did not simply mean more goods; it also meant the emergence of universal or democratic goods that were consumed by capitalist, manager, and worker alike.

No product better exemplified the new age than the car. Whereas the first cars were a toy of the elite, the Model T was designed to be affordable to Henry Ford's farmer father. Ford was not the first metal-

---

[7] A firm's culture, a close relative of a firm's concept, is examined in chapter 3; the idea of strategy is further developed in chapter 5.

fabricating firm to manufacture a universal product. Singer's sewing machines and Pope's bicycles were designed for a mass market. But Ford's Model T became the symbol of the potential of mass consumption. At a time when luxury cars were selling for over $4,000, Ford dropped the price of the Model T from $950 in 1909 to $360 in 1916 while sales expanded from 12,000 to 577,000 cars; over the same period Ford's market share surged from under a tenth to nearly a half (Hounshell, 1984, p. 224). Ford ushered in an enterprise strategy that was alien to economic theory, for that theory held that the evil of monopoly and monopolistic competition was that it restricted output to hold prices up. Ford, instead, relentlessly expanded output and reduced prices.

But Chandler's description of these developments denies any contingent features to business and industrial organization. If the American economy was to be modernized it had to fit the imperatives of Big Business. While Chandler addresses issues of class, his class analysis is derivative of a deeper efficiency imperative which drove the organization transformation.[8] Whereas Chandler's analysis is institutional, ironically, the Chandlerian perspective has no space for institutional diversity. Instead, the efficiency imperative is imposed by an organizational logic: administrative coordination transcends market coordination because it is more efficient in the marketplace. Chandler's perspective implies a teleological sequence of stages dictated by ever more efficient means of economic coordination.

The competing market control account stresses the emergence of Big Business as a particular response engineered by top management to counter a late nineteenth century profit squeeze between cutthroat competition on the one hand and organized labor's resistance to wage reductions and new production methods on the other. But the market control story does not explain why Big Business took the particular form it took in terms of the organization of work, of hierarchy, or of supplier relations. Furthermore, while Big Business may have been designed to bring market stability to mass production industry, it did not solve the problem of capitalist instability. In fact it created new sources of instability not addressed by Chandler.

The reason is that the high fixed cost structure of mass production alters the dynamics of market adjustment: prices can plummet much further and still exceed variable costs.[9] Scale economies present firms

---

[8] Chandler describes the rise of the managerial class and the decline of owners and financiers that accompanied the spread of the modern business enterprise. He does not draw out implications for the working class and, with it, the strategic limits to Big Business. This matter is examined in chapter 5.

[9] For a diagrammatical illustration see Scherer (1979, pp. 205–8). Naomi Lamoreaux (1985) specifies the conditions under which cutthroat competition is likely to occur.

with the strategic opportunity to drop prices and expand production. The gamble is that profits can be sustained by selling greater volume at lower prices. But the pursuit of greater sales in a static or declining market must reduce the market share of rivals which, in turn, can trigger a price war.

Thus the same production methods that generated increased throughput and market share also altered the self-regulating mechanism of prices in the market and increased the vulnerability of whole sectors to market downturns. The new potentially destructive dynamics were quickly understood by the participants. The guiding idea became to supersede or control markets wherever possible. Vertical integration was but a first step.

As we shall see in the next chapter, the creation of the corporation was only one means of regulating supply and demand. The desire for market control led to institutional innovations in the form of inter-firm cooperation as well. This implies that an understanding of internal business organization is incomplete without accounting for interrelationships between specific forms of inter-firm coordination, or market regulation, and productive organization.

Finally, did the rise of Big Business solve forever the problem of production as implied by the efficiency paradigm? I will argue later that the limitations of the institutional matrix known as Big Business only became apparent with the rise of the New Competition in the mid-twentieth century. American Big Business found itself incapable of responding to competitive strategies of continuous improvement and product quality based upon flexible production methods. The production organization of American Big Business was designed for another purpose: high throughput of standardized products.

Both the Chandlerian organizational evolution and the market control accounts offer something crucial to understanding the organization of the American economy: Chandler offers an unmatched description of the organization and efficiency of Big Business, and the market control perspective gives independent explanatory power to the struggle for stability by business managers and for a higher standard of living by the working class. In short, American Big Business meant both efficiency and the pursuit of market control; neither its accomplishments nor its failings can be explained in terms of one alone.

Postscript on Economies of Time in Economics

The notion of economies of time begins with Adam Smith. Ironically, the first pages of Adam Smith's *The Wealth of Nations* describe the gains in productivity from specialization by price coordination not within the market but by administrative coordination within the firm. From one angle, it is a description that fits the American System in that the source of productivity gain is specialization as opposed to throughput, the hallmark of mass production.

Chandler's visible hand of managerial coordination has a different function from Smith's invisible hand of market coordination. Administrative coordination is not a backup that swings into action because of market imperfections; it is a superior form of organization which enhances economies of time.

But Smith could be interpreted within the throughput paradigm as well. Smith did not ignore time. For Smith one of the three sources of productivity gain ensuing from the division of labor was "the saving of the time which is commonly lost in passing from one species of work to another. . ." (Smith, 1970, p. 112). Ironically, this simple insight goes some distance to making sense of the New Competition described in chapter 5. But Smith's economies of time became defined in economics in terms of specialization and not throughput, for the criterion of competitive success in conventional economic theory is not throughput but allocative efficiency. The timeless dimension of optimal allocation theory makes it blind to both the Chandlerian and the New Competition's sources of time economies.

3
Big Business and Sector Regulation

Between 1850 and America's entry into the First World War, 12 recessions can be identified in which output dropped 10 percent below its long-term trend (Best and Connolly, 1982, pp. 150–1). Employees and owners alike suffered during downturns waiting for the next upswing. Each downturn left in its wake unemployment, bankruptcies, and depressed communities. But upswings always came.

Capitalist reality was consistent with competitive market theory. Imbalances between demand and supply in a market automatically set in motion self-correcting forces. A key assumption for the self-correcting principle to work is rising marginal costs which act as a constraint governing the behavior of firms. For example, a firm facing rising marginal costs has no choice but to respond to a reduction in market prices with a reduction in production levels, a response that counters the original pressure pushing prices downward. In the theoretical model, firms have no strategic options: they are constrained by the competitive structure to engage in stabilizing behavior.

Big Business, however, is inconsistent with the assumptions required by the theoretical model of a spontaneous self-regulating market. Mass production relaxes the constraint of rising marginal costs which, in turn, creates a strategic possibility not open to the firm in the perfect competition model: the mass producer can react to a condition of excess supply by increasing supply. The strategy would be to increase market share and compensate for lower margins with higher volume. The first problem is that increased sales and lower costs would come at the expense of rivals' market share. The second problem is that rivals would not likely sit by while their market share dwindled: they too would turn to a strategy of higher volume and lower prices.

The laws of supply and demand are profoundly altered with the new cost structure and demand conditions. The "law" of supply assumes that each price has a unique output level which is governed by rising costs. But any such unique mapping of cost to supply is denied if costs do not rise with increases in production levels. Under the new conditions firms can make strategic choices that were denied them under the assumption of rising marginal costs and perfect competition. Firms may react to lower prices with lower, the same, or higher production levels: it depends upon their strategic choice which, by definition, will be related to the actual or expected strategies of rival firms.

The inclusion of strategy into the analysis of output decisions renders meaningless the textbook supply curve derived by mapping costs to output and output to price. One far-reaching real world implication is that prices are no longer sufficient to coordinate demand and supply and ensure that markets are self-regulating. The claim is not that Big Business meant market instability; it is that stability cannot be explained in terms of the price adjustment model of conventional theory. A second implication is that an explanation of Big Business and market stability requires an alteration in the most fundamental presumption of conventional economic theory – the presumption that individual action is sufficient to achieve private interest.

Mass producers are confronted with an environment analogous to that characterized by the tragedy of the commons. In the case of the commons, the fear of overgrazing can induce pre-emptive grazing by neighbors. The tragedy is that the mere threat of a free rider will induce free-rider activity. In the case of competition amongst mass producers, the awareness that a rival can respond to unsold goods in the market by expanding supply and dropping prices, may be enough to engender a pre-emptive price drop and lead to a price war. For the follower will be at a double disadvantage: the early bird will enjoy economies from increased market share, and the follower will suffer diseconomies with reduced sales.

The tragedy of the commons and the potential for cutthroat competition both stem from the same logic: a split between private and collective rationality. While it may be privately rational to overgraze or drop prices, it is collectively irrational because of the effects it has on the actions of others. In both cases collective well-being depends upon private responsibility to act in the collective interest and against the immediate private interest. Administered regulation is about establishing rules to guide private action when market competition does not ensure that private and collective rationality converge.

In the last chapter, intra-firm organizational responses to the tendency to overproduction were explored. In this chapter, I argue that the pursuit of stability by Big Business led managers beyond the integration of mass production and mass distribution, standard volume pricing, and product diversification to interfirm modes of organization or sector regulation. The term "regulation" connotes administrative methods of balancing supply and demand in a market; the term "sector" signifies that such administrative methods apply to producers selling a similar product in the same market.[1]

A variety of forms of sector regulation succeeded the emergence of Big Business. One – dominant-firm regulation – occurs when a dominant producer establishes and enforces informal rules which guide the pricing decisions of rivals and thereby governs the adjustment process in a sector. In this case the dominant firm possesses the power to enforce the rules by the threat of financial ruin to violators.

A second means of sector regulation is inter-firm cooperation by means of collective action. Cooperation can be formal as in cartels, or informal as in the establishment of norms amongst firms that share a long-run stake in an industry. The idea behind collective inter-firm action is also to alter the dynamics of market adjustment. Government regulation, in the form of corporate law, antitrust policy, and regulatory agencies, is yet a third form of inter-firm organization to pursue stability in the age of Big Business.

In this chapter, I will examine each of the new forms of regulation associated with mass production. I will then turn to two foreign examples, the case of rationalization cartels in Germany and the persistence of spontaneous market adjustment in the United Kingdom. The German example is presented to introduce the argument that the form of sector regulation reacts back upon the firms within the sector and shapes their development. The British example supports the contention that the decline of Great Britain's industrial leadership is explained, in part, by the continued dominance of either spontaneous market adjustment or price cartels, neither of which was a catalyst for industrial restructuring.

---

[1] A sector, for example, the furniture sector, can be divided into subsectors like kitchen cabinets, upholstery, or living-room furniture. A sector evolves over time as the competitive strategies of firms and the needs of purchasers change: for example, the furniture sector may evolve into what would be better described as an interior design and furnishings sector. Finally, a sector can be considered vertically as well as horizontally, particularly for industrial policy purposes. Here the wooden furniture sector might include makers of metal accessories such as hinges and handles for cabinets. My point is that the definition of any particular sector depends upon the purpose of analysis and the state of its development and that the definition of a sector, like that of a market, must never be considered static, for the purpose of strategic competition is to redraw market and thereby sector boundaries.

Dominant-firm Regulation

Businessmen have forever attempted to control markets. But historically the means of controlling markets were either the exploitation of a natural monopoly or the establishment of barriers to competition. Mass production, combined with the organizational innovations of Big Business, created new possibilities for market-controlling strategies.

The term "dominant-firm regulation" refers to inter-firm coordination, formal or informal, amongst a group of firms that are dominated by a single firm. The actions of the subordinate firms are constrained by the presence in the market of a powerful rival that, in effect, establishes the rules of the game. Enforcement power derives from the capacity of the dominant firm to punish a defiant rival severely without risking ruin itself. Three examples follow.

US Steel and the Control of a Raw Material Market

Carnegie's strategy of competing by driving costs down with permanent technological upgrading was disruptive to both his competitors and their bankers. After Carnegie Steel Works was bought for $420 million by J.P. Morgan and Company, Morgan's goals of "harmony" and "community of interest" were established in the industry.[2] Carnegie Steel Works became part of US Steel.

US Steel, unlike its predecessor, did not pursue the expensive and disruptive strategy of technological leadership; instead it implemented a strategy designed to limit the independence of competitors by the control of iron ore inputs. After a string of investments in firms and land, US Steel owned over 50 percent of the iron ore in the Lake Superior region (Lamoreaux, 1985, p. 147). Another 20 percent was held by other large steel firms and much of the rest was controlled by James Hill, a railroad owner. In 1906, US Steel leased Hill's holdings, hence capturing control of 70 percent of the regional supplies of iron ore.

Naomi Lamoreaux compares the response of the steel firms to the Panic of 1907 with the downturn in 1893. The earlier decline in demand ushered in price wars that left the whole industry bleeding. The Panic of 1907 led to the first of the Gary dinners: periodic meetings of steel industry top executives. The steelmakers learned of the potentially devastating consequences of independent action given their cost structures from experience of the 1893 downturn. In 1907 they jointly limited production and held prices up. But success depended upon an enforcer

---

[2] The sum that Morgan paid Carnegie was equivalent to half of the national savings of the United Kingdom at the time (Best and Humphries, 1986, p. 225).

with the market power of a US Steel. Only then could high profit margins preclude expanded supply.

Judge Gary, the chief executive of US Steel, did what Carnegie's competitors had never been able to do: ensure that technological change was secondary to the protection of profit margins in the *sector as a whole*. US Steel was the vehicle: with Gary in charge the leading firm in the sector pursued a strategy of securing a high rate of return on past investments as opposed to a strategy of permanent innovation. Profit margins were no longer used to push out the frontier of steelmaking production methods. Dividends to stockholders became the priority. In the process the organizational capacity to innovate no longer held a privileged place as in the days of Carnegie. As the strategy of the leading firm shifted so did the organizational characteristics of the firms in the sector. But undermining the organizational capacity to innovate was to render the sector ill equipped to compete with developing sectors elsewhere that organized around strategies of permanent innovation.

Ford and Market Expansion

As noted, Henry Ford had a populist side to his character. The concept of the Ford Motor Company was to produce a universal product that everyone could afford. Ford understood that the transition of the car industry from an upper class to a universal product created a problem of demand.[3] His solution was not to buy up or make deals with competitors, but to expand market size.

Ford's approach to sector regulation was to establish Ford Motor Company as the lowest cost producer and dominate the industry to such an extent that he could ignore competitors. Ford's concern, in the early and mid-1920s, was not rivals but inadequate consumer purchasing power. In this Ford looked beyond sector regulation to macro-economic demand management. His attempted solution was to balance mass production with mass consumption by increasing the income of workers. Ford linked the prosperity of the Ford Motor Company to the prosperity of the nation. But even here he saw a private solution. In Ford's words:

> An unemployed man is an out-of-work customer. He cannot buy. An underpaid man is a customer reduced in purchasing power. He cannot buy. Business depression is caused by weakened purchasing power. Purchasing power is weakened by uncertainty or insufficiency of income. The cure of business depression is through purchasing power, and the source of purchasing power is wages. (Ford, 1926, p. 151)

[3] For an analysis of universal goods see Best (1982, pp. 56–9).

This reasoning was deployed to defend Ford's break with tradition in doubling the prevailing wages. But the $5 day was not enough. The integration of mass production and mass consumption was a problem that Ford, acting alone, could not solve. If he had not known before, Ford found out in 1931 that macro regulation was beyond the power of individual firms, even giants such as the Ford Motor Company. Ford lost $50 million in that year when the River Rouge plant was shut down and 75,000 workers were sent home for an "indefinite vacation" (Hounshell, 1984, p. 296). Without a means of linking wages to productivity in the economy as a whole, a system for balancing mass production and mass consumption did not exist. Ford was adamantly opposed to one institution which later came to play this role, collective bargaining (Piore and Sabel, 1984, pp. 78–82).

The Ford example demonstrates the difficulty of going it alone in an industry in which new entry cannot be controlled. His mass production methods were imitated by others and his production-based concept of standardization was countered by General Motors' mass–class concept which Ford eventually had to imitate. Advertising that promoted the car as a symbol of status and lifestyle undermined the utilitarian appeal of Ford's standard product, and the marketing ideas of a down payment and instalment credit reduced the competitive edge of lowest price (Olney, 1988).

Henry Ford, like the railroad managers before him, did not adjust to the new environment. The Ford Motor Company was quietly rescued by the government during the Second World War. After the war and under the leadership of Henry's grandson, Henry Ford II, the company slipped quietly under the General Motors umbrella. Ironically, it was General Motors that saved the Ford Motor Company. First, General Motors provided an organizational model (described in chapter 2), a price umbrella, and a training ground for automobile managers. Henry Ford II understood this and used it to rebuild his company in the shadow of the new giant of American industry. But a strategic investment program of General Motors, described below, had as much to do with the revival of Ford as anything done within Ford Motor Company.

General Motors and Market Formation

The strategic planning of General Motors was extraordinary, not only in the persistence with which it pursued the concept of mass–class but the width of its gaze which extended to an inter-sectoral orientation. General Motors perceived the automobile sector as one amongst several competing sectors in a continuously evolving pattern of industries, and it acted to influence this evolution to secure a favorable position for automobiles. General Motors' planners perceived less threat from other car companies than from the development of alternative modes of transportation. In this General Motors was partly right and partly wrong. As argued in chapter 5, General Motors did not plan for the New Competition.

General Motors suffered no such myopia to the competitive threats of the 1920s, a critical time in which irreversible choices were being made about the formation of the ground transportation system of the United States. It was clear that the future of the automobile industry was dependent upon the progress of alternative collective consumption modes of ground transportation. For in those years the United States had extensive trolley transit and rail systems which had the potential to meet the needs of a growing urban population. The possibility of American transportation being defined in terms of trains and mass transit was the threat that induced a massive strategic investment by General Motors. The following, based upon the account of Bradford Snell, is the ugly side of General Motors' strategic activities. For obvious reasons it is not described by Alfred Sloan, and General Motors disputes Snell's version. However, it demonstrates a strategy analogous to that which lay behind General Motors' withdrawal from the aircraft industry which is described in chapter 2.[4]

During the mid-1920s General Motors, often in conjunction with Standard Oil of California and Firestone Tire, launched an investment program enabling it first to control and then to dismantle the electric trolley and transit systems of 44 urban areas in 16 states. Often operating through a holding company, National City Lines, the three corporations acquired electric rail systems, uprooted the tracks, and substituted diesel-powered bus systems. After acquisition and conversion, the systems were sold back to local groups, but only with a contractual clause precluding the purchase of new equipment "using any fuel or means of propulsion other than gas" (Snell, 1974, p. 37).

The investments of National City Lines were not made in pursuit of profit in the usual sense of the term. Their purpose was strategic. It was to enlarge the markets for cars, oil, and tires by blocking other modes of transportation, private or public. Once the transit and rail options were precluded by strategic action, the market for ground transportation became defined as a market for cars.

The power of highly organized and strategically oriented firms to shape markets and define consumer options is, like vertical integration,

---

[4] The same example is developed more fully elsewhere (Best, 1982, pp. 56–8).

but one aspect of securing control of supply. But whereas vertical integration limits the opportunities for excluded suppliers of intermediate goods, the actions of National City Lines pre-empted the opportunities for existing and potential suppliers of competing forms of the final product.

Once this irreversible choice was made in favor of cars, General Motors, Ford, and Chrysler could compete amongst themselves for transportation demands in the market. The automobile firms had a superior sector strategy to that of the railroad firms; the leading firm within the sector made strategic investments that led to the definition of transportation needs in terms of a car-based system. The whole automobile sector benefited. The American railroad industry, however, acted passively and without a strategic orientation.

General Motors was not against using the government as a resource to consolidate the position of the automobile industry. Fews firms have been more effective in vying for government dollars. General Motors played a leading role in organizing automobile-related groups including the American Road Builders Association, the American Trucking Association, and the American Petroleum Association, as well as the car companies, to lobby in Congress. In fact, Congress diverted its entire transportation budget to roads between the years 1944 and 1961 (O'Connor, 1973, p. 105). The resulting $156 billion between 1945 and 1970 gave the car companies an enormous advantage over the railroads and other forms of mass transit.

These examples are not exhaustive. They are merely meant to illustrate that strategies for pursuing dominant-firm regulation extend beyond horizontal combination.

Cartel Regulation

In the deflationary 1870s national trade associations were formed in most American industries. Their purpose was to establish rules for production quotas and price-setting to counter the tendency to overproduction and price-cutting. But such rules were notoriously difficult to enforce. The next step, for some, was the formation of cartel-like associations with a formal governance structure. The railroads and the lumber industry provide two examples.

The Eastern Trunk Lines Association

The railroad industry was the first to experience high fixed costs. In 1914 the capital to output (or gross operating revenues) ratio in railroads was nearly 6, compared with roughly unity for manufacturing as a whole (Scherer, 1979, p. 209). Fixed costs were approximately two-thirds of total costs.

Not surprisingly, the early history of the industry was characterized by cycles of price wars followed by informal agreements reverting to price wars. For example, in the early 1870s the two carriers on the New York City to Chicago run, the Pennsylvania and the New York Central, had an arrangement that set prices at $0.56 per hundredweight of grain. But with the entry of the Baltimore and Ohio in 1874 a price war broke out and prices skidded down to $0.20 per hundredweight in 1876, $0.15 in 1877, and $0.075 in 1879 until a new pricing agreement was established (Scherer, 1979, p. 209). But like the previous agreement it was short lived.

Not by coincidence the cost accounting pioneer, Albert Fink, was also a leader in the movement to establish a formal association amongst independent railroads. Fink, a civil engineer who rose to senior vice-president of the Louisville & Nashville Railroad, understood the economies of railroading. For him, the railroads had two choices: consolidation or cooperation. But only cooperation would secure the long-term development of the industry. Formal association, in Fink's words, "makes separate, individual existence of these roads possible, and puts a check on the consolidation of these roads. . .[It] secures all the advantages of consolidation without its disadvantages" (Chandler, 1977, p. 140).

With the collapse of informal pools during the depression of 1873, the railroad men set up formal associations. Fink headed the largest, the Eastern Trunk Lines Association. The annual conventions of the association served as the legislative branch at which rules, procedures, and resolutions were agreed. A central office with a staff served as the executive branch by gathering information, implementing resolutions, and conducting inspections. The weak branch was the judicial. Fink appointed Charles Francis Adams, the successful head of the Massachusetts Board of Railroad Commissioners, as Chairman of the Board of Arbitration (McCraw, 1984, p. 49). It was not enough.

Fink failed to obtain Congressional support for a means of legal redress to violators of association agreements. Without legal sanction, as Fink put it, "the only bond which holds this government together is the intelligence and good faith of the parties composing it" (Chandler, 1977, p. 140). This bond was not enough when challenged by desperate firms attempting to ward off bankruptcy, or by speculators who gained control of railroad companies. By the late 1880s the Eastern Trunk Lines Association was in ruins following a series of price wars. Railroad associations were put out of business formally with the Supreme Court rulings that the Sherman Antitrust Act of 1890 restricted loose combinations.

But the railroads did not give up on government intervention. As we shall see, railroad executives were the leading advocates for the first federal regulatory agency, the Interstate Commerce Commission, established in 1887 (Kolko, 1963, p. 59). Federal commissions were to become a bulwark against both potentially troublesome state commissions and congressional interference.

Fink's fears of the ill effects from consolidation were well founded. The great innovative enterprises of the mid-1800s did not adapt to the changing environment of the times, particularly the coming of the automobile and the truck. Failing to act collectively and strategically, the once proud industry that had been the wellspring of creative organizational ideas and training ground for American business managers went into near terminal decline. In a precarious financial position, the industry was temporarily taken over by the government during the First World War.

Hoover Associationalism and the Lumber Industry

The First World War was a watershed for sector regulation. The war mobilization effort was facilitated by the trade associations which both represented Big Business and shared power with government in establishing production quotas, setting prices, and coordinating investment and modernization programs.

The associations and individuals that had planned and implemented the war effort were not simply disbanded and sent home in the postwar period. Instead, those in the "problem" industries in particular were given a boost under the leadership of Secretary of Commerce Herbert Hoover. In the postwar debates over regulatory reform, Hoover stressed two points: first, economic order demanded administrative regulation; second, industrial self-government was superior to both monopolistic and statist regulation. The concentration of power in either private or public hands could only be checked by creating intermediate institutions between business and government with the purposes of bringing order and promoting the development of the sector. The primary function of government would be to facilitate the organization of these institutions.

Ironically, under Herbert Hoover the US Department of Commerce was developing an industrial policy, in the sense of creating sector-specific policy instruments, at the same time that the Japanese Ministry of Commerce and Industry was beginning its experiments with similar specific industrial policy initiatives.[5] One of Hoover's more ambitious efforts, organizing the lumber industry, has been examined by William Robbins and Ellis Hawley.

Lumber industry activities were a public issue in the 1920s. The lumber companies were caught between users, such as the housing construction and paper industries, complaining about a lack of standards, high prices, and inefficient production methods, and the conservationists, organizing to stop the rapid depletion of America's forests. While mammoth mills such as Mill B of Weyerhaeuser Timber Company built in 1915 in Everett, Washington, were turning out lumber on a mass production scale, the industry remained highly fragmented. Lumber giants were not as successful in using scale to drive down costs and establish market dominance as Carnegie and Ford had been in their industries. While US Steel's strategy of gaining control of the basic raw material was pursued by the large lumber companies, the greater dispersal of resources made it ineffective as a means of controlling entry and stabilizing demand for the large mills. The conditions required for monopolistic regulation were not present.

The industry lacked a means of protecting its own lifeblood, namely the forests. Instead, a "tragedy of the commons" was being acted out as companies cut and burned without regard to rapid deforestation. The tendency was exacerbated in hard times as lumber companies were driven by the threat of bankruptcy to savage the forests and flood the market with lumber. For Hoover the solution was a policy of business cooperation to control cutting and to encourage reforestation. The way to do this was industrial self-government by industry association. An association of producers could establish rules for cutting, set standards, seek exports, stabilize markets, and promote a brand of scientific management which, in this case, included the promotion of conservation.

To create a vehicle for self-government Hoover joined with the leaders of the National Lumber Manufacturers, an industry association. At a conference held under the auspices of the Department of Commerce in May 1922, Hoover unveiled a plan to create a self-government agency, the Central Committee on Lumber Standards, to be overseen by a board composed of representatives from the lumber industry and other constituencies related to the industry including manufacturers, wholesalers, architects, railroads, retailers, and wood users (Hawley, 1981, p. 104). The agency could use Department of Commerce facilities, but would be independent of government officials. Voluntary agreements amongst "industrial statesmen" would enable the industry to collectively

---

[5] Japanese industrial policy is examined in chapter 6.

set standards and regulate supply in response to demand and the need to conserve the resource base. As with the Eastern Trunk Line Association, the agreements were to be monitored by an association-directed staff.

The reforestation and conservation provisions of the Central Committee on Lumber Standards were not deemed adequate by critics, or even by Hoover himself. Hoover reacted by creating two more self-government agencies, the National Committee on Wood Utilization and the National Timber Conservation Board. For Hoover these agencies were "Exhibit A of government by cooperation" and provided an alternative to regulatory agencies run by government officials.

The Great Depression, however, wreaked havoc with Hoover's model of industrial self-government. Lumbermen responded to the market decline as they always had. Cutting and supply increased, standards and prices plummeted, and conservation pleas were ignored. Interestingly, many lumbermen officials drew the lesson from the failure to control production by cooperation and voluntary agreements that only compulsory agreements overseen by a governmental enforcement agency could save the industry from itself (Robbins, 1981, p. 130).

The election of Franklin D. Roosevelt in 1932 presented the lumbermen with such an opportunity. The *American Lumberman* praised an early fireside chat in which the president proposed to cure "sick industries by the excision of certain evils. . . such as overproduction, cutthroat competition and other unfair practices" (Robbins, 1981, p. 131). A Lumber Code Authority was established under the auspices of the National Industrial Recovery Act. Not surprisingly, the National Lumber Manufacturers Association drafted the lumber code, and its provisions were remarkably similar to those of Hoover's private associations with one exception: a federal regulatory authority would compel adherence to the code. Clearly, the trade association had greater potential power over the industry under the statist regulatory regime than under cooperative self-regulating authority vested in Hoover's associational agencies.

In practice, however, the government was no more successful at policing the various articles of the Code of Fair Competition for the Lumber and Timber Products Industries. The articles were openly flouted by numerous small-scale operators who argued publicly that the provisions were unfair. In 1934, officials of the Lumber Code Authority took one such violator to court. William Belcher was accused of violating various provisions of the code, but the Northern District Court of Alabama dismissed the government's indictment. The Court ruled that the National Industrial Recovery Act was unconstitutional because it violated the First Article of the Constitution by granting legislative powers to an administrative agency. The Lumber Code Authority did not, according to the Court decision, have the power to establish laws over the citizens of the nation, such as Mr Belcher. Before the case could be heard in the Supreme Court, an official in the Justice Department, perhaps at President Roosevelt's request, recommended that the Supreme Court dismiss the appeal (Robbins, 1981, p. 142). Thus ended the short history of official cartelization of the lumber industry.

A variety of lessons could be drawn from the failure of cartelization in the lumber industry. It certainly illustrated the difficulties of enforcing inter-firm agreements by either voluntary self-government or by government authority in an industry as fragmented as the lumber industry. Also, it added ammunition to those who held that cartels are simply means of protecting insider large firms against outsider small firms, whatever the rhetoric about serving the public interest. Others saw support for the claim that cartels cannot, by their nature, promote the development of an industry.

Government Regulation

In effect, the American public and Congress accepted the claim that mass production undermined the self-regulating market. Regulatory agencies were set up to influence supply and prices in most sectors that Big Business came to dominate. Examples include the Interstate Commerce Commission for railroads, the Federal Reserve System for banks, the Texas Railway Commission for oil and gas, the Securities and Exchange Commission for securities markets, the Civil Aeronautics Board for airlines, the Department of Agriculture for farms, and the Nuclear Regulatory Commission for nuclear power. Each of these agencies, departments, or commissions became part of a fourth, administrative, branch of government.

But United States government regulatory activity is not limited to the actions of regulatory agencies. These agencies operate within a framework of corporate and antitrust law that shapes the organization and actions of firms. I will look first at regulatory features of corporate law followed by antitrust law and practice, before turning to product- or sector-specific regulatory agencies.

Corporate Law[6]

Corporations were not always able to buy other firms. In fact, before 1886 a corporation could only be established by an Act of Congress,

---

[6] The material in this section draws heavily from Morton Horwitz (1985).

either national or state. This practice harked back to the chartered trading companies that received their right to trade from Royal assignment. As such their privileges and responsibilities were granted by the sovereign and written into their charters. Early corporations, following tradition, were "artificial" entities, or creatures of the state.

However, in 1886 the Supreme Court held in *Santa Clara Co. v. Southern Pacific Railroad* that the corporation was a person under the Fourteenth Amendment of the Constitution and entitled to its protection. The significance of the case was that the Supreme Court moved from an artificial to a natural entity concept of the corporation. For the first time the corporation had "natural" rights which preceded those of the state.

The 1889 New Jersey Incorporation Act was the next step in the break with the artificial entity doctrine: corporations could own shares in other corporations. Thus trusts and holding companies had a legal basis.[7] The upholding of the New Jersey Act by the Supreme Court introduced a further twist: only states were judged to have the power to charter corporations. Given the freedom of a corporation to choose the state in which it was chartered, a corporate charter now meant little more than public registration in the state of either New Jersey or Delaware where the responsibilities of "corporate" citizenship were non-existent.

A third set of interpretations of the Supreme Court opened the floodgates for corporate merger activity. Over a series of decisions the Supreme Court ruled that the corporation, unlike the partnership, was not subject to the unanimity rule (Horwitz, 1985, p. 201). This meant that important corporate actions only required a simple majority vote of stockholders. The American corporation was now streamlined for action. It had become a legal person that could devour and be devoured by other legal persons. In this the American corporation was not only a person but a cannibal.

As noted, the Supreme Court decisions were not intended to centralize economic power; if anything, the concern of the Supreme Court justices

---

[7] The trust was a short-lived organizational form in the history of American business. It originally meant an organization in which all of of the governance rights (as distinct from the ownership rights of purchase and sale, and receipt of profits) of a firm were turned over to one or more trustees. The trustees then held all the voting power of the stocks which they used to hire and fire officers and otherwise manage the firm. A key idea behind the formation of a trust was to centralize the management of a group of firms so that they could operate as one. A holding company, in comparison, did not involve the separation of voting from owning rights; consequently, it did not allow for the same unification of management. A corporation was the next stage, following the trust form, in the separation of ownership and management, in that owners could be completely anonymous as the shares are freely bought and sold in the stock market.

was to decentralize the power of government. But granting the power to charter corporations to the states in tandem with the New Jersey incorporation ruling, meant that a virtual free rein was given to corporate merger activities, including horizontal expansion. Firms could no longer be characterized as passive responders to the market signals of textbook economics; they were active shapers of markets according to corporate strategy. Curbing the new potential for abuse of economic power became the task of antitrust, a topic we turn to next.

Antitrust Law and Practice

The first national antitrust legislation was the Sherman Antitrust Act of 1890, enacted to define illegal business practices. Section I declared illegal "every contract, combination in the form of trust or otherwise, or conspiracy, in restraint of trade or commerce" and Section II declared criminal "every person who shall monopolize, or attempt to monopolize, or combine or conspire with any other person or persons, to monopolize any part of the trade or commerce among the several states, or with foreign nations".

Since Congress did not prescribe how the new law was to be implemented, responsibility for enforcement was taken up by a new antitrust division within the Justice Department. The challenge to the enforcement officials was to establish criteria that made economic sense and were legally enforceable. The Sherman Antitrust Act turned on the criteria for determining "restraint of trade" and "attempt to monopolize", neither of which had clear economic meaning.

The job of the antitrust division was not simplified by a 1911 Supreme Court decision in which Standard Oil and American Tobacco were found guilty of monopolizing "unreasonably". The new "rule of reason" criterion increased the difficulty of prosecuting under the Sherman Antitrust Act: firms had to be guilty of restraint of trade or attempting to monopolize, and of having done so unreasonably.

Not surprisingly, the passage of the Sherman Antitrust Act did not counter the trend to concentration in American business.[8] In 1914 the US Congress tried again to reinvigorate antitrust activities with the passage of the Clayton Act and the Federal Trade Commission Act which called for the establishment of the Federal Trade Commission (FTC) as an independent specialized enforcement agency.

---

[8] One view of the relationship between corporate and antitrust law is stated by Morton Horwitz: "Corporation law and antitrust law are as one" (statement made at a seminar at the University of Massachusetts, March 23, 1987). In this Horwitz means that both, however unintentionally, have promoted the rise of Big Business.

Louis Brandeis was arguably the principal intellectual figure standing behind the Federal Trade Commission Act (McCraw, 1984; Zacharias, 1988). Brandeis' sympathies were toward small business, and he favored the creation of a regulatory commission that would attack Big Business and provide information that would aid small business. It did not work out that way. In the words of the Secretary of Commerce in a letter to the White House, "Instead of striking at the things we mean to hit, it [the bill] does, as a matter of fact, seriously injure the small businessmen whom we are aiming to help" (McCraw, 1984, p. 121).

It was not the intention of either the Congress or the Supreme Court justices to single out loose combinations as illegal and consolidation by merger as legal. Nevertheless, antitrust law has rarely been directed against consolidation. Instead, as concluded by Richard Posner, ". . .a large proportion of the Department's cases – and an even larger proportion of the FTC's – are brought in industries not normally regarded as highly concentrated" (Posner, 1970, p. 410).

The question is: why has antitrust, like corporate law, resulted in consequences which are often the reverse of official intentions? A part of the answer is that the terms "restraint of trade" and "to monopolize" are inherently ambiguous, and efforts to formulate unambiguous criteria for purposes of legal enforcement only bogged down the enforcement agencies in endless legal hassles over definition, with one notable exception.[9] The act of combining to set prices was defined as a restraint of trade. In this case, antitrust officials did not have to demonstrate that trade had been restrained, only that an act to combine prices had occurred. Consequently, the criteria for enforcement became one of legal feasibility: antitrust officials concentrated their energies on activities for which court cases could be won. Ironically, the easiest target of all was organized labor for the crime of fixing wages. In fact, between 1890 and 1929, ten antitrust cases led to imprisonment and in every case the accused was a trade union official (Posner, 1970, p. 391).

The ambiguity with respect to antitrust and monopolization was deepened with the *US Steel* case of 1920, in which the Chief Justice of

---

[9] The key terms in the Sherman Act are "essentially contested concepts" in that both "restraint of trade" and "monopolization" are theory dependent. Limiting price competition in industrial districts, for example, is a means of countering the "bacilli of depression" in Schumpeterian theory and can be done for purposes of increasing the long-run competitiveness of the industrial district relative to foreign rivals (see the example comparing the North London furniture makers with the furniture-making industrial districts of the Third Italy described in chapter 8). Or, what is seen as monopolization by the market control perspective can be the promotion of productive efficiency by the Chandlerian throughput perspective (see chapter 2). The idea of "essentially contested concepts" is developed by Connolly (1974, chapter 1).

the Supreme Court wrote: "The law does not make mere size an offense." Combined with the earlier "rule of reason" cases involving American Tobacco and Standard Oil in 1911, the burden of proof shifted from Big Business to prove they were not in violation, to the antitrust officials to demonstrate both that a company had engaged in an act of monopolization and that the act had harmful effects.

Thomas McCraw has argued that the reason for the gap between intention and practice of antitrust was that anti-Big Business officials like Brandeis did not understand the economics of size: Big Business, he argues, succeeded because it could produce at lower prices than small business (McCraw, 1984, pp. 97–101). If economics had been able to offer a theory of the firm or a conceptual apparatus for analyzing business organization, it might have been possible to define criteria of restraint of trade. But conventional economics was lodged in a static equilibrium framework and lagged behind the rapidly developing organizational revolution. Consequently, Big Business could often claim, without effective rebuttal, that they were acting for reasons of efficiency and not monopolization.

The way out for Brandeis, according to McCraw, would have been to jettison the procedural due process approach to regulation for a disclosure and publicity, or "sunshine", approach which seeks consensus, makes broad policy, and advises in advance rather than prosecutes after the violation (McCraw, 1984, pp. 130–1).[10] McCraw argues that the most successful agencies, including the Securities and Exchange Commission (SEC), pursue the sunshine approach and the least successful regulatory agencies, such as the Interstate Commerce Commission and the FTC, pursue the due process approach.

Instead, Brandeis was instrumental in the formation of the FTC according to a legalistic adversarial philosophy of regulation (McCraw, 1984, pp. 122–5). He actively promoted the enforcement approach to regulation without attention to the difficulty inherent in developing clear-cut criteria for distinguishing the harmful from the beneficial effects of size. This inherent ambiguity was amplified by the constitutional restrictions on the FTC to act as a lawmaker. For any effort by the FTC to develop legally enforceable criteria for defining acts such as "restraint of trade" or "monopolization" always risked constitutional conundrums and either a paralyzed or an unsympathetic judicial branch.

McCraw concludes that antitrust policy became, unintentionally, anti-small business because of the lack of an economic theory of Big Business and a legalistic due process concept of enforcement. Terms such as

[10] The sunshine concept of regulation is developed more fully in the following section.

"restraint of trade" and "monopolization" were both rooted in the paradigm of *allocative* efficiency and the ideal of perfect competition. Consequently, when Big Business could demonstrate that it was the champion of *productive* efficiency it is little wonder that courts did not find it guilty of monopolization which meant, in textbook economics and antitrust law, that such firms were producing fewer goods at higher prices than if they had less market power. Faced with these obstacles in developing operational criteria and the obvious ability of Big Business to "deliver the goods" should we find it surprising that young antitrust officials, themselves trained in law, turned to the cases of price fixing amongst groups of small firms which were easier to convict?

John Kenneth Galbraith offers a different interpretation of why antitrust law has only rarely been applied to Big Business which implies a different concept of antitrust altogether. Galbraith is critical of any analysis of Big Business, such as that of McCraw and Chandler, that does not account for corporate power. Galbraith argues that the unstated purposes of antitrust law is to reinforce the conventional economic doctrine that defends capitalism on the grounds that it denies power to anyone. It gives the impression, desired by the powerful, that market power is challenged by trustbusters when, in fact, antitrust laws are a ". . .cul de sac in which reform can easily be contained" (1973, p. 209). But Galbraith does not stop here: the concept of antitrust is based upon the erroneous presupposition that price competition is the regulating mechanism of industrial capitalism when, in fact, the real regulating mechanism of Big Business is countervailing power.

Galbraith's concept of countervailing power presumes the prior existence of market power exercised by dominant firms or quasi-cartels associated with Big Business. To the extent that Big Business is disciplined, it is disciplined not by other firms selling similar products at lower prices but by countervailing power organized by buyers from or sellers to Big Business. Mass retailing enterprises, farmer selling cooperatives, consumer buying cooperatives (most successful in Scandinavia), and labor unions are Galbraithian examples of countervailing power. Whereas the competition of conventional economic theory originates in the existence of rival firms on the *same side of the market*, countervailing power derives from rivals on the *other side of the market* (1952, chapter 9). Antitrust activity that breaks up organizations of small firms is not simply ironic; it risks undermining countervailing power, the self-generating regulatory mechanism crucial to capitalism.

But there is more to the story of antitrust and regulatory mechanisms. McCraw's critique of Brandeis for lacking an adequate economic analysis can be turned against McCraw as well. For McCraw, following Chandler, accepts the conventional view that price competition is the only regulatory mechanism. The problem begins with Chandler's distinction between center and peripheral sectors. In McCraw's words "[t]hese peripheral firms compete with one another very much in the fashion of Adam Smith's classical model, which remains the model of competition described in economics textbooks" (McCraw, 1984, p. 73). By denying the possibility of alternative regulatory mechanisms, McCraw does not consider the concept of regulation that would have been most consistent with Brandeis's call for government support of small firms, namely the idea of an industrial district as networked groups of small firms engaging in complementary production activities and sharing common services. The inadvertent industrial policy of the Springfield Armory could have served as an example. Admittedly, Brandeis saw potential government services in support of small firms primarily in terms of information; the Springfield Armory engaged in technological transfer and provided collective services including labor education.

In recent times the idea of an industrial district is stretched to account for competitive strategies based upon production flexibility and product innovation. I argue in the chapters on the New Competition that this orientation to regulation has been developed successfully by local governments in post-Second World War Italy and is increasingly being pursued in Japan. These ideas do not deny a role for antitrust, but seek to integrate a concept of antitrust with one of industrial policy.

Regulatory Agencies

American antitrust and corporate law were both conducive to the rise of Big Business, but they did not solve the problem of the potential for cutthroat competition created by high fixed costs. Furthermore, the rise of Big Business itself created a target for populist political campaigns against concentrated economic power which was not disciplined by competition or government.

The concept of the sector-specific regulatory commission was based upon the reality of Big Business and the potential for abuse of concentrated economic power. But whereas the pressure to reduce economic concentration was diffuse and mediated by a political movement, the pressure from Big Business for institutions to promote sector stability was concentrated. Regulatory commissions did not escape this pressure, but lacking an economic theory of regulation neither the architects nor the implementers had concepts by which to channel these pressures. The first federal regulatory commission set the trend.

The Interstate Commerce Commission (ICC) was established by the 1887 Act to Regulate Commerce. The Act was designed to create a public administrative agency to govern the railroads. It forbade cartelization, pooling, and rebating, prescribed that rates be "just and reasonable", and established an administrative agency. Five commissioners were appointed to six-year staggered terms by the President and confirmed by Congress. The commissioners hired a staff to implement their policies. Defining these policies raised a host of unforeseen constitutional problems associated with the ambiguous role of administrative agencies within the American Constitution.

The ICC, like all regulatory agencies, must fit within the constitutional doctrine of separation of powers. Regulatory agencies are part of the executive branch of government in that the comissioners administer laws passed by Congress, but, unlike departments of the executive branch of government, they are not subject to Presidential directive. The regulatory commissioners are appointed by the executive office with the approval of Congress but, once in office, their actions are dictated not by the President but by the charter of the regulatory agency as articulated in the legislation. The legislative charter as well as the rules and practices, both formal and informal, of the regulatory agencies are subject to the test of constitutionality by judicial review. In a sentence, agencies of the executive branch of government cannot pass laws or act as a court of law.

The first problem facing the ICC was a familiar one in the history of antitrust and regulation: the range of its activities was not clearly defined by the framers of the legislation. But a second problem was equally serious: activities that were prescribed, in particular rate fixing, were not based upon sound regulatory principles.

The rate-fixing approach to regulation has never effectively dealt with the ambiguity inherent in establishing "objective" costs. The cost of machinery, for example, can be calculated in historic costs, replacement costs, or market value. But since there is no single definition of "true" capital costs, an opening is created for endless arguments amongst lawyers for and against specific measurements in an arena ill suited to the development of substantive criteria or procedures.

Instead of facing up to the inherent limitations of a rate-setting concept of regulation, Congress identified the problem as a lack of regulatory power which it sought to rectify with the Transportation Act of 1920. This Act "gave the commission power to set minimum railroad rates, to supervise the issuance of railroad securities, to approve the previously forbidden practice of pooling, and to begin comprehensive planning for a systematic national transportation network" (McCraw, 1984, p. 63). Consequently, both railroad and regulatory officials focused on disagreements over costs to the neglect of more important matters including strategic planning and innovation. In fact, sector strategic planning has never been a task of the ICC. It was powerless to stop the unprecedented merger boom amongst railroads that followed the passage of the Sherman Antitrust Act. Likewise the ICC did not question or call to the public's attention the market-reshaping investments of General Motors.[11]

The apparent failures of the ICC have led some to reinterpret the underlying purpose behind its creation. Gabriel Kolko argues that the ICC was created by the railroad companies as a counter-strategy to state commissions which could be dominated by anti-Big Business groups. Railroad executives were stunned when, in a general railroad strike in 1877, local militia called out by the Governor of the State of Pennsylvania to protect the Pennsylvania Railroad yards instead joined forces with the striking workers (Friedman, 1989, p. 14). Kolko quotes a 1885 statement of one railroad executive who warned ". . .all popular forms of government. . .[will] be attended by the growth and development of communistic ideas" (Kolko, 1963, p. 161). To the extent that Kolko is right it was a short-term victory for the railroad executives. The form of regulation that emerged did not equip them to deal with the real challenges facing their industry.

The legalistic–adversarial concept of regulation is not the only one. A relatively successful regulatory commission in the United States, the SEC, is based upon a disclosure-consensual concept of regulation. James Landis, the author of the major securities legislation, was acutely aware of the tendency for prevailing regulatory practices to generate unintended consequences.[12] To escape this tendency, Landis perceived the proper role of the regulatory commission less as an enforcer of rules, and more as a shaper of the definition of the market itself. This calls for a different definition of the tasks of the commissioners and the staff. First, it demands an intimate knowledge of the industry and the people in it. Second, it demands a creative orientation to propose and develop means of self-enforcement.

Landis pursued alliances within the industry amongst groups that shared his views about definitions of what constituted acceptable and unacceptable actions. The primary responsibility of the commissioner was to account for the otherwise unrepresented general public in these

[11] McCraw argues that the ICC sought to promote "fairness" amongst competing modes of transportation: "The commission regulated transportation rates in such a way as to ensure that each industry – rail, highway, or water – received not those portions of the total traffic most appropriate to its routes, but instead a fair share" (McCraw, 1984, p. 64). An industrial policy based upon an extension of such a fairness principle across industries is precisely the opposite of a strategic industrial policy as pursued by the New Competitors (see chapter 6).

[12] My treatment of James Landis and the SEC draws heavily on McCraw (1984).

deliberations. The commissioner might seek to form or reconstitute industry associations to generate a consensus in the industry around these definitions. They could then be used as parameters in the legislation.

One powerful weapon of self-enforcement is disclosure: the Securities Act of 1933 and the Securities Exchange Act of 1934 required that any firm using the new issues market and the stock market disclose financial statements and a range of other pertinent information relevant to investors and whistle-blowers (McCraw, 1984, p. 173). Any firm that failed to supply all such information routinely would forfeit its rights of access to the securities markets.

In other cases Landis created a new market to facilitate self-enforcement. For example, the securities Acts required corporations to provide audited financial statements performed by independent accountants. This freed commission staff members for other activities. Landis counted on the professional ethics of accountants to go some distance to ensuring honesty in disclosures, but professional ethics were reinforced by the threat of the loss of license. The auditing standards established by the SEC required the development of a common accounting language. This task was also the preserve of the professional association of accountants. Without such a language the auditing task would be impossible.

Thus Landis' method was to guide industry officials towards a definition of what actions were acceptable and unacceptable within the "market" and then to find means of enforcing this behavior with a minimum of direct government involvement. Properly designed, the legislation would focus the enforcement energies of the regulatory staff on the intended targets. Secondly, it would establish incentives for self-enforcement. Thirdly, the legislation would define violations in legally enforceable terms. For example, a firm would be penalized for failure to disclose information, auditors' actions would be judged by criteria required for professional licensing, and brokers would be held accountable to association rules.

The SEC is an example of the sunshine approach to regulation which depends upon making information available to the public. Before the SEC disclosure requirements, financial information about corporations was dispersed to investors by investment banks. The securities Acts broke the monopoly control of financial information in order to restore confidence in securities markets, but a side effect was to establish a basis for monitoring the activities of corporations by commission members, or by anyone else for that matter.

Despite its attractiveness, the sunshine approach has rarely been the basis for regulatory activity in the United States. Ironically, it might be more threatening to Big Business than the legalistic–adversarial approach.

For while the SEC has never demanded internal management accounting information such as the benefit–cost analyses used to make decisions about, for example, product safety or environmental impact, the principle of disclosure provides a basis for requiring such information. Furthermore, the sunshine concept creates pressures for the commission to develop independent sources of industry expertise. For without such information and people, the whistle-blower will be unable to assess effectively the substantive content of the information that is provided.

For whatever reasons, the legal–adversarial concept dominated the regulatory activities of the US government until the emergence of the deregulation movement in the 1970s. By this time the interactions between Big Business and the regulatory commissions were often bound up by layers of rules and judicial decisions that could only be understood by specialist lawyers. At a time of stagflation, regulatory agencies were easy prey for attack from both the left and the right. From the right, regulation was seen as a failed liberal experiment that was hobbling American business with governmental restrictive practices. From the left, the regulators were perceived as captured by the corporations they were supposed to be regulating. From the New Competition perspective, a "regulatory miasma" had emerged that was as choking to flexibility in government–enterprise relations as scientific management was to management–worker relations.[13]

Both sides agreed that the legalistic–adversarial approach to regulation had not been resoundingly successful. In fact, both regulation and scientific management had become elements of the social inertia that has limited the response of business enterprises to the challenge of the New Competition. But the deregulation school was successful in two ways: first the attack focused on regulation rather than Taylorism, and second the issue was defined in terms of regulation or deregulation and not in terms of the forms of regulation.

To widen further the scope of the debate, I turn next to a third, corporatist concept of regulation that is distinguished by the purpose of promoting industrial modernization. The case of inter-war German rationalization cartels provides an example.

Rationalization Cartels in Germany

As in America, prices in Germany fell between 1873 and the mid-1890s. But unlike in America, cartels were a legal means of market regulation.

---

[13] The term "regulatory miasma" is from Robert Reich (1987, chapter 18).

Consequently, German mass producers were forming cartels contemporaneously with the merger boom at the turn of the century that created American Big Business. In 1887, only eight of Germany's largest 100 manufacturing and mining firms belonged to cartels; by 1907, 61 out of 100 were cartel members (Kocka, 1980, p. 80). The term "syndicate" referred to cartels with joint marketing agreements, which according to Jurgen Kocka (1980, p. 88) were the most successful such combinations. Kocka (p. 89) estimates that firms that belonged to cartels accounted for roughly 25 percent of German industrial output in 1907, doubling to around 50 percent by 1938.

If the purpose of cartels had been merely to push up profits by controlling prices, they would most likely have been unsuccessful. But German cartels sought more than price control. Often price control was a means to another goal: rationalization of production. According to Robert Brady, the term rationalization, to the Germans, meant a union of two ideas: "universal application of scientific methods and techniques, and cooperative effort in all phases of investigation, production and distribution" (Brady, 1933, p. 6). The application of science to the economy embraced first the organization of production, including plant, equipment, and methods, second synthetic raw material discovery and supply, third technological advance, and fourth economic organization (Brady, 1933, p. 3).[14]

The implications for competition policy of the efficiency and rationalization perspectives are diametrically opposed. Cartels, according to conventional economic theory and American and British antitrust policy, interfere with markets and thereby protect outdated production methods and work practices from the modernizing influence of price competition. Worse still, in the words of a leading economics textbook, the ". . .object [of a cartel] is the monopolistic domination of the market". The result is allocative inefficiency.

Cartels, in German economic thought, are perceived as possible instruments for the promotion of rationalization and economic growth. Robert Liefmann states: "Cartels. . .were in some of the most important German industries actually a principal cause of the rapid economic development which has characterized the last decades" (Liefmann, 1932, p. 87). Liefmann argues that cartels were a means for promoting the

---

[14] In the German language the term for the study of natural sciences does not include a word, such as science, that separates it from the study of humanities. Thus the natural sciences and humanities are translated as *naturwissenschaften* and *geisteswissenschaften* and social science as *sozialwissenschaften*. Science means, in this context, disciplined inquiry and is not conflated with a formalist research methodology (McCloskey, 1985, p. 54).

transition from cottage industry to modern business enterprises: "cartels. . .led above all to the emergence of firms from the shells of the domestic system" (Liefmann, 1932, p. 64).

From this perspective, cartels can provide the financial and managerial breathing space to enable rationalization of production. Here the term rationalization is extended to imply a structural link between the form of competition amongst firms and the organization of production within firms:

> [Rationalization] connects the processes of works reorganization . . . with the industrial combination movement in both its aspects of financial amalgamation and price control. The novelty consists in the combination of the two ideas – re-grouping as a preliminary to re-organization; that is it excludes on the one hand specialization or standardization carried out by the individual firm, and cartel and trust formation alone on the other. (Warriner, 1931, p. 29)

Given the premise that mass production and perfect competition are incompatible, particularly in an economy as small as that of turn of the century Germany, the right of firms to form cartels was not an issue in economic thought. In 1897 the legality of cartels was confirmed by the Reich's highest court (Kocka, 1980, p. 88). The debate was about the role of government oversight. Until the imposition of government controls during the First World War, when certain sectors were forced to form cartels, the government's stance towards cartels was one of passive observation (Michels, 1928, p. 37).

Immediately after the First World War, governance of the economy became a major issue. The ambitious Wissel–Mollendorff program proposed combining all enterprises and industry associations in a "public law corporation", an economic parliament supervised by the ministry of industry. It failed in the Reichstag but was immediately followed by a more active cartel policy (Michels, 1928, p. 37). In 1919, in cooperation with national trade associations, the government established a code of cartel ethics and the Cartel Mediation Board to settle disputes at the sector level which, in turn were organized by private boards. Still the government was not involved in supervision or enforcement and the Cartel Mediation Board had no legal means of enforcing its decisions.

Cartel excesses were blamed, in part, for the inflation that led to the Stresemann government assuming semi-dictatorial powers on October 13, 1923.[15] The Cartel Law of November 2, 1923, was issued by

---

[15] Most accounts attribute the German inflation to other factors. Galbraith, for one, argues that the large overhang of spendable assets combined with a fear of inflation, the large reparations payments, and mismanagement all contributed (1975, pp. 186–95).

government decree without Reichstag enactment (Michels, 1928, p. 43). The Cartel Law strengthened the private boards, not by replacing the personnel with government officials or even vesting the private boards with direct governmental authority, but by converting the Cartel Mediation Board into an official cartel court of final judgement on any disagreements within the private boards.

Cartels, however, were only one form of inter-firm organization created to promote economic rationalization. The Kaiser Wilhelm-Gesellschaft was created by the Reich in 1911 for the purpose of establishing sector-specific scientific laboratories. Laboratories were established in many industries including coal, metallurgy, rubber, metals, textiles, leather, aviation, electrical and hydraulic power, and "psychotechnics" (Brady, 1933, p. 16). Support for the laboratories came from the Reich, state governments, private individuals, and firms.

Cartels and scientific laboratories were key elements in an economic governance structure that judiciously integrated the market and the plan for the purpose of modernizing production. The ideal of a self-regulating economy did not guide governmental economic policymaking. But clearly, rationalization was not the only goal of the government, and the institutions designed to promote rationalization also created an economic governance structure that could be used for other government purposes.

The potential that Germany's industrial structure offered for purposes of top-down state control did not go unnoticed by observers of the German rationalization process. In Brady's 1933 book the potential of the system for political dictatorship is evident:

> Any group capable of developing and carrying through a national economic plan in Germany would find much of the necessary machinery already available for use. The Kaiser Wilhelm Society and the Institute for Business Cycle Research would be able to centralize and coordinate scientific research on a national basis. The German Standards Committee could easily expand its activities to include the elaboration of a complete body of national standards and coded practices. The various committees of the National Board for Economy and Efficiency would shortly be able to supply guiding rules for internal organization of all phases of management in all the various branches of industry and commerce. The National Association of German Industry possesses a machinery which could be readily adapted for the purpose of centralizing policy-forming powers for the major industries. Similar adaptations could be made of existing central organizations in agriculture, retail and wholesale trade, banking and finance, shipping, trucking, and railroad transportation, communication, handicrafts, and other fields. (Brady, 1933, pp. 61–2)

In short, the German industrial structure was propelled by privately directed enterprises which engaged in a variety of private but collective actions, including the creation of active production associations, cartels, and scientific laboratories. Sometimes these actions were purely voluntary, and at other times they were pressed upon unwilling participants. When such organizations were backed by powerful enterprises they had considerable clout in influencing state and banking policies. But the fact that the organizational structure of the economy created a basis for the state to control firms and cartels does not mean that state personnel had either the theoretical understanding of capitalist modernization dynamics or the capability to organize enterprises and inter-firm organizations.

The point is not that cartels lead inevitably to political domination. Cartels were and are commonplace in the Scandinavian countries and Switzerland. Table 2 demonstrates the extent of cartels (defined as an "agreement fixing prices or allocating markets" (Chamberlin, 1933, p. 170) and single-firm monopolies in Sweden. Before and after the Nazi period, European governments have used cartels as an instrument for promoting economic development: ". . .the price-fixing authority turns out to be a general and powerful Rationalization Board" (Brems, 1954, p. 178). In many countries this "rationalization board" function was taken over by the State. Norway, for example, made cartels compulsory in many industries. The reason can be found in Norway's antitrust law of 1926, which stated: ". . .price control is necessary as a permanent element in the industrial organization of the economy' (Brems, 1954, p. 176). Price controls were a means of encouraging "rationalization. . .by allowing efficient firms more profits. . .[and] quality goods if particularly profitable prices are fixed. . .[and saving] superfluous costs if the price authorities refuse to fix the level which covers such costs" (Brems, 1954, p. 176).

Not surprisingly, in post-Second World War Germany the concern was again less about allocative efficiency than about rationalization, including productive modernization and resource mobilization. For Germany, price competition was associated with fragmentation, and the effort of the Allied powers to impose American-type antitrust was perceived by the public as an effort to ". . .harm Germany's competitive position in world markets" (Brems, 1954, p. 148). Freedom in the European context means the "freedom by managers to choose monopoly or competition" (Brems, 1954, p. 155). Cartels were banned in 1945 by the victorious powers, but it comes as little surprise that exceptions and evasion existed. Nevertheless, in the case of Big Business, mergers and vertical integration had reduced the role of cartels (Kocka, 1980, p. 89).

Thus, unlike the British, the continental Europeans sought to make the transition to the principles of mass production and saw market

Table 2 Extent of cartels and monopolies in Swedish industry, 1935

| | Value of total domestic sales (million kroner) | Percentage controlled by | |
		Cartels	Cartels plus single-firm monopolies
Mining, iron, steel, and metal works	279.9	39	41
Iron, steel, and metal products	256.5	24	28
Mechanical shops	462.3	16	26
Electrical industry	117.2	54	72
Instruments, gold, and silver	29.6	3	16
Stone and clay	157.1	55	56
Wooden products	228.9	10	11
Paper, pulp, and graphical industry	289.5	23	24
Food	1,188.1	28	74
Textiles	579.3	9	9
Leather, hair, and rubber industry	192.5	–	–
Chemico-technical	206.7	18	35
Total	3,987.6	23	39[a]

[a]Weighted averages.
Source: cited in Brems, 1954, p. 171.

control as indispensable to this process. It was a model of development that was neither Smithian nor Marxian, but Schumpeterian and mercantilist. It clearly emerged out of a different intellectual and political tradition with respect to the role of the state in the economy. Perhaps the late unification of the German state, in 1871, and its role as the creator of a single national market contributed to a public image of the state as a liberator for economic activities. For the first time, Germans could freely trade across the entire nation. This is in contrast with Britain and America, where public anxieties about excessive state power have been central to democratic struggles over the centuries.

Market Regulation and the Decline of British Industry

Perhaps the drop of Britain's share of world exports of manufactured products from 33 percent in 1899 to 23 percent in 1929 merely reflected a catching up of the newly industrializing countries of the day, mainly the United States and Germany. But the postwar drop from 25 percent in 1950 to under 8 percent in 1984 could not be so easily dismissed (House of Lords, 1985). Over the same period British per capita income had dropped to roughly half that of her major competitors. Why?

Bernard Elbaum and William Lazonick argue that British firms never adequately responded to the organizational innovations that propelled mass production into both the staple industries such as textiles, steel, and shipbuilding, and the new sectors, including cars and electrical products. Instead, firms remained small, vertically specialized, and coordinated by the market at a time when firms in similar industries elsewhere were vertically integrating and introducing managerial hierarchies to achieve economies of time. Thus the industrial organization of Britain, created in an age before mass production, was ill equipped to restructure production according to the new principles. Collectively, British firms were ill equipped to confront the invasion of foreign products and firms based on the new principles of production and organization.

Modern managerial enterprises came late to Britain. The central office, functionally departmentalized organizational form created in the United States to carry through the strategy of vertical integration was never widespread, and the multidivisional organizational form suited to the diversification movement in the United States of the late 1920s and 1930s was not adopted in Britain until the 1960s (Hannah, 1980, p. 60). Imposing a multidivisional form on firms that had already established mass production, as occurred in the United States, was one thing, but imposing it on a holding company structure that had not implemented production rationalization was another. The benefits of divisional decentralization were likely to be lost on organizations that had not been administratively centralized.

Multidivisional firms are not the only institutional rationalization agent; banks too can develop and implement sector rationalization strategies. In Germany, banks led in the promotion of industrial combination and rationalization in key sectors such as mining, machinery, steel, and electrical products. The objects of sector reorganization were, as Riesser put it in 1911, ". . .to get rid of troublesome competition, to combine the successive stages in the process of production, or to diminish the costs of production" (Riesser, 1911, p. 369). In the United

States J.P. Morgan played a key role in converting cutthroat competition into the "harmony" and a "community of interests" of Big Business via mergers that created giant oligopolies such as American Telephone and Telegraph, General Electric Company, International Harvester Company, Mercantile Marine Trust, and US Steel (Winkler, 1930, p. 168; Sinclair, 1981).

Montagu Norman, the head of the Bank of England, unsuccessfully attempted a similar sector rationalization project in the British steel industry in 1931–2. He organized a Bank of England subsidiary, the Bankers Industrial Development Company, to create a source of equity capital to finance the amalgamation of the industry (Tolliday, 1986). It did not work. Historically the British merchant banks had financed governments, trade, and the staple industries including railroads, but were never seriously involved in promoting sector rationalization as in either Germany or the United States (Best and Humphries, 1986).

In the United Kingdom the task of sector restructuring was eventually taken up by the government after the Second World War. A number of staple industries and automobile manufacturing were nationalized. But industrial reorganization in the nationalized sectors was based on the assumption that big was efficient. Production irrationalities would be solved by changing ownership and creating large companies with market power.

Economists in the Keynesian tradition identified Britain's economic problem as a lack of demand that could be solved by fiscal and monetary policies, including exchange rate adjustments and, if required, trade controls. The organization of production was an abandoned topic in academic circles. Within the business world, management and much of the business press blamed labor unions for restrictive practices on the shopfloor. Nowhere was the misorganization of production itself an issue. As long as the problem was defined in terms of the sphere of circulation or distribution institutional rigidity persisted.

Conclusions

The first conclusion to be drawn is that the emergence of mass production altered coordination mechanisms. In chapter 2 we saw that the rise of Big Business meant the integration of mass production and mass distribution. In this chapter we examined the next step: the sectoral regulation of Big Business. Since cartels were outlawed in the United States some combination of mergers, government regulation, price leadership, and tacit collusion was established. The term "regulation" signifies that the coordination of supply and demand in a sector is not by either price or administration alone, but by some combination of the two.

The second conclusion is that the effects of federal government antitrust policies tended to be plagued by unintended consequences. Antitrust, by penalizing loose combinations, gave incentives to merger activity and the consolidation of activities within a single firm. In fact, to the extent that antitrust policy gave incentives to develop vertically integrated enterprises McCraw (1986, p. 41) has argued that US antitrust policy has been an inadvertent but powerful industrial policy.

Corporate law, as well, has been an inadvertent industrial policy, for it shapes the strategic options available to firms and affects the dynamics of sector evolution. America's official public policy toward industry has been preoccupied with the issue of *allocative* efficiency; its inadvertent industrial policy has promoted *productive* efficiency. The official policy signalled to enterprises that either market or hierarchical coordination are legal but that inter-firm cooperation is subject to criminal offense. We can now account for what has been a paradox: namely, that United States antitrust activity was created, in theory, to counter economic concentration but worked, in practice, to promote economic concentration. Public policy towards industry did both: official policy countered Big Business while a second inadvertent policy promoted Big Business.

The third conclusion is that the form of inter-firm coordination affects long-run sector dynamics. In some cases the regulators consciously shaped the accumulation dynamics of the industry; in other cases they did not. In all cases there was a temptation for the regulated and the regulators to establish a cosy relationship. But cosy relationships were not in the best interests of the sector as a whole, for long-term vitality of a sector requires both cooperation and competition. Cooperation alone can remove the cutthroat competition that erodes the financial resources required for the long-term development of the sector; competition alone can ensure the competitive tension required for a large organization to remain innovative and responsive to new challenges and opportunities. We can say that public policy towards industry should administer a paradox (as opposed to establishing an ideal): it should promote both competition and cooperation.

The fourth conclusion is that the concept of regulation in conventional economic discourse is defined in terms of price competition or governmental regulation of industry. This is hardly surprising: both micro-economics and Keynesian theory are largely silent on the internal organization of the business enterprise let alone organized inter-firm relationships. While Galbraith's concept of countervailing power is a step in the right direction, he, like Chandler and McCraw, stops with the large firm: the assumption of passive undifferentiated enterprises spontaneously and anonymously regulated by price in the market re-emerges to explain non-Big Business parts of industry (the market system for Galbraith, the periphery for McCraw). In this both Chandlerian and Galbraithian perspectives overplay the notion of a dual economy and thereby conceal a constitutive feature of the New Competition: consultative inter-firm relations between large and small firms organized into supplier networks. But this is part of a larger critique of both perspectives for treating American Big Business as the single ideal form of business organization. Neither perspective accounts for the limited strategic capabilities of Big Business or the possibilities of other organizational forms. In this, the New Competition came as a surprise to more than the managers of Big Business.

4
Theoretical Perspectives on the Firm

The previous chapters have focused on the historical transition from market to managerial capitalism, and the associated developments in production, consumption, and regulation. By the First World War the visible hand of administrative coordination had replaced the invisible hand of market coordination and new forms of inter-firm regulation had been established in many sectors of American industry. This chapter chronicles the evolution of the theory of the firm that accompanied the transformations in economic organization.

One aim of economic theory is to elucidate the basic forces driving an economy: to explain the relationships amongst these forces and how they relate to the polity and society. A second is to suggest ways of propelling and harnessing such forces for the common good. The capability of business enterprises to innovate and adapt is one such basic force.

Three economic perspectives on the firm are examined: the neoclassical, the Schumpeterian, and the Penrosian. Neoclassical theory does not attempt to explain the rise of mass production, the relations between competitive strategy and business organization, or the dynamics of a capitalist system. A neoclassical and institutional hybrid, the Williamson transaction costs framework, does tackle such issues but, I argue, is limited by remaining wedded to the neoclassical presumption that firms are a consequence of market failure. The Schumpeterian perspective, by abandoning an equilibrium theory of price, propels economic change by incessant innovative thrusts of the entrepreneurial enterprise. But it offers less insight into the organization of production itself. Only the Penrosian perspective suggests conceptual categories for exploring the internal dynamics of enterprise growth, the forces propelling a transition from mass to flexible production, and new forms of regulation.

Equilibrium Theories of the Firm

R.H. Coase wrote the seminal neoclassical article on the theory of the firm. Coase suggested two criteria for judging a theory of the firm: realism (consistency with reality) and tractability; consistency with "two of the most powerful instruments of economic analysis developed by Marshall, the idea of the margin and that of substitution, together giving the idea of substitution at the margin" (Coase, 1937, pp. 331–2). Close attention to the tractability criterion has been a defining feature of efforts to construct an equilibrium theory of the firm. It has been taken for granted that the two tests are compatible. If the arguments of this chapter are right, such a claim is mistaken. We will look first at Marshall followed by Coase and Williamson as leading proponents of the equilibrium approach.

Marshall and the Representative Firm

Alfred Marshall and Leon Walras are both credited with constructing equilibrium theories of price based upon the interaction of supply and demand. But Walras's general equilibrium framework did not include a theory of production. He described a pure exchange economy without any consideration of production. Marshall's partial equilibrium theory was more ambitious: he attempted to integrate a theory of exchange with one of production by exploring the costs of production which lie behind the supply curve.

In Marshall's theory of production, businessmen or "undertakers" set up firms to transform inputs into outputs. But the relation between inputs and outputs is determined by "laws of return" specific to each industry. Diminishing returns means higher costs and an upward-sloping supply curve; increasing returns means decreasing costs and a downward-sloping supply curve. In Marshall's words: "...the part which nature plays in production shows a tendency to diminishing return, the part which man plays shows a tendency to increasing return". And, "[t]he *law of increasing return* may be worded thus: – an increase of labour and capital leads generally to improved organization..." (Marshall, 1920, p. 318). Marshall suggests that the law of increasing returns will dominate in many industries: for example, "...in most of the more delicate branches of manufacturing, where the cost of raw material counts for little, and in most of the modern transport industries the law of increasing return acts almost unopposed" (Marshall, 1920, p. 319).

However, for the purposes of the "statical theory of equilibrium" Marshall assumes that decreasing returns dominate. Furthermore, his

Principles of Economics is about statical equilibrium. At one point Marshall states that a static analysis is merely an introduction to economics:

> The Statical theory of equilibrium is only an introduction to economic studies; and it is barely even an introduction to the study of progress and development of industries which show a tendency to increasing return. (Marshall, 1920, p. 461)

From this statement it would appear that Marshall's elaborate price theory was but a special case to which he did not attribute much real world relevance. But Marshall's attention to industrial organization suggests that he sought to stretch the statical theory, or at least develop concepts for a theory of the firm that would stretch across the static and dynamic divide. Was he successful?

The idea of increasing returns to scale is attractive for explaining the rise of large-scale industry. The difficulty lies in integrating the concept with equilibrium value theory. One approach is to posit increasing returns as a function of technical progress over time. Thus returns diminish in the short run which limits the size of the firm. But such a long-run supply curve is a function of time, whereas the demand curve is a function of output. Consequently, demand and supply cannot be put together on the same graph, or used to explain equilibrium price, as they are not measured in the same units.

Marshall sought a different solution. He posited a biological theory of the firm. After addressing cost advantages of large-scale production Marshall argued that firms, like trees, ". . .gradually lose vitality; and one after another they give place to others, which. . .have on their side the vigour of youth" (Marshall, 1920, p. 316). Even joint stock companies, which can retain the ". . .advantages of division of labour, of specialized skill and machinery" will likely stagnate against the force of "younger and smaller rivals". Inevitably the original founders will be forced to turn over the reins to people with "less energy and creative genius, if not with less active interest in. . .prosperity [of the business]" (Marshall, 1920, p. 316).

But even if the biological theory of the firm is entertained, the "laws" of return put pressure on the assumptions required for Marshall's value theory for reasons pointed out by Piero Sraffa (1926). The problem this time is an asymmetry between demand and supply. While movements along a demand curve will not affect the position of the demand curve, the same cannot be said of movements along either an upward-sloping or a downward-sloping supply curve. A movement along an upward-sloping curve, for example, means that the costs of at least one factor have increased. This implies that the costs of production (and the related supply curves) of other commodities that use the same factor will also increase, inducing a change in the equilibrium prices of other products. These price changes will react back on the demand for the original product. Thus it is impossible to isolate the demand and supply conditions of a single industry without making the assumption that inputs in the supply curve do not figure in the costs of other products. If they do, demand and supply are interdependent, as any movement along the supply curve will shift the position of the demand curve. The common textbook diagram showing demand and supply intersecting to determine price is not meaningful except as a special case of constant returns to scale.

Sraffa suggested two possible escapes. One was to save the theory of price by abandoning Marshall's partial equilibrium for Walras's general equilibrium framework. But for early general equilibrium theory, as with its modern descendant, "the firm is a shadowy figure" (Hahn, 1981, p. 131). The problem once again is the requirement that increasing returns be absent if we are able to derive equilibrium prices. To establish the existence of an equilibrium, theorists assume that all goods, present and future, have perfectly competitive markets and a determinate price.

The second option was to abandon the assumption of perfect competition and assume that firms can set prices within margins. Chamberlin and Robinson initiated a research project that would account for increasing returns within an equilibrium framework, but, again, the results foundered on Marshall's dilemma: the very effort to construct concepts that give substance to a theory of the firm puts pressure on the assumptions required for the theory of price. In this case increasing returns undermine the assumption of perfect competition, and with it an equilibrium price theory, or at least a theory of price that can be explained within the neoclassical conceptual framework. In the words of one modern textbook: "It is a pity that noncompetitive theory is in such a primitive state as regards tested propositions, and this is why the rest of the book is concerned with competitive markets" (Layard and Walters, 1978, p. 255).

The assumption of perfect competition is a means of escape from a conundrum raised first by Cournot's treatment of duopoly in 1838 (Chamberlin, 1933, chapter 3). Cournot's conundrum is that under conditions of imperfect competition, an explanation of price depends upon what rivals assume about competitors' reactions. In the case of duopoly, models have been constructed that generate monopoly prices, competitive prices, determinate and indeterminate prices between monopoly and competitive outcomes, and oscillating prices (Chamberlin, 1933, chapter 3). The absence of perfectly competitive markets creates theoretical difficulties which "will only be resolvable by a managerial theory of production" (Hahn, 1981, p. 134). To date the project of intergrating a theory of either management or production with that of price remains beyond the scope of static theory.

In conclusion, Marshall's effort to integrate a theory of the firm with an equilibrium theory of price was not successful. We turn next to a third effort to escape Marshall's dilemma which is based upon a new concept. Ronald Coase attempted to overcome the problem by explaining the determinants of the size of the firm with Marshall's concept of substitution at the margin.

Coase and Transaction Costs

Coase suggests that the economic activities of individuals in a capitalist economy are coordinated in one of two ways: spontaneously, by the price mechanism in the market, or planned via an authority relationship within the firm. Coase quotes D. H. Robertson's analogy of firms as "islands of conscious power in this ocean of unconscious cooperation like lumps of butter coagulating in a pail of buttermilk" (Coase, 1937, p. 333). Whereas the market spontaneously coordinates self-directed individuals, the firm administratively coordinates both directing and directed individuals. In the words of Coase:

> Outside the firm, price movements direct production, which is co-ordinated through a series of exchange transactions on the market. Within a firm, these market transactions are eliminated and in place of the complicated market structure with exchange transactions is substituted the entrepreneur–co-ordinator, who directs production. (Coase, 1937, p. 333)

The firm, for Coase, is the existence of an "entrepreneur–co-ordinator" who complements Walras's auctioneer in the market as a coordinator of people's activities. The firm makes possible the substitution of an employment contract by which boss-directed individuals produce as yet unspecified products and services. The market mediates a series of contracts among self-directed individuals for delivery and receipt of specific products and services at specific future dates. Thus an individual desiring products in the future has two options: contract for specific products and services in advance in the market, or become an entrepreneur–coordinator and hire labor to provide products and services as and when desired.

The employment contract is unspecified in terms of what the employee will produce. It only specifies that he or she will agree to submit to the employers directives. In Coase's terms, "It is the fact of direction which is the essence of the legal [and economic] concept of 'employer and employee'. . ." (Coase, 1937, p. 350).

In effect, Coase generates a rationale for a firm by relaxing one of the assumptions of general equilibrium theory, namely that a market exists for all goods whether delivered now or in the future. Real world markets may not exist for products or inputs desired in the future because of an epistemic difference between present and future. While the present already exists and current demands and supplies are knowable, the future is inherently unknowable and future demands and supplies are uncertain. Because futures contracts are difficult to specify in unambiguous terms, entrepreneurs substitute employment contracts for product contracts. An employment contract allows greater flexibility in responding to the actual conditions as they emerge. As Coase put it: "It seems improbable that a firm would emerge without the existence of uncertainty" (Coase, 1937, p. 338).

Coase's next task was to explain the dividing line between coordination in the market and in the firm, in a manner consistent with the criteria of realism and tractability. Previously, Coase charged, economists had barely addressed the obvious fact that within a firm the price mechanism is superseded, let alone explained the basis on which the choice between market and planned coordination is made.

Coase's innovation was to explain the proportions of market and firm coordination by measuring the administrative costs of each in the same unit, namely transaction costs. Both modes of economic coordination carry costs of administering a transaction: the costs of discovering relevant prices and of negotiating, implementing, and enforcing a contract in the market, and the managerial costs of organizing transactions in the firm. Firms exist where the cost of conducting a transaction within the firm is less than the cost of conducting the same transaction in the market. Deploying Marshall's concept of substitution at the margin, Coase concluded that equilibrium between the firm and the market existed where the costs of each mode of transaction, firm and market, were equalized. This equilibrium also explained the size of the firm:

> . . .a firm will tend to expand until the costs of organizing an extra transaction within the firm become equal to the costs of carrying out the same transaction by means of an exchange on the open market or the costs of organizing in another firm. (Coase, 1937, p. 341)

Thus, with Coase, the firm was put on equal footing with the market. The firm could no longer be ignored or assumed to be constituted by a bundle of exchange relations directed by household choices. Coase pointed the way ahead by identifying a "special class springing up who direct the activities of others to whom they give guaranteed wages" (Coase, 1937, p. 346). He also distinguished between initiative or enterprise and management, a distinction to which we will return in another context.

But Coase's analysis is very schematic. The transaction costs framework is tautological unless the distinctive costs of market and firm coordination are explained. For example, rather than explaining what limits the size of the firm, Coase states: "Naturally, a point must be reached where the costs of organizing an extra transaction within the firm are equal to the costs involved in carrying out the transaction in the open market. . ." (Coase, 1937, p. 340). Coase adds that because of diminishing returns to management ". . .a point must be reached where the loss through the waste of resources is equal to the marketing costs of the exchange transaction in the open market. . ." (Coase, 1937, p. 340). But without ever spelling out the causes of diminishing returns to management Coase simple asserts: "When we are considering how large a firm will be the principle of marginalism works smoothly. The question always is will it pay to bring an extra exchange transaction under the organizing authority?"

But what if it continued to pay until an industry was monopolized? If so, serious doubts would be raised about the competitive theory of price, including the process of continuous substitution at the margin. We are therefore led back to Cournot's conundrum about the determinancy of price and Marshall's dilemma about the determinancy of the size of the firm. Terms like diminishing returns to management are wheeled in to limit the size of firms without analyzing what they turn on and if they are subject to transcendence by organizational innovations. Hicks, for example, after demonstrating that rising marginal and average costs are conditions of production equilibrium, states that ". . .the only reason why marginal costs should increase is the increasing difficulty of controlling an enterprise, as its scale of production grows" (Hicks, 1939, p. 83).

In summary, we are not home free. By dropping the assumption of perfect information about the future, Coase is able to create a basis for distinguishing between the market and the firm as alternative modes of coordination. Market coordination is no longer synonymous with efficiency; under certain conditions planned coordination within a firm could be more efficient. This is certainly a step ahead in terms of the realism test. But after an encouraging start much is left unsaid and unanalyzed. It appears that Coase, like Marshall, was constrained from developing promising concepts for analysing business organization by the second test, namely the specter of inconsistency with the equilibrium theory of price.

But Coase did open up a new research agenda for economic theory. The introduction of transaction costs meant that organizational form, in this case market or firm, depends upon administrative costs of coordinating economic activities. Principal–agent or agency theory is one such post-Coasian elaboration on the firm which seeks to integrate a theory of the firm with the neoclassical theory of price.

Agency Theory

The Coasian authority relation within the firm is based upon an employment contract in which the performance of the employee can be readily monitored and measured. But under certain circumstances only the employee can judge work effort. An employer may hire a specialist who alone knows if his/her work effort is diligent. Or the interdependent nature of the tasks performed may make monitoring of work effort costly. For example, the performance of an assembler in a manufacturing process may depend upon his/her accounting for the quality of materials and components supplied; once the defective product has been assembled the source of the defect may be too costly to locate.

Under such circumstances of information asymmetry the principal–agent theory holds that "incentive-compatible" payment systems will replace the more costly monitoring systems of rewarding agents. The worker could receive, for example, a bonus for achieving a target level of defect-free products. The employee will then have a pecuniary incentive to check diligently for material or component defects, even though he/she could never be singled out as responsible.

Agency theory, then, explains why organizations exist under circumstances in which performance cannot be efficiently monitored, and it does so in terms that are consistent with individual optimizing behavior. It is a neoclassical theory of organization consistent with neoclassical price theory in that it requires no additional assumptions beyond those required for utility-maximizing behavior. The theory clearly has appeal in terms of explaining how individual employers could create an incentive system in the case of asymmetrical information without escalating monitoring costs. But it also implies that free-rider problems could emerge once the organization included a large number of employees. Agents who are assumed to shirk responsibility unless financially rewarded would look for ways to avoid effort unless the disutility of their effort was rewarded by output effects. In an interdependent production process changes in individual effort are not likely to have sizeable output effects.

Not surprisingly, agency theory runs up against the same problem of externalities within the firm that private contracting does in the market. Just as *homo economicus* will free ride in the case of public goods he/she will seek to avoid effort in the workplace. The result is that agency theory needs space for collective action as a means of achieving allocative efficiency, or even competitive success. To date the theory has not been applied to explain the rise of Big Business and the separation of management from ownership. It is more appropriate to suggesting the pressures towards the decentralization of Big Business of the 1980s. We turn next to another post-Coasian approach which has been deployed to understand the rise of Big Business.

Williamson and Markets versus Hierarchy

Williamson is critical of the conventional conception of the firm in terms of a production function (the positing of a purely technical relation between inputs and outputs) and seeks to replace it with a notion of the firm as a governance structure. He modifies the standard behavioral assumptions by positing opportunism and bounded rationality (limited knowledge) and he relaxes the assumptions of complete knowledge of the future and perfect competition.[1] These behavioral propositions are central to Williamson's rationale for the existence of the firm: "But for the simultaneous existence of both bounded rationality and opportunism, all economic contracting problems are trivial and the study of economic institutions is unimportant" (Williamson, 1981, p. 1545).

Because information is limited and opportunism does exist, the study of economic institutions is important. Williamson focuses on the decision of a firm to make (produce within the firm and administratively coordinate by managerial hierarchy) or to buy (purchase in the market) across a "technologically separable interface". The firm will internalize activities (make as opposed to buy) under conditions of asset specificity and/or demand externality.

Asset specificity means that production requires investment by the maker in specialized equipment that, once in place, cannot be used for producing any other goods. By introducing specialized or dedicated machinery Williamson relaxes the neoclassical assumption of homogeneous inputs that can be purchased and sold in perfectly divisible amounts in the market. Under these conditions, perfect competition reduces to bilateral monopoly once the contract is signed and the product-specific investment has been made. Bilateral monopoly makes the establishment of an equilibrium price problematic. The upshot is that a futures contract may be subject to price haggling; therefore the firm makes, as opposed to buys, in order to avoid becoming either a hostage to an opportunistic seller or bogged down in price negotiations.

Williamson suggests that firms internalize activities for a second reason, namely market coordination under certain circumstances does

---

[1] Opportunism is "self-interest seeking with guile" (Williamson, 1985, p. 30).

not ensure product quality. For example, a manufacturer that sells to a retailer cannot ensure that the retailer will provide the proper service for the manufacturer's product. The manufacturer's reputation with consumers can suffer from actions by the retailer over which the manufacturer has no control. In such cases of "demand externality" the manufacturer's lack of control over distribution will undermine the quality image of the product in the market by activities that cannot easily be precluded by market contract.

The reason for firms, then, is market failure. Firms emerge to counter market imperfections caused by bounded rationality and opportunism. The individual firm is responding to transaction costs of market exchange which surpass those of administrative coordination. The purpose of the corporation is to economize on transaction costs. The model suggests that market contracting is lessened and the size of the firm increases as asset specificity and/or demand externalities increase.

Williamson breaks with the neoclassical theory of price in that he does not attempt to derive a supply curve from costs grounded solely in utility and technical coefficients of production, but he holds to the notions of substitution at the margin and the view that firms owe their existence to imperfect markets. The existence of conglomerates is explained by Williamson in terms of imperfect capital markets.

It is an advance to envisage the firm as a governance structure as opposed to a production function, but Williamson's concept of governance structure is not given much force. The production activities themselves are independent of the governance structure. Governance refers simply to administrative coordination. But Big Business is about more than coordination of, in Williamson's words, "technologically separable entities" (Williamson, 1981, p. 1544); it is also about inter-relations amongst mutually interdependent units. Establishing the principle of flow, scientific management, or line and staff functions, for example, within one department will have reverberations throughout an organization and lead to its reconstitution. A theory of the firm for purposes of understanding industrial policy issues must move beyond considerations of coordination with concepts that allow for links between governance structure and production performance of the type identified by the institutional studies referred to in chapters 2 and 3. Herbert Simon is a starting point.

Simon and the Organizational Economy

Herbert Simon does not explain firms in terms of markets but markets in terms of firms. America has an organizational economy and not a market economy. Most people are employees of organizations and organizations are connected to one another and to consumers by markets. The question, for Simon, is not which is more efficient, but what makes organizations work. To make progress on this question Simon abandons the Coasian authority relation as the defining character of the firm. For an organization to work employees must do more than accept commands from managers: "What is required is that employees take initiative to advance the achievement of the organization's objectives, and apply all their skill and knowledge to make good decisions to that end" (Simon, 1988, pp. 8–9). Why, asks Simon, do employees contribute much more to organizations than could be spelled out in employment contracts?

Simon answers that it is evident that employees take pride in their work and in the quality and success of the organization in which they work. Organizations that are not successful in inculcating an orientation of "we" as well as "I" amongst employees will fail to tap a source of motivation that leads to employees assuming responsibility for results as opposed to simply following the rules spelled out in the employment contract.

Thus, for Simon, an organization is a means of establishing enabling rules as well as rules of authority. Enabling rules encourage individual responsibility so that the gains of collective action can be realized. To take an old example, if the prisoners decide upon a rule in advance, and trust one another to stick to it, the end result is an improvement in outcome for both. Organizations are means of establishing enabling rules that allow people to cooperate. In cases of interdependence of choices market coordination is simply an inferior means of establishing enabling rules.[2]

The idea of enabling rules extends the notion of innovation. Firms that develop new rules that enable cooperative actions are engaging in organizational innovation. Thus the "line and staff" concept enabled staff personnel to specialize with unambiguous lines of authority. The advantage of organizational over market specialization is that it internalizes the positive externalities: each participant can count on the other to follow the rules. Without such rules, the indeterminacy of the actions of others reduces the possibility of specialization in an interdependent system.

Firms, as means of generating net benefits by cooperating rather than contracting individually, do not imply an absence of power relations or solve the problem of motivation. But this analysis does suggest that organizations depend upon some element of community involving

---

[2] For one example of the application of game theory to these issues, see Robert Axelrod (1984).

reciprocity amongst members over time. Without elements of community, the power relations integral to hierarchy will likely be unleashed and, in time, undermine the basis for cooperation upon which the organization depends.

Simon breaks with neoclassical equilibrium theory and opens the door to the study of economic organization. Before considering others, I offer some conclusions on the dominant perspective.

Conclusions on Equilibrium Theories

Marshall, Coase, and Williamson develop concepts for a theory of the firm but within a framework that gives primacy to the equilibrium theory of price and the assumptions required to sustain it. One of these assumptions is that of substitution at the margin; another is the utility theory of human motivation which holds that human economic action can be explained in terms of exogenously determined self-interest.[3] Consequently, potential concepts to explain economic developments such as strategy, production, management, organization, culture, and regulation are suppressed by the Coasian test of tractability to "substitution at the margin". The role of beliefs, purposes, and norms in human action is reduced to the pursuit of interests by individual action. A high price is paid for remaining wedded to theories that seek to explain the firm in terms of imperfect and costly markets. Why has it remained the dominant paradigm within economic theory?

A part of the explanation is that introducing the possibility for ideas to shape action undermines the greatest accomplishment of neoclassical economic theory: an explanation of how atomistic individuals seeking their own self-interest can, by operating within a system of free markets, act in ways that promote the public interest. Harmony is assured by individuals acting only to pursue their self-interest without consideration of the effects of their actions and without cooperation or collective action. The presumed identity between private and collective interests implies that the economy is self-governing, hence providing a rationale for the separation of the sphere of the economy from that of the polity in theory and practice.

The roles of ideas, of notions of cooperation and community, or of

---

[3] Williamson, in particular, does not hold to such a narrow concept of the person. He argues that "capitalism is prone to undervalue dignity and that safeguards can sometimes be forged that help correct the conditions" (Williamson, 1985, p. 271). My point is that while more complex notions of the person can be found in economic discourse, once the effort is made to fit such descriptions into equilibrium price theory, they are reduced to the utility assumption of *homo economicus*.

rule-enabling institutions complicate the claims of allocative efficiency which are so central to neoclassical theory. However, accounting for rule-governed actions or the existence of strategic capacities within the economy extends the possibilities for instability and limits the faith anyone can have in the automatic adjustment mechanisms of the market or the self-governing capacity of the economy. For if the market is itself an object of strategic reconstitution, then issues of the potential abuse of economic power must be addressed. For this reason a theory of production depends upon a complementary theory of regulation of which market coordination is a special case. We turn next to perspectives of the firm which, like that of Simon, break with the equilibrium theory of price and point us toward a more general framework for understanding economic organization.

The Schumpeterian Firm

Joseph Schumpeter responded to Marshall's dilemma in the opposite way to equilibrium economics. Whereas equilibrium economics, in the pursuit of an ideal of permanence, ignores structural change and denies a role for competitive strategy, Schumpeter perceives permanence as stagnation and posits an ideal of perpetual innovation and change. The virtue of the market system, in this view, is not efficiency but innovation. The power of innovation to drive down costs and prices, with or without monopoly, dominates the savings associated with economizing on transaction costs.

Schumpeterian and equilibrium economics would not represent competing paradigms if dynamic analysis rooted in a Schumpeterian theory of the firm could be grafted onto static analysis without violating the assumptions on which the equilibrium theory of price is based. But even if static theory were modified to account for disequilibrium and imperfect competition, it would remain ill equipped to comprehend Schumpeterian competition and the capitalist process. I will illustrate by comparing the two perspectives for a number of issues.

Price Competition versus Creative Destruction

Price competition only captures a thin slice of economic dynamics. In Schumpeter's words:

> . . . in capitalist reality as distinguished from its textbook picture, it is not [price] competition which counts but the competition from the new commodity, the new technology, the new source of supply, the new type of organization (the largest-scale unit of control for instance) – competition

which commands a decisive cost or quality advantage and which strikes not at the margins of the profits and the outputs of the existing firms but at their foundations and their very lives. (Schumpeter, 1942, p. 84)

Because product design, technology, organization, and market structure are subject to disruption they must be targets for strategic action by business enterprises, and they are included within the boundaries of Schumpeter's economic analysis. Here capitalism is not driven by consumers choosing among pre-existing products so as to equate ratios of marginal utilities with parametric price ratios, or by entrepreneur-coordinators choosing between making or buying at the margin, but by the pressures of Creative Destruction: a "... process of industrial mutation . . . that incessantly revolutionizes the economic structure *from within*, incessantly destroying the old one, incessantly creating a new one. This process of Creative Destruction is the essential fact about capitalism. It is what capitalism consists in and what every capitalist concern has got to live in" (Schumpeter, 1942, p. 83, original emphasis). Clearly, Schumpeter's focus on discrete historical jumps is not compatible with substitution at the margin. Marshall's edict is misleading: *natura non facit saltum* (nature makes no leaps) (Marshall, 1961, 9th (Variorum) edn, title page).

Efficiency versus Innovation

Schumpeter's purview is the upheaval and breaks associated with innovation:

> . . . what dominates the picture of capitalist life and is more than anything else responsible for our impression of a prevalence of decreasing cost, causing disequilibria, cutthroat competition and so on, is innovation. (Schumpeter, 1939, p. 91)

Schumpeter defines innovation as the setting up of a new production function. Whereas equilibrium theory is concerned with variations in output as inputs vary, Schumpeter focuses on variations in the form of the function. But he does not restrict the analysis to shifts in a given production function, for this would imply that the product stayed the same, whereas competition over new products, new processes, and new organization are all part of the capitalist process and subject to strategic design.

To locate his notion of innovation in a dynamic context, Schumpeter assumes that innovations entail the construction of New Plant, are often, but not always, embodied in a New Firm, and are associated with the rise to leadership of New Men. Thus the concept of innovation reinforces Schumpeter's image of a capitalism in which new products, firms, and whole industries come to replace older counterparts and are, in turn, subjected to obsolescence themselves by carriers of new ideas. The threat of obsolescence, and not price competition, is what disciplines the capitalist.

The Administrative Coordinator versus the Entrepreneur

Economic theory fails to shed light on the capitalist process because it assumes away the very factors that drive the capitalist system. What is needed is an analysis which focuses on structural change and not equilibrium processes. As Schumpeter put it: "Current economic theory is almost wholly a theory of the administration of a given industrial apparatus. But much more important than the manner in which capitalism administers given industrial structures is the manner in which it creates them" (Schumpeter, 1942, p. 84).

To understand how capitalism creates industrial structures the firm must be perceived as an agent of economic change and the entrepreneur as the source of new ideas. New firms carry new ideas. In the words of Schumpeter:

> Most new firms are founded with an idea and for a definite purpose. The life goes out of them when that idea or purpose has been fulfilled or has become obsolete or even if, without having become obsolete, it has ceased to be new. That is the fundamental reason why firms do not exist forever. (Schumpeter, 1939, p. 94–5)

The entrepreneur is an originator, carrier, and/or implementer of new ideas, and every firm is based upon a particular idea. Thus the entrepreneur is crucial to Schumpeter's perspective, and he examines the organizations within which the entrepreneur acts in terms of whether they facilitate the tapping of entrepreneurial energies or stifle them.

Thus, by focusing attention on the entrepreneur, Schumpeter downplays the administrative coordinator who with the consumer is the *persona dramatis* of equilibrium theory. The entrepreneur is not driven to maximize profits by substituting amongst homogeneous factors of production for a given product, but to revolutionize existing product designs, production processes, and organizational forms. Whereas the assumption of profit maximization presupposes the existing rules of the game, the entrepreneurial assumption presupposes a drive to establish new rules if not new games.

The Ideal of Perfect Competition versus Regulation

Schumpeter makes a radical break with the ideal of perfect competition. In his words, "perfect competition is not only impossible but inferior, and has no title to being set up as a model of ideal efficiency" (Schumpeter, 1942, p. 106).

Perfect competition leaves firms ill equipped to seize opportunities. From a Schumpeterian perspective, timing is crucial. Firms that do not build into their organization the capacity to anticipate change and seize opportunities will lose out to competitors who do, no matter how efficiently they allocate resources within the prechange conditions. The successful firms will be those that set aside resources for research and development, have vigorous planning departments, and enjoy sufficient profit margins to finance such overheads. The firm that is idealized in neoclassical economic theory, however, wastes opportunities because it lacks the profits and scale necessary to finance the overhead expenditures required to anticipate change.

Anticipating change takes resources, and the form of inter-firm competition within a sector affects the resources available to anticipate and promote change organizationally and to create what Schumpeter called "future values". Thus the concept of regulation developed in the last chapter is consistent with Schumpeter's dynamics. While the demise of an individual firm may be simply part of the process of creative destruction, a perfectly competitive industry that allocates efficiently in line with the neoclassical ideal is vulnerable to complete destruction. In Schumpeter's words: ". . . a perfectly competitive industry is much more apt to be routed – and spread the bacilli of depression – under the impact of progress or of external disturbance than is big business" (Schumpeter, 1942, p. 106).

Schumpeter's analysis is also consistent with the concept of a sector as more than a collection of identical firms producing substitute products. Firms in a sector or industrial district can enjoy what are external economies to one another but internal economies to individual firms by specializing in complementary products, processes, activities, or services. While Schumpeter does not examine the relationships between alternative forms of inter-firm coordination and firm strategies, the notion of alternative forms of competition creates the conceptual space for a theory of regulation.

Credit: A Veil versus a Source of Future Value

In neoclassical theory, physical capital is a factor of production which the administrative coordinator employs along with labor to produce goods. Capital can be substituted for labor to produce any given output, and will be as the relative price of labor rises.

For Schumpeter, capital is "that sum of means of payment which is available at any moment for transference to entrepreneurs" (Schumpeter, 1934, p. 122). He adds, "The money market is. . .the headquarters of the capitalist system" (Schumpeter, 1934, p. 126). It is in the money market that economic projects are compared, that development is financed, and the "system of future values first appears" (Schumpeter, 1934, p. 125). Thus for Schumpeter, like Keynes, the money market affects "real" variables such as output and income. But as "the monetary complement of innovation" (Schumpeter, 1939, p. 111), credit creation and its allocation shape not only the level of output but "future values". Bankers, who are in charge of the "headquarters", can either finance innovation, expand output, and shape values or retard the workings of the system. Retardation can be caused by not distinguishing projects that represent innovation from those that seek to preserve the status quo. Schumpeter's bankers can play a strategic role in promoting the competitiveness of a nation's firms or they can passively react to proposals without seeking to generate "future values". Without the provision of credit, "future values" will be endangered.

The Schumpeterian notion of value cannot, as in equilibrium theory, be reduced to the tastes, endowments, and technical coefficients of production. For value is not the equilibrium solution to a system of utility-based demand and supply equations; rather, values represent the creation of new products, processes, and organizations by strategic decisions and investments.

Profit, takes on a new meaning as well. Instead of being a return to a factor, capital, it represents a return to successful innovation. It is also a source of finance for two types of (dynamic) costs: prepaid costs for future products in the form of current investment in innovation, and deferred costs in the form of funds available for implementing innovations in the future. Profits, in short, are costs of staying in business (Drucker, 1980, p. 33), for a firm that does not invest in the future will lose out to those that do.

In the neoclassical theory of production, substitutability between labor and physical capital is assumed. The manager maximizes profit by substituting one for the other until the ratios of marginal products to factor prices are equated for all factors. However, in Schumpeter's firm it is not meaningful to link individual factor productivities to factor prices for the simple reason that factors of production are not substitutable. Schumpeter's manager has to unite employees around the idea or vision of the firm, pursue innovation, and ensure that the capacity of the firm to meet the competitive requirements is met out of current revenues plus credit.

Economic Stability versus Capitalist Disruption

Schumpeter's interactive dynamic between firms and markets is loaded with a contradiction destructive to capitalism itself: Big Business both promotes and expropriates the source of entrepreneurship, the bourgeois class. It does so by ousting small and medium-sized firms in competition and by placing the control of the giants in the hands of hired management. The place of the bourgeoisie is taken by a managerial class and a coupon-clipping rentier class, neither of which embodies the entrepreneurial spirit required to carry through waves of creative destruction. The inevitable outcome of capitalist growth is the destruction of the capitalist system and its replacement by socialism, even though the gravediggers are not the ". . .intellectuals or agitators but the Vanderbilts, Carnegies and Rockefellers" (Schumpeter, 1942, p. 134). The modern corporation ". . .relentlessly narrows the scope of capitalist motivation. . .it will eventually kill its roots" (Schumpeter, 1942, p. 156). The one barrier that is resistant to strategic action by the entrepreneur is that of inadequate motivational resources. "Capitalism loses its ability to secure emotional attachment to the social order. . .the very thing capitalism is constitutionally unable to produce. . ." (Schumpeter, 1942, p. 145).

Thus the collapse of capitalism will come not from a crisis of legitimacy, but from one of motivation:

> Dematerialized, defunctionalized and absentee ownership does not impress and call forth moral allegiance as the vital form of property did. Eventually there will be nobody left who really cares to stand for it – nobody within and nobody without the precincts of the big concerns. (Schumpeter, 1942, p. 142)

The support system for entrepreneurship is further undercut by the erosion of the bourgeois family. In the post-bourgeois family, the standard of consumption replaces that of accumulation and in the process a different *homo economicus* emerges, stripped of capitalist ethics. Schumpeter summarizes the sources of disintegration of the entrepreneurial drive as follows:

> Thus the same economic process that undermines the position of the bourgeoisie by decreasing the importance of the functions of entrepreneurs and capitalists, by breaking up protective strata and institutions, by creating an atmosphere of hostility, also decomposes the motor forces of capitalism from within. (Schumpeter, 1942, p. 161–2)

Schumpeter resolves Marshall's dilemma by constructing a theory of the firm which breaks with equilibrium value theory, but creates an analogous dilemma of his own. His theory of the capitalist process is rooted in the tensions between innovating and stagnating firms, but giving conceptual integrity to the firm puts pressure on the assumptions Schumpeter employs to explain the business cycle. Schumpeter's analysis of the inevitable decline of capitalism is not integrated into his theory of overlapping business cycles. He became trapped between a methodology required to explain the creative act of innovation and one that establishes an underlying logic of permanence. Marshall's permanence was one of equilibrium prices to which the "representative" firms and the whole economic system would ultimately adjust, and Schumpeter's is one of virtually mechanical business cycles that form the parameters constraining entrepreneurial actions.

Schumpeter's analysis is undeniably rich in sociology and historical dynamics. Furthermore, his emphasis on innovation and accumulation transformed the theoretical role of the firm from that of profit maximizer within given constraints to one of strategic agent seeking to overcome constraints. He also provides a critique of the ideal of market coordination thereby creating space for a more general theory of regulation. But Schumpeter is also schematic. The focus on big bang events and sudden unexpected dislocations is a welcome antidote to substitution at the margin. However, is his prognosis of the inevitability of the decline of capitalism consistent with a perspective that gives effectivity to entrepreneurial or strategic action? Is there not a role for institutional as well as technical innovation by entrepreneurial activity? And cannot entrepreneurial activity be pursued by managerial or other collective agencies? Schumpeter's analysis of innovation would suggest yes; his analysis of business cycles and his prognoses about the capitalist enterprise would suggest no. Schumpeter might have elaborated a theory of capitalist dynamics that juxtaposes such contradictory tendencies, but he did not.

The Schumpeterian perspective is much more promising than the equilibrium perspective for understanding the reasons for the decline in competitiveness of American business enterprises. The firm is given conceptual integrity, business strategy is given effect, technology is organizationally embodied, and a basis exists for assessing the potential for industrial policy. To carry out such an assessment we must escape the confines of mechanical and biological metaphors, and treat the individual, the firm, and their environment as inherently paradoxical and contradictory. Schumpeter's focus on innovation has certainly pointed us in the right direction.

In the next section we descend from these Schumpeterian peaks, useful as they have been for viewing the grand historical contours, to focus on the minutiae of firms engaged in mundane competition. We take leave of the great theorist wrestling with the issues of the inevitability or not of socialism. If the trip to the top of the mountain was successful in shifting our attention from substitution at the margin to structural shifts, it was a trip well worth taking.

Penrose and Internal Growth Dynamics

Penrose shares with Schumpeter the opposite reaction to Marshall's dilemma to that of the equilibrium theorists. By defining the problem not as one of allocative efficiency but in terms of the causes of, and limits to, growth of the firm, she makes a small but far-reaching move. She sidesteps entirely the plan versus market dichotomy which has played a double role in economics: it fuelled the socialism versus capitalism debate over whether planning or market systems were more efficient, and it explained the boundary between administrative and market coordination in neoclassical economic theory. Both of these issues are static; Penrose moves directly into dynamics. I start with her definition of the firm and then draw a series of distinctions that will be used in ensuing chapters to explain the New Competition.

The Firm as an Administrative Unit with Boundaries

Penrose's theory of the growth of the firm is based upon two assumptions: everything cannot happen at once, and a person cannot do everything alone. She then defines the firm as an administrative unit with boundaries. The assumptions give weight to the concept of administrative unit and boundary. An administrative unit implies teamwork amongst individuals, and teamwork takes time to establish. Thus the boundaries can only be extended with time. Managers cannot hire other managers or workers in the market who possess experience in the firm. Firms, then, are limited in growth by the boundaries of teamwork. A holding company or a trust, for example, can acquire other companies, but by Penrose's definition the firm has not grown. In the terms of chapters 2 and 3, Big Business is different from a holding company or a trust in the same way. Penrose goes on to enrich her theory in a number of important ways.

Productive Resources and the Services of Resources

Penrose distinguishes resources from the services of those resources, ". . .it is never *resources* themselves that are the 'inputs' in the production process, but only the *services* that the resources can render" (Penrose, 1959, p. 25, emphasis in original). Resources can be defined independently of their use while services cannot be. The term "service" implies a specific joint activity or purpose. In Penrose's words:

> The services yielded by resources are a function of the way in which they are used – exactly the same resource when used for different purposes or in different ways and in combination with different types or amounts of other resources provides a different service or set of services. (Penrose, 1959, p. 25)

This service–resource distinction is reminiscent of the use value–exchange value distinction of classical political economy and the labor–labor power distinction of Marx. The labor–labor power distinction defines profits in terms of the difference between the use value of labor as an activity to the capitalist and the exchange value of labor power (the cost of reproducing labor equated to the wage by competitive markets).

Penrose's distinction, however, is different in crucial ways. The distinction does not, like the labor–labor power distinction, imply that the source of value can be reduced to a single factor of production. For Penrose the collectivity has an independent effect:

> . . .when men have become used to working in a particular firm or with a particular group of other men, they become individually and as a group more valuable to the firm in that the services they can render are enhanced by their knowledge of their fellow-workers, of the methods of the firm, and of the best way of doing things in the particular circumstances in which they are working. (Penrose, 1959, p. 52)

Thus the firm is more than a collection of resources. Instead, Penrose makes interpersonal relations, what others might call culture, an independent explanatory variable. The "optimal" combination of resources cannot be deduced from "market" prices. Furthermore, the productivity of resources depends, in part, on each firm's specific culture. Consequently, the neoclassical notion of a marginal product to a single factor, independent of use, makes no sense. The marginal product to a factor is firm specific; it is affected by the unique combination of services within the firm in which it is employed.

Not surprisingly, Penrose's conceptualization of the firm leads to a divergence between the value of a productive service and its price and, in turn, a different interpretation of the virtue of markets. The market determines the price (the outside value) of a productive resource, i.e. the amount that a firm has to pay to hire a productive resource. But this price is not a measure of the (inside) value of the service to the firm. The value (inside price) of a productive service is unique to each firm; value is not equalized across firms by competition in the "market". Furthermore the market price is not a measure of the value of the resource to society if employed elsewhere. Thus the market price is not a measure of the opportunity forgone by employing the resource in one activity as compared with another.

This is a serious problem for neoclassical economics. It undermines the theoretical claim that a free-market system spontaneously creates an efficient allocation of resources. Allocative efficiency theorems depend upon resource prices indicating the value of resource employment elsewhere – the opportunities forgone. It is apparent why neoclassical economists have been so determined to define the firm in terms that are consistent with equilibrium price theory. The point is not that dynamic theories of the firm have superior criteria for settling issues with regard to allocative efficiency; they cannot. It is that introducing the firm undermines the presumption that market prices contain all the information required for a criterion of allocative efficiency. Prices are but one imperfect indicator of allocative efficiency.[4]

Objective and Experiential Knowledge

Penrose, like Veblen, distinguishes between two different types of knowledge, objective and experiential. Objective knowledge is independent of particular individuals or groups and can be transmitted by book, blueprint, or statement to everyone on equal terms. Experience, however, cannot be so transmitted: "it produces a change – frequently a subtle change – in individuals and cannot be separated from them" (Penrose, 1959, p. 53). Experiential, practical, or "tacit" knowledge may be embedded in habit, skills, routine, practices, or "teamwork" (Polanyi, 1967).

A firm, as already stressed, is more than a collection of individuals: "it is a collection of individuals who have had experience in working together, for only in this way can 'teamwork' be developed" (Penrose, 1959, p. 46). But experience includes more. In Penrose's words:

> Experience. . .develops an increasing knowledge of the possibilities for action and the ways in which action can be taken by. . .the firm. This increase in knowledge not only causes the productive opportunity of a firm to change . . .but also contributes to the 'uniqueness' of the opportunity of each individual firm. (Penrose, 1959, p. 53)

Experience, as distinct from objective knowledge, limits the capacity

---

[4] The theory of the second best holds that if the optimality rules are violated anywhere, then the welfare effects of reallocating resources elsewhere according to the optimality rules are ambiguous. The point being made in the text is different. There the argument is that the mapping of prices to benefits is ambiguous; the use of the resource in different employments generates different benefits to the consumer depending upon how it is used.

of management to plan in ways that are taken for granted in both the Coasian theory of the firm and scientific management. Experiential knowledge cannot be shifted from the worker to the manager and returned in the form of instructions (see Hodgson, 1988). The failure to account for, or to tap, experiential knowledge in production has left managers dumbfounded as to why their firms underperform. It has not been ignored by firms that make up the New Competition, as we shall see in the next chapter.

Penrose's notion of experiential knowledge yields a different interpretation of planning in the firm: "Extensive planning requires the cooperation of many individuals, and this requires knowlege of each other" (Penrose, 1959, p. 47). Planning is not simply an alternative to the market with regard to coordination of otherwise identical resources, with the purpose of reducing transactions costs. For Penrose, planning involves cooperation, which takes time and affects the particular pattern of productive services. As noted above, managers cannot purchase in the market the labor time of individuals with experience in the firm.

Economies of Size and Economies of Expansion

Penrose identifies various endogenous pressures for growth of the firm. One stems from the fact that firms produce products *and* knowledge. In Penrose's words, "the very process of operation and of expansion are intimately associated with a process by which knowledge is increased" (Penrose, 1959, p. 56). And knowledge increases the productive capacity of a firm. In Penrose's words, ". . .the process by which experience is gained is properly treated as a process creating new productive services available to the firm" (Penrose, 1959, p. 48). Hence Penrose's theory is a learning theory of the firm.

Second, new managerial services are continuously being created in the process of growth. Growth means that managerial resources are being used to develop new systems. But each time a new system is in place and procedures become routinized, idle managerial resources appear. Unless the firm is to underemploy such resources, managers must seek new applications for them. Thus managers are under internal pressures to seek new avenues for growth and innovation.

The growth rate of the firm is limited in the short run by the management services either available or absorbable into the existing organization. But Penrose does not pose limits to the ultimate size of the firm. In her words:

> It is this capacity of the firm to alter its administrative structure in such a way that non-routine managerial decisions requiring real judgement can be made by large numbers of different people within the firm without

destroying the firm's essential unity, that makes it so difficult to say with confidence that there is a point where a firm is too big or too complex to be efficiently managed. (Penrose, 1959, p. 18)

But the fact that a limit to the size of the firm cannot be stated does not imply that larger firms are more efficient than their smaller counterparts. Larger firms enjoy economies of expansion which are to be distinguished from economies of size: "The great prestige of the large firm rests on its ability to explore, to experiment, and to innovate; it is this ability, together with the market position. . .which give rise to many of its economies of expansion" (Penrose, 1959, p. 262). But economies of expansion do not translate into economies of size. Once the expansion has occurred the larger firm has no necessary economies of size and the new plants can often be spun off without loss of efficiency. For example, a firm that builds a highly qualified process engineering staff will enjoy lower costs in setting up new production processes but once the production is routinized its cost advantage will disappear.

In fact the economies of expansion and economies of size may be in contradiction if expansion undermines a firms "basic position" based upon its unique combination of productive resources:

> In the long run the profitability, survival, and growth of a firm does not depend so much on the efficiency with which it is able to organize the production of even a widely diversified range of products as it does on the ability of the firm to establish one or more wide and relatively impregnable "bases" from which it can adapt and extend its operations in an uncertain, changing and competitive world. It is not the scale of production nor even, within limits, the size of the firm, that are the important considerations, but rather the nature of the basic position that it is able to establish for itself. (Penrose, 1959, p. 137)

The necessity of maintaining "impregnable bases" or "defenses in depth" implies that firms will be forced to specialize; consequently opportunities will open up in the "interstices" for smaller firms. Thus, for Penrose, interstices emerge because the rate of growth of any firm is limited and no firm can take advantage of all profitable opportunities for expansion (Penrose, 1959, p. 222). When opportunities for expansion increase faster than they can be seized by large firms, interstices develop which can be filled by small firms, some of which will eventually become large firms themselves.

Interstices, by creating growth opportunities for medium-sized firms, limit the degree of industrial concentration and lead Penrose to conclude ". . .in a steadily growing economy. . .the process of concentration will come to an end and eventually reverse itself" (Penrose, 1959, p. 258).

Competition: the God and the Devil

The "new competition" of the 1950s referred to competition among large firms, a competition that often took the form of new products, processes, and organizational forms and not competition over price. Penrose joins Schumpeter and John Kenneth Galbraith in arguing that a capitalism composed of small firms would be slow to innovate (Galbraith, 1952, p. 88).

The reason is that only large firms controlled markets, and market control was necessary for the innovators to be able to recoup their costs. Without market control, free-riders could imitate the innovation and sell it without accounting for development expenses. In Penrose's words, ". . .the control of output, the control of markets, and the control of price must remain in the hands of those who bear between them the 'development cost' required for constantly increasing output and continuously improving products" (Penrose, 1959, p. 233). The problem with small firms is that they do not control markets but are controlled by them. At the same time, if the "new competition" restricted the entry of new competitors, the interstices would become a barrier to growth. This is because, as noted, the large firms cannot pursue all of the opportunities for growth.

Thus, whereas Schumpeter anticipated an industrial organization dominated by fewer but larger firms, and Marshall one of homostasis in which average firm size remained constant like trees in a forest, Penrose's analysis implies a variety of possibilities. For her the actual composition of large relative to small firms is not biologically or technologically determined. This is because, in her closing expression, "competition is at once the god and the devil" (Penrose, 1959, p. 265).

The basic dilemma, she writes, is that

> Competition is the essence of the struggle among the large firms that induces and almost forces the extensive research and innovation in which they engage and provides the justification for the whole system; at the same time the large firms expect reward for their efforts, but this expectation is held precisely because competition can be restrained. (Penrose, 1959, p. 264)

The point is not that large firms are good or bad for the economy. It depends on the circumstances and the actions of firms. The problem is that because large firms require sufficient control over prices to generate an overhead for financing product innovation, that very same power can be used to erect barriers to entry and thereby blunt the competition required to spur innovation. It also implies that regulatory or industrial policy cannot be based on simple rules about optimal firm size.

Inter-firm Cooperation: Neither Plan nor Market

The Penrosian enterprise depends upon developing a distinctive capability in one or more activities. Richardson (1972) makes the distinction between similar activities that utilize the same capability and complementary activities that utilize unrelated capabilities. In so doing he extends Penrose's theory of the firm to give conceptual underpinning to inter-firm cooperation as an alternative to either extra-firm (market) or intra-firm (hierarchical) coordination.

The similarity or complementarity distinction allows a reconceptualization of the boundaries of the firm and of the notion of a sector. Neoclassical theory draws the boundary of the firm by comparing the transactions costs of market and administrative coordination. Price competition in the market would select those firms with the optimum internalization.

The Richardson vision, however, suggests that firms will internalize similar activities and externalize complementary activities. To benefit mutually from specializing in complementary activities the firms must develop collaborative relationships with producers of complementary components. Collaboration creates channels for consultation on investment plans and the shaping of designs, new products, and processes across functional specialties without a corporate hierarchy.

An analysis of comparative transactions costs misses the point, because the comparison is between different products and production organizations. The choice for a firm is not simply whether to make or buy, but whether to make, buy, or collaborate. Collaboration depends upon the establishment and nurturing of inter-firm consultative institutions.

For example, a metalworking job shop will require general tools and skilled craftspeople capable of creating prototypes for a diverse range of customers. To maintain a distinctive competence such firms will continuously update skills and machines that enhance prototyping and small-batch capabilities. Organizational flexibility can be enhanced by developing workers' capacities to operate, maintain, set up, and modify a variety of metalworking machines, to be aware of the capabilities and limits of the whole production system, and be able to anticipate opportunities. Firms that periodically require prototyping facilities will be better placed by maintaining a collaborative relationship with, rather than owning, such a job shop. The reason is that a specialist shop will have machines and capabilities developed in the supply to a variety of customers that an in-house shop could not possess.

The Richardson distinction between similar and complementary activities substantiates an image of a sector as a networked association of producers of complementary products. Sectors in which firms specialize by activity will have a different dynamic from sectors composed of identical firms engaging in the same activities. The first requires collaboration and information flows across firms; the second fits the formal plan–market dichotomy of economic theory in which firms are linked by markets.

This has implications for the regional rise and fall of industrial sectors or regionally based sectors. For competition within a sector does not ensure that inter-firm specialization will emerge and, in fact, market competition can thwart the emergence of specialization according to activity. The reason is that a single firm that specializes by activity is dependent upon firms specializing in complementary activities. If complementary products are not available or are only available from firms that seek to exploit short-run market advantages, then the firm will likely fail in the market.

A sector in which firms are coordinated by the market alone can persist even though firms have not specialized by activity as long as the sector is insulated from competition. But market-coordinated districts will come under competitive pressure from collaboratively coordinated districts once the barriers to trade are relaxed. It follows that a specific industrial district can be outcompeted in the international marketplace, even though individual firms within it have organized themselves according to minimum transactions costs.

Thus business and sector organization is not determined by technology or transactions costs but negotiated within a context of competing and collaborating firms. The following two chapters provide illustrations that coordination and coherence across activities can be by market, by inter-firm institutions within a sector, or by inter-departmental hierarchy within an enterprise. In this vision, sectors and the firms that constitute them are shaped, in part, by the specific forms of inter-firm collaboration that are developed.

Conclusions and Critique

The Omission of Organization in Economic Theory

The import of Penrose's substitution of hetergeneous and firm specific services for homogeneous inputs is a denial of the complete market assumption even in theory. For Penrose all goods and services do not have a price and cannot be bought or sold in the market. Their value to an organization depends upon experience and teamwork within the organization. This modification has far-reaching effects. The function of management is not as a functional equivalent to the invisible hand for coordination.

For Schumpeter and Penrose, management shapes a company's vision, organization, and culture, anticipates change, designs competitive strategies, and searches for opportunities in a future for which no crystal ball or probability functions exist. With the inclusion of management as an explanatory variable the grip of static equilibrium theory gives way to that of the dynamics of adjustment to environmental change, and the notion of profits as a return on capital is replaced by profit as, on the one hand, a quasi-rent received for superior organizational capability and, on the other, a financial resource for innovation, investment, and organizational development.

Perhaps the largest casualty of the abandonment of equilibrium theory is the normative appeal of formal models of allocative efficiency regulated by the "invisible hand". The fact remains that every society does choose how to allocate its resources and that every choice involves social opportunity costs; what is lost is the presumption that such choices can be made spontaneously, impersonally, and efficiently in the "market". But by abandonment we gain understanding of capitalist processes. The Schumpeterian and Penrosian firms are more illuminating with respect to the transition to managerial capitalism than the shadowy firm of equilibrium economics. No theory can fully explain a Colonel Metcalf, an Andrew Carnegie, a Frederick Taylor, or a Henry Ford, but theory can account for the application of new organizational ideas that altered the dynamics of the capitalist production processes. The point is not that the history of industrial capitalism would have been profoundly different without them, but that they represented new methods of conducting business which shaped the organization of industry.

The Omission of Labor in Management Theory

We have come a long way from the plan or market dichotomy of neoclassical economic theory. Schumpeter extends the notion of competition from price to product, process, and organization. Penrose gives us concepts for understanding the uniqueness of every firm and the crucial role of teamwork and cooperation.

But the organizational innovators and the theorists of business innovation share a lacuna which is crucial to understanding the limits of American Big Business and the success of the New Competition. The lacuna is a hidden assumption that the motivations, development, and activities of managers and workers are conceptually different and not subject to the same analysis. Just as the virtues of decentralization for Thomson and Sloan stopped at the level of divisional management, the importance of teamwork and knowledge creation to the organization of non-managerial work is ignored by Chandler and Penrose. In America and Britain the void has been sustained by scientific management both in practice and in theory. The new competitors, in contrast, have transcended the void by redefining the relations between management and worker so that both are subject to the same conceptual analysis.

The result is a learning-firm paradigm with distinct organizational variants. The learning firm is examined within the context of the Japanese production system in chapter 5. In chapters 7 and 8 the learning firm is explored within the institutional framework of the Third Italy. Both versions of flexible production share a critical element that distinguishes them from the archetypal American Big Business: the integration of thinking and doing within the labor process itself. This integration of thinking and doing has a crucial implication for managerial hierarchy and power relations within the firm. Thinking and planning *by* workers requires horizontal information flows across functional boundaries; thinking by management and the planning *of* worker activities by management requires vertical information flows coordinated by middle management. Thus relations of teamwork are superimposed on relations of hierarchy. But teamwork demands relations of trust between managers and workers that are antithetical to the top-down power relations between manager and worker that are built into the scientific management paradigm.

In short, the integration of planning and doing facilitates the absorption and development of innovation; the failure to integrate planning and doing is what freezes the mass production plant. The new competitors have exploited this rigidity.

Part II

The New Competition

5

The Entrepreneurial
Firm in Japan

Introduction: Schumpeterian Competition and the Penrosian Firm as Engines of Growth

The contrast between prewar and postwar Japanese national development strategies is striking, in both content and results. Before the war the Japanese did not seek economic advancement by competitive superiority of business enterprises in the international marketplace but by imperialist domination. The imperialist strategy left a humiliated nation occupied by the American Army. The competitive enterprise strategy drove a fiftyfold expansion in the Japanese economy between 1946 and 1976.

The success of the postwar economic strategy is remarkable given the paucity of internationally competitive prewar Japanese firms. In contrast, postwar Germany could build on business organizations and human resources that had produced world leaders in dynamic sectors such as chemicals, electrical products, and machine tools. Whereas German products had long been at the top of the quality spectrum, Japanese products were at the bottom.

An explanation of postwar Japanese economic growth has lagged behind the reality. Top managers and the consultants of Western business enterprises, in particular, have been forced to seek an understanding of why Japanese business enterprises are so effective in the marketplace. For while outdated economic theories live on, outdated business enterprises do not.

The response came too late for whole sectors including motorcycles, consumer electrical products, and steel. Why did it take Western business managers and economists so long to address the issue? One reason is that they lacked categories to explain it. But a second is that even where telling explanations were available they were ignored because they did not offer solutions amenable to existing management instruments of either the firm or the government. In these cases an effective response demanded that managers abandon organizational principles that had earlier made them successful and restructure business enterprises according to entirely different production concepts.

In this chapter the economic success of Japan will be explained in terms of the emergence of business enterprises capable of competing on new grounds. Building on the last chapter, three interrelated dimensions of the Japanese business enterprise will be examined: strategy, culture, and productive organization. In the second section I elaborate on the concept of strategy as a means of institutionalizing Schumpeterian organizational innovation. Four postwar general strategies are discerned, each of which guided an organizational transformation. In the third section the Penrosian notion of teamwork as a means of developing distinctive productive services is discussed in terms of the idea of a learning culture. Each firm has a distinctive culture (or firmality, if such a word existed) like each person has a personality. The development of a learning culture aims to implant the idea of continuous improvement throughout the organization. A learning culture means that everyone is capable of contributing to organizational development. In the fourth section I examine a series of innovative production concepts that illustrate the learning capacity of leading Japanese firms.

The main theme is that the successful Japanese firm has combined Schumpeter and Penrose, and thereby altered the notion of entrepreneurship from "big ideas by individuals" to a social process of learning within which individual contributions can come from the bottom up, as well as from specialist staff. In the final section, I relate the origins of the Japanese entrepreneurial firm to the institutional resolution of deep political conflicts (and national humiliation) by wartime defeat, and the specific resolution of immediate postwar class struggle.

Clearly, postwar Japanese economic growth cannot be explained in terms of these analytical concepts alone. But they are a starting place and, combined with the complementary developments in regulation examined in the following chapter, provide a basis for management, unions, and governments seeking to respond to the New Competition just as an explanation for the rise of Big Business in turn of the century America was required by those seeking to defend themselves against the new competition of those days.

Competitive Strategies and Enterprise Practices

Strategy

The concept of strategy can be contrasted with the profit maximization assumption of economic theory. Textbook firms have one goal, profit maximization; one strategy, price competition; and one organizational means, cost minimization. The theory conforms to the real world obsession of American managers with improving internal efficiency and reducing the unit costs of labor, capital, raw materials, and purchased components. But price competition is but one form of competition.

The idea of strategy implies that a task of top managers is to choose the form of competition and develop an appropriate organization. For example, firms may compete on the basis of minimum costs or they may pursue Schumpeterian competition in the form of "the new commodity, the new technology, the new source of supply, the new type of organization" (Schumpeter, 1942, p. 84).

Thus the concept of competitive strategy implies that the goal of absolute efficiency in production is not universal but contingent. A firm with the lowest cost of production may or may not win in the market. It depends upon the strategies adopted by competitors. For this reason real world firms must weigh their relative strengths and weaknesses against those of their competitors in a shifting environment that will be reconstituted as the form of competition shifts. The idea of strategy also implies that organization is critically important for the success of firms, much like it is for teams in sports contests, politicians in political campaigns, or armies in the field of battle.

Economic historians have not ignored the role of strategy in American business history. Chandler's history of mass production made profit maximization dependent upon strategy and structure. The strategy of vertical integration led managers to develop the central-office functionally departmentalized structure, and the strategy of product diversification subsequently led to the multidivisional structure. But strategic planning, for Chandler, is about moving to an ideal type of internal structure after which strategic planning is no longer necessary. For example, in Chandler's words: "After 1900. . .when the systems were completed and *strategic planning was no longer of major significance*, the American railroads nearly all came to have much the *same type of structure*" (Chandler, 1977, p. 148, my emphasis).

While Chandler's strategy–structure paradigm illuminates the history of mass production it also, like the profit maximization paradigm, posits the notion of an ideal invariable structure and omits any analysis of continuous improvement in product and process design, the motivating theme of the entrepreneurial firm. Finally, the concept of strategy of relevance here is one of production, as opposed to marketing strategy (which does not imply business reorganization). For example, the investment described in chapter 3 by General Motors to establish the car as the dominant mode of transportation by eliminating potential competitors was a strategic move made to preserve a particular business organization. The General Motors investment was a marketing strategy to shape or design a market; it was not a shift in production strategy, which remained one of Taylorized mass production.

Production Strategies in Postwar Japan

James Abegglen and George Stalk write that the competitive strategy of the archetypal postwar Japanese firm evolved from one of low wages, to scale economies, to focused production before arriving at the strategy of flexible production and the associated organizational innovations described in the fourth section of this chapter. The first three strategies were cost dominated, but the emphasis shifted from conserving costs of direct to indirect labor.[1] The second and third strategies were propelled by the absorption of foreign technologies but the fourth is distinguished by an endogenous capacity of Japanese firms to improve continuously. The latter three have all been quality conscious with persistent attention to process and product improvement. A brief description of each strategy follows.

LOW WAGE

In the immediate postwar period Japan had virtually no resources except labor. To generate the foreign exchange required to finance food and raw material imports Japanese industrial planners channelled financial and material resources to labor-intensive industries such as textiles, toys, and footwear. Exports were low-priced goods made by low-paid workers and labor-intensive processes.

SCALE ECONOMIES

Industrial policymakers were aware that labor-intensive industries and processes were not the basis for building a high growth economy and sought to redirect resources toward high volume capital-intensive processes. At a time when Japan had virtually no capital a decision was

---

[1] People that alter the physical characteristics of the material as it is transformed into a product are counted as direct labor. People who perform support functions to direct labor activities such as maintenance, scheduling, inspection, and supervision are counted as indirect labor.

made to build large capital-intensive steel plants.

The results were stunning. In 1950, the United States produced over 70 percent of world steel and Japan virtually none. But by 1980 Japan had eight of the world's ten deepwater steel plants of capacity over 10 million tons (excluding the USSR); the United States had none. In 1977 Japan had 25 blast furnaces with over 2 million tons capacity, the USSR had nine, the European Economic Community (EEC) had seven, and the United States had none (Magaziner and Hout, 1980, pp. 13ff).

In a little over two decades, the Japanese steel industry did what Carnegie had done a hundred years before: international production leadership was established by investing heavily in the latest steel-making technologies which enabled it to drive costs below the competition. In blast furnaces, for example, it is estimated that every doubling in scale led to a 30 percent reduction in production costs (Magaziner and Hout, 1980, p. 15). The return on steel-making assets for the largest five Japanese steel-making companies was a mere 1.8 percent for the period 1966–72; they were 3.8 percent for the largest eight US companies.

The Japanese investments, like Carnegie's, would not have been justified on a discounted cash flow rate of return basis. They were long-term strategic investments to penetrate markets. In the early years of high investment, the cash flow was negative and the steel makers went heavily into debt. Nevertheless, after many years they began to pay for themselves because cost economies were sufficient to establish market dominance. American competitors who invested on the basis of rate of return for given production methods found themselves, too late, with declining market shares and loss-making operations. The lesson of Carnegie's overwhelming of the British Steel industry had been forgotten in America. The common strategy of the US steel makers in the postwar period, like that of the British steel makers a hundred years before, was incrementalism: invest in bits and pieces as opposed to new plants. It works only as long as everyone in the industry is operating within the same production paradigm.

The strategy of scale economies, high capital investment, and market penetration was followed in a range of other industries where by 1976 Japan enjoyed the following shares of OECD exports (Magaziner and Hout, 1980, p. 9): motorcyles, 90 percent; televisions and radios, 70 percent; ships, 43 percent; watches, 23 percent; cars, 20 percent. In each of these cases debt was the major source of financing and finance capital was channelled in their direction by industrial policy, as we shall see in chapter 6.

FOCUS AND OVERHEAD ECONOMIES

When Japanese firms first penetrate foreign markets they often find that they are competing against firms with an array of product lines. But instead of competing with a similar array, the Japanese competitor focuses on the high volume segment and establishes a production facility that minimizes complexity. This strategy is based upon the fact that manufacturing overheads in Western companies are usually between 150 and 250 percent of direct labor costs. The New Competitors targeted overhead costs for substantial reductions by minimizing product lines and getting the production fundamentals right (Abegglen and Stalk, 1985, p. 81; Telesis, 1986, p. 137).

Manufacturing overheads include costs of materials handling, inventory, quality control, inspection, changeover, warehousing, and resource planning. But each of these costs increases more than proportionally as the number of product lines increases, and a proliferation in products leads to increased numbers of parts, defective parts, and general complications involved in production. All these costs plus distribution and marketing expenses are generally allocated in proportion to direct labor time. By focusing on few product lines Japanese companies greatly reduced the amount of indirect labor time per unit output. Abegglen and Stalk (1985, p. 84) estimate, based upon studies of limited number of industries, that overhead costs per unit can be expected to increase by 30–40 percent for every doubling of the number of families of products produced in a factory.

Faced with Japanese competitors that were undercutting prices by substantial margins in the volume markets, Western producers retreated to high value added segments. This counter-strategy of "segment retreat" was often shortsighted. Western firms set prices equal to direct costs plus average overhead costs which all too often signalled withdrawal from volume markets (Telesis, 1986, p. 138). But the Japanese, whose economies were based on lower overhead costs, realized high profits and eventually followed into the lower volume markets as well.

The problem of segment retreat is one manifestation of a deeper problem rooted in the management accounting systems common to Big Business. When product costing systems for diversified firms were first developed, overhead costs were a small percentage of direct labor costs. Consequently it was reasonable, as a rule-of-thumb estimate, to weigh the overhead costs to each product division as a proportion of the division's direct labor costs. However, in recent years the overhead functions have expanded enormously (direct labor rarely accounts for more than 15 percent of costs), and the old rule of thumb no longer makes sense. But since it is still commonplace for product divisions and "profit centers" to be charged overhead costs in proportion to direct labor costs, division managers concentrate on reducing direct labor because that generates a multiplied reduction in overhead costs charged to the division.[2]

Thus accounting systems geared to Big Business have led Western firms to identify the problem of lack of competitiveness in terms of direct labor productivity and excessive direct labor costs. Since labor rates are established by collective bargaining, individual managers sought to adjust other instruments over which they have more control. Two directions in which they could move were to cut back on volume production or add new product lines. Both responses exacerbated the real problem. Output decreased and overhead increased. Western accounting systems which were designed to measure costs as opposed to solve problems, contributed to wrongheaded responses to the competition.

FLEXIBLE PRODUCTION

It was not until the 1970s that Japanese firms developed the plant flexibility to produce a range of products on the same production lines without driving up indirect labor costs. The new plant flexibility emerged out of the focused system and the refinement of associated production activities which together established the organizational preconditions for the "just-in-time" (JIT) production system. JIT is not simply an inventory management system; if anything, reduced inventories have been a consquence of sharply reduced changeover times and lead times, source inspection methods, and self-stopping machines. Each of these production innovations is examined in the fourth section. It will become apparent that the development of flexible production methods depended first upon the integration of planning and doing on the shopfloor and associated redefinition of the roles of both management and labor, and second upon consultative supplier relations.

Perhaps the most obvious indicator of redefined labor and management relations is the link between flexible production methods and fewer tiers of middle management. Abegglen and Stalk estimate that two-thirds of the labor productivity advantage of flexible producers is in indirect labor which, as shown in table 3, can exhibit productivity differentials of 5:1. At the same time the preoccupation of much of American management has been on the much smaller direct labor advantage. But given the organizational advantage, no amount of direct labor economizing could

---

[2] See Johnson and Kaplan (1987, chapter 8) for a complete treatment of these matters, including examples. As is clear from chapter 2, I have drawn heavily from their individual and collective works on management accounting and the organization of production.

Table 3 Labor productivity differences between two automobile factories

	Japanese competitor	American competitor	Difference
Units produced per day	1,000	860	140
Total factory workers	1,000	2,150	1,150
Workers per unit per day			
Direct	0.79	1.25	0.46
Indirect	0.17 ⎫	1.0 ⎫	1.04
	⎬ 0.21	⎬ 1.25	
Salaried, other	0.04 ⎭	0.25 ⎭	
Total	1.0	2.5	1.5

Source: Abegglen and Stalk, 1985, p. 106.

make American firms competitive when under attack from the New Competition.

In summary, the New Competition, in the industries identified here, is not about maximizing profits for a given material, product, process, and organizational method, but about seeking a competitive advantage by continuously upgrading product, process and organization. The New Competitor is a business organization that pursues a strategy of continuous improvement by integrating thinking and doing.

Culture and Teamwork

Chandler integrated the concept of strategy with that of structure in explaining the source of competitiveness of a business enterprise. But Chandler's concept of structure is a purely organizational one. What is missing is the inter-subjective dimension of structure that is inherent in human organization. Inter-subjective refers to the role of shared ideas and beliefs that constitute practices and norms which guide and give meaning to the activities of individuals within an organization.

Many business leaders attach great importance to the role of beliefs in explaining success. An example is the following quote from Thomas Watson Jr of IBM:

This then is my thesis: I firmly believe that any organization, in order to survive and achieve success, must have a sound set of beliefs on which it premises all its policies and actions. Next, I believe that the most important single factor in corporate success is faithful adherence to those beliefs. And, finally, I believe if an organization is to meet the challenge of a changing world, it must be prepared to change everything about itself except those beliefs as it moves through corporate life. In other words, the basic philosophy, spirit, and drive of an organization have far more to do with its relative achievements than do technological or economic resources, organizational structure, innovation, and timing. (Watson, 1963, p. 5)

The set of shared beliefs to which Watson refers can be described as a company's culture. Culture implies the existence of mutual understandings that allow individuals to transcend the individualism of economic man, where self-interest is pursued by individual actions alone. Culture derives from mutual reciprocity which gives the individual the resource of trust to overcome the prisoner's dilemma, the tragedy of the commons, the tyranny of small decisions, and all such formulations of the predicament of individual decisionmaking in a world without trust, culture, and community. Culture is also the basis for collective identity or a sense of self that derives from membership of a group, team, community, or nation. It expands the source of meaning in life from "I" to "we" and the notion of community from the summation of private interests to the establishment of the common good. Finally, culture is the wellspring of teamwork, the resource so critical to the Penrosian firm.

While culture is not a concept in conventional economic analysis it is often deployed to explain what cannot be explained by economic categories. Thus culture is introduced to explain the success of the kaisha when traditional categories of economic analysis fall short. But used in this way, the concept of culture is rarely explanatory. To explain the competitive success of Japanese firms by the existence of an exceptional Japanese culture of cooperation, for example, leaves unexplained the numerous examples of failed Japanese firms, the class struggle that followed the Second World War, the intense competition amongst Japanese firms, and the comparatively poor performance of Japanese firms before the 1950s.

Such explanations fail to capture the institutional specificity of culture. A better place to begin is with the set of beliefs referred to by Watson. What are the links between beliefs and business enterprise success?

Teamwork comes, in part, from a shared commitment to the beliefs described by Watson – beliefs that are reinforced by actions on a day-to-day basis, not beliefs embodied in company slogans. Managers like

Watson understand that people are intrinsically motivated, for example, by involvement in the production of useful products, and they shape company strategy accordingly. Thus a commitment to quality products resonates with pride of workmanship and gives meaning to work. But a commitment to quality will not be pursued spontaneously by employees; it demands a commitment (in words *and* deeds) on the part of company leadership. It is this interaction of beliefs and commitment that supplies, replenishes, and reinforces culture, the raw material for teamwork.

Thus culture is important in explaining the success of Japanese firms, but it cannot be taken for granted. It is an accomplishment of individual enterprises to develop their cultural resources. To explain culture's role in the competitive success of Japanese enterprises requires an analysis of the specific strategies and beliefs of individual enterprises.

Undoubtedly, links can be established between a country's historical experience and the types of meaning systems that a successful manager can use to motivate people in work. For example, the humiliation of the loss of the Second World War and the occupation of Japan by foreign armies undoubtedly goes some way towards explaining the appeal of the goal of many Japanese firms to "beat America" in international markets. But how can this motivation explain the success of Japanese firms located in America and employing Americans?

Culture is a missing concept both in the conventional economic formulation of the firm and in Chandler's conception of structure. Accounting for enterprise culture partially explains the notion of social inertia. Firms are restricted from shifting strategic plans by the "basic philosophy or beliefs" of the enterprise. Changing these beliefs is, in turn, limited by their constitutive role in the work, management, technical, and regulative practices of the enterprise. A bureacratic firm based upon scientific management in which trust is at a minimum cannot readily decentralize power to workers without risking chaos; the existence of tiers of management devoted to monitoring activities implies the absence of enterprise culture, just as the need for a large police force suggests a lack of political culture or community. Thus changing a production paradigm is analogous to changing religious views: it involves alterations in ways of life.

The relations of trust that exist between managers and permanent workers do not extend to all workers outside or even inside the Japanese corporation. Japan has a large underclass that does not benefit from the job security and "family style relations" of permanently employed workers. Corporations regularly employ temporary and part-time workers who, like the employees of many subcontracting firms, older workers, and women, are outside the enterprise culture described here.

The Japanese kaisha have not eliminated class relations. They have greatly reduced the difference in material rewards between managers and permanent workers compared with their American and European counterparts. Furthermore, they have extended the notions of knowledge creation and absorption beyond those of the Penrosian approach in which these processes are stimulated by a growth-induced imbalance between managerial resources and production capabilities. For this reason the Schumpeterian–Penrosian perspective must be extended to account for an analysis of the relation between work organization and the capacity to innovate. I do this by examining a series of organizational innovations that have been implemented by leading Japanese firms.

New Production Concepts

Strategy and culture, however, are not enough to explain competitive success. To understand the New Competition we must examine a series of new production concepts. Taken together they suggest that the Japanese firm is a production organization with an unprecedented capacity to solve problems and innovate; thus the appellation, the entrepreneurial firm.

Process over Operation Efficiency

The members of a visiting French delegation from Citroen to the Washing Machine Division of Matsushita was dumbfounded to find that the process time between the first and last operation in the production of a washing machine was about 2.5 hours compared with a week in France (Shingo, 1985, p. 13). They were surprised because they had noted that many of the machines in the Citroen factory were more efficient. What was an anomaly to the French was obvious to the Japanese, namely that operational and process efficiency are two different things.

In effect, the Japanese distinguish between productive and unproductive time. Operational efficiency is about productive time – the time during which material is being transformed by machining operations. Process efficiency includes both productive and unproductive time. Unproductive time is the time materials spend in inventory or other non-operational activities such as handling, moving, inspecting, reworking, recording, batching, chasing, counting, and repacking. *Operational* throughput efficiency, the indicator of success for mass producers, is measured in terms of productivity per labor or machine input hour. *Process* throughput efficiency is the ratio of the time a product is being transformed to the time it is in the production system.

Process efficiency has led to the creation of a new set of success indicators. One indicator is the work-in-process (WIP) turn: the ratio of WIP to annual sales.[3] The WIP turn is analogous to the stock-turn ratio used as a measure of efficiency by the first mass retailers (Chandler, 1977, p. 223).

Toyota was at the forefront in driving up WIP turns. In the late 1970s when Western automobile companies had WIP turns of around 10 and rarely as high as 25, Toyota's WIP turn was greater than 300 per year (Abbeglen and Stalk, 1985, p. 114). Abbeglen and Stalk estimate that every doubling of the WIP turn increases labor productivity by 38 percent. Few Japanese companies can match Toyota's performance but many have improved dramatically in short periods of time. Mazda, for example, increased its WIP turn from about 12 times a year in 1976 to over 50 times in 1981 (Abbeglen and Stalk, 1985, p. 113).

Ford's Model T assembly line also realized high WIP turns. In fact, Henry Ford produced only one car on the line to achieve the overhead economies of focused production. What is remarkable about Toyota is that it has been able to move from a strategy of focused production to one of flexible production without dramatic declines in WIP turns, increases in cumulative changeover times, or a mushrooming in indirect labor time. In comparison, the American multidivisional firms tended to proliferate middle management positions for coordinating, monitoring, and planning with each added product.

Whereas operational efficiency focuses the attention of management on increasing the productivity of workers and machines, emphasis on process efficiency focuses attention on a series of activities that absorb much more time (in the flow of the product from the entry to the exit point of the plant) than the time that the product is being machined. Workers can work twice as fast and still only increase throughput efficiency by miniscule amounts. Why? The amount of time that workers are actually transforming material is a small percentage of the total production time. While serious statistical studies do not exist, rough indicators do. One such indicator is the ratio of the time a product is being transformed to the time it is in the plant. Colin New has estimated that in UK and US production systems these ratios are as low as 1 to 2.5 percent, and rarely higher than 20 percent even in plants with "high volume assembly processes" (New, 1988, p. 1).

---

[3] WIP is the value of inventories that a plant requires to maintain production. It does not include inventories of produced goods waiting to be shipped. Hence it is a subcategory of inventories as shown in chapter 2, figure 1. It is readily ascertained from a company's balance sheet.

Put differently, whereas mass production emphasizes operations engineering – the reduction of time required per machine or labor hour – the New Competiton emphasizes process engineering – the reduction of time required to move materials from plant entry point to plant exit point, and to transform new product ideas into products. Mass production cost accounting systems are again misleading for highlighting sources of uncompetitiveness. In this case, they measure operations time but ignore processing time. Consequently they do not highlight the cost-adding activities that restrict (process) throughput efficiency. As noted above, cost reduction measures in Big Business mistakenly focus on the intensity of labor and machine usage and obscure the non-operational time-adding activities.

Just-in-Time for Material Resource Planning

Whereas Ford symbolized the triumph of mass production, Toyota symbolizes the emergence of the JIT production system. Both revolution-ized production methods and enjoyed incredible rates of growth. When Toyota first entered the US market in the late 1950s with the Toyopet it was a failure. It was unreliable, unattractive, unsafe, and it did not sell. But Toyota did not abandon automobile production; instead they retreated to the drawing board before re-entering the market nearly a decade later. By the mid-1980s, Toyota had become the third-largest car company in the world, behind General Motors and Ford. In early 1988, the market value of Toyota was about $40 billion compared with Chrysler's $4 billion. How did Toyota make the transition?

According to Taiichi Ohno, the creator of the Toyota production system, the basic concept of the system is "thorough elimination of wasteful practices" (Ohno, 1984, p. 87). He adds that this concept is supported by two fundamental principles: "right on time" and "automation". But the story begins before Ohno.

The inspiration behind JIT, the idea that inventories can be virtually eradicated in the production process, came from Kiichiro Toyoda, the founder of Toyota Motor Works, two years before the production of the first Toyota car in 1937 (Nayak and Ketteringham, 1986, p. 212). His idea was that the assembly line should be modelled after the American supermarket. The idea of a supermarket is that production orders for replacement supplies are governed by purchases off the shelf, the last stage of the production system. Thus instead of the *planned* coordination by a material resource planning staff to assure that each stage in the production process was supplied with the requisite materials at the right time, coordination would be *spontaneous*. That is, suppliers would produce *ex post*, to sales figures, and not *ex ante*, to preplanned production orders.

The JIT communication system is in the form of actual consumption figures of the following stage, and not of orders from a planning staff anticipating future demands. Hence the analogy that mass production pushes products through the production system while JIT pulls them through. The amount and kind of information is incomparable. Instead of middle management coordinating millions of downstream decisions about when and what to produce, each unit is produced to order from the succeeding unit.

The supermarket analogy, like interchangeability of parts, was a simple idea but one that took decades to put into practice. Also like interchangeability, it was revolutionary for reasons that could have been only dimly foreseen even by its earliest proponents. It was the catalyst for the creation of a new production paradigm. To carry the analogy a final step, both new systems were implemented to conserve on the scarcest factor that firms faced in their specific circumstances but both carried the seeds of an entirely new set of principles of productive organization that overwhelmed any cost advantages from factor abundance. In both cases rival firms were faced with reorganizing to implement the new principles or facing a future of steadily declining market share.

Single-Minute Exchange of Dies for Economic Order Quantities

JIT in a multiple product plant without flexible production methods is no different from mass production. In both cases assemblers seek to cut costs by having suppliers hold inventories and deliver as needed. What makes JIT revolutionary is the capacity of production facilities to produce a range of products economically with short changeover times. In contrast, the record for the longest changeover time is probably the nine months of shutdown time that it took to convert from the Model T produced at Ford's Highland Park plant to the Model A produced at River Rouge.

Long runs tend to be operationally efficient but process inefficient. The reason is that while any other product is being assembled, the materials for all of the other products are being produced for inventory. Process efficiency is enhanced by short runs. Short runs reduce the time that materials are stored and level out production runs in supplier firms, making them more process efficient.

The barrier to short runs in mass production firms is the time required to change over the configuration and settings of the machinery from product to product. Long runs minimize changeovers, during which

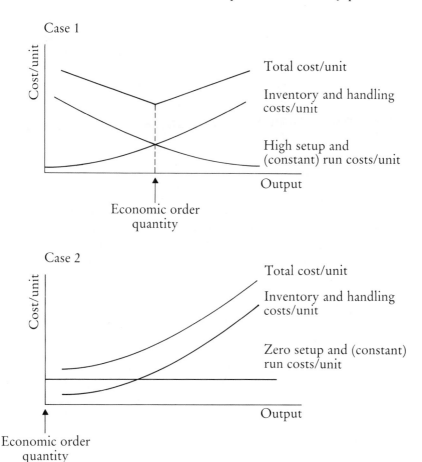

Figure 2 Setup times and economic order quantity: case 1, high setup and constant non-setup costs: case 2, zero setup and constant non-setup costs.

production is stopped, but generate rising non-production costs. Under mass production, changeover times were generally treated as fixed constraints and batch sizes were determined by economic order quantities or, as shown in figure 2, by the quantity of output at which the rising cost of inventories was equated to the unit decreasing changeover costs.[4]

Multiproduct mass producers developed the concept of economic

---

[4] A tension exists in every multiple product firm between optimal production runs and consumer orders. Put differently, consumer purchases do not come in batches that match optimal production runs. Instead, consumers, as a group, are simultaneously purchasing the whole range of a company's products. This is the problem that JIT addresses.

order quantities to determine the minimum total cost after factoring in the production economies with the inventory diseconomies. The equations are based upon the premise that changeover times are an invariable constraint.

The concept of inventory as wasteful overproduction and the drive to eliminate waste led Japanese producers to seek alternatives to long runs. The solution was to drive down changeover times so that small batches could be run with minimal interference with the principle of flow (see chapter 2). What had been an invariable constraint to the mass producers became a challenge to the entrepreneurial firm.

Again, the concept of reducing changeover times is simple. But the capacity of the Japanese to increase production flexibility and product variety radically is illustrated by an example from the General Motors–Toyota joint venture plant in Fremont, California, where a typical die change was reduced from 12 hours to 15 minutes. Toyota is reportedly installing flexible lines that will enable switching from four to six cylinder engines in minutes, a changeover that has historically been restricted to annual model time frames by American companies (*Business Week*, November 4, 1985, p. 43).

Ohno gives credit to Shigeo Shingo for the concept of "single-minute exchange of dies" (SMED). In Ohno's words:

> . . .we began to study the question of how setup changes could be performed in a very short period of time. Shigeo Shingo, of the Japan Management Association, was advocating "single-minute setup changes" and we felt this concept could be of great service to us. . . . We are now looking into cutting setup times down to a matter of seconds. (From *Management*, June, 1976, a journal of the Japanese Management Association, cited in Shingo, 1983, p. 26)

The basic idea behind SMED is to distinguish between internal and external setup activities and convert what had been internal to external activities. External setup activities are those that can be done while the machine is operating. For example, transporting old dies to storage is external, whereas mounting dies is an internal setup activity. Shingo's contribution was to develop both a procedure for distinguishing between internal and external activities, and techniques for converting what had seemed to be the former into the latter. Furthermore, in conjunction with the Japanese Management Association, he developed handbooks that illustrated the concepts and which were widely distributed. Shingo's book provides over 40 examples, many detailed, of changeover time reductions from between 30 minutes and several hours to minutes measured in single digits (Shingo, 1983).

SMED often means an alteration in a die, or adding a special fixture which is specially designed to facilitate setups. It does not mean new machines or sophisticated machines, hence the distinction again between focusing on operational and process efficiency. Toyota's production engineers systematically pursued a policy of driving down changeover times and production runs by investing in extra tooling and fabricating jigs to move tools quickly as an alternative to investing in inventories (Abegglen and Stalk, 1985, p. 96). The result is more general machines (in that each machine can produce a greater variety of products in less time), inventory reductions, more efficient utilization of space, higher capital turnover rates, and "level scheduling" with suppliers. Level scheduling allows suppliers to even out production over time which reduces their inventory costs as well.[5]

Thus JIT depends upon, and is a consequence of, flexible production based on short runs and changeover times. Otherwise, JIT would simply mean pushing inventories upstream to suppliers.

Automation for Automotion

Ohno distinguishes automation from automotion. Whereas the Ford assembly line was "self-moving", the Toyota line is "self-working" (Ohno, 1984, p. 90). A self-working machine is a machine that is designed to detect abnormalities and stop automatically before any defective products are produced. For Toyota, automation meant machines with a built-in capacity to stop.

The idea of a self-stopping machine is attributed to Sakichi Toyoda (1867–1930) the inventor of automatic (self-stopping) looms and the founder of Toyota. Toyota began as a textile loom company and became successful because of the guiding idea of a self-stopping mechanism which revolutionized weaving. Early machines at Toyota were equipped with sensors that anticipated machine breakdowns before it occurred so that the machine could be repaired before any defective products were produced. According to folklore, Sakichi Toyoda's motivation came, in part, from a desire to relieve the tension faced by his mother who was a loom operator (Nayak and Ketteringham, 1986, p. 217). The result, in Ohno's terms, was machines "equipped with human intelligence" (Ohno, 1984, p. 91).

Automatic machinery, in Ohno's sense of the term, revolutionized the organization of production in several ways. First, it liberated the machine operator from constant attention to a single machine. A single worker could now oversee several machines without fear that defective

---

[5] The concept "level scheduling" is explained by Abegglen and Stalk (1985, pp. 103–4).

products would go undetected or that an expensive machine might be damaged because a part entered at a wrong angle. Consequently, Toyota developed the concept of multimachining based upon machines laid out in U-shapes with a single worker overseeing a group of machines around him/her as opposed to a straight line layout with one person per machine. Thus the Toyota system permitted a discrete increase in labor productivity that was not based necessarily or simply on worker speedup but on organizational innovation.

Second, the fact that machines shut themselves down every time an abnormality occurred focused worker and staff energy on detecting the problem and developing a solution. Increasingly the task of workers shifted from being mere operators of a single machine to maintaining machines and seeking process modifications so that machines would not shut down. Thus workers became problem solvers as opposed to merely machine minders. To facilitate this new role, the internal mechanisms of machines were deliberately made visible so that they could be more easily understood and modifications could be considered. In the words of Fujio Cho, a Toyota production manager, "Mr. Ohno said if a production line cannot be understood with your own eyes, then it is not a good production line" (Nayak and Ketteringham, 1986, p. 221).

The idea that workers could alter machines or suggest means of modifying the production system to prevent recurrence of abnormalities became part of the system. Instead of machine breakdowns being perceived as the cause of chaos as on the mass production line, they became an opportunity for improvement in the process. The worker, instead of being perceived as merely a factor of production, became an active force in the continuous upgrading of the productive system.

To repeat, JIT is more than a system of inventory management. Ohno uses a baseball analogy to illustrate the link between JIT and automation. The analogy also illustrates the link between teamwork and skills:

> How can I best express the connection between the two pillars of the Toyota production system, "Right on time" and "Automation"? Using metaphors from baseball, I would say that "right on time" represents teamwork. . .it displays the essence of cooperation. "Automation" enhances each individual player's skills. When "right on time" has been implemented, every player in the field will show good timing in catching balls, and base runners will be put out through cooperative teamwork. Each section can systematically develop good team play. Again to use baseball terms, supervisors and directors are like hitting, fielding, and running coaches. A good baseball team uses system plays, perfecting their teamwork so they can respond to any situation. A plant where "Right on time" has been thoroughly understood is like a baseball team with good teamwork. (Ohno, 1984, p. 93)

Sashimi (Layered) for Sequentially Staged Product Development

Several years ago, Xerox Corporation executives found themselves in a situation that has become almost commonplace. Their market share was being eroded by Japanese competitors who were developing new products twice as fast and at half the cost. It allowed the competitors to charge a premium price for exclusive products, to incorporate the latest technological developments in their products, and to target emerging market niches (*Wall Street Journal*, February 23, 1988, p. 1). Xerox responded effectively to the New Competition. But most such challenges have gone unmet. The reason? The challenge of the New Competition cannot be met from within the confines of the traditional multidivisional organizational structure. To understand why, I will compare the organization of new product development of mass producers and the New Competitors.

Product development by mass producers was (and is) done sequentially by functionally specialized departments. The production design department signed off as it turned the new product prototype over to manufacturing; production engineers designed the required modifications in plant layout and machines and turned the actual production activities over to manufacturing managers and unit engineers. Once the new product was coming off the assembly line it was turned over to the sales department. Individuals in each department did not work with individuals in other departments; it was the task of management to coordinate across departments. At Chrysler, for example, the manufacturing department was not represented on the product design committee until 1981. With hindsight it is not surprising that American mass producers avoided new product development except for superficial changes.

In a study of five major Japanese companies Ken-ichi Imai, Ikujiro Nonaka, and Hirotaka Tekeuchi describe product development as a "dynamic and continuous process of adaption to changes in the environment" (Imai et al., 1985, p. 340). Three organizational features of the product development process stand out: "self-organizing" development teams, overlapping development phases, and a commitment to continuous learning.

Project teams are assigned by top management to pursue a broad strategic product development goal as opposed to being presented with a specific new product concept. "Self-organization" refers to the autonomy given to the groups to define their own activities. The groups are composed of members with diverse functional backgrounds who work together. Product designers, process engineers, manufacturing personnel, and marketers, for example, work together from the birth of a new idea to its maturity in the new product. In addition, the phases of product design, development, and commercialization are overlapped so that problems are being tackled simultaneously.

The product development group faces challenges collectively rather than in the isolation of distinctive specialist departments; information is shared across functional boundaries as common languages are developed and responsibility is shared. In the process a segmented division of labor is replaced by a shared division of labor. Imai et al. (1985, p. 353) quote a Mr Watanabe, of Honda, who contrasts team members in a relay where each member says, "My job is done, now you take it from here", with rugby, where "every member of the team runs together, tosses the ball left and right, and dashes toward the goal". The rugby approach allows the cross penetration of ideas from each functional specialty in the design phase; thus knowledge that will affect the ultimate success of the product is brought to bear on product design at any early stage from each of the departments.

The third feature of the new product development process identified by Imai et al. (1985, p. 353) is "an almost fanatical devotion to learning – both within organizational membership and with outside members of the interorganizational network". Taking these three features of new product development together, it is clear that nothing short of a major reorganization of a conventional mass production organization is required if it is to hope to match the New Competition. The New Competition illustrates the application of the principle of flow to the new product development process; such an idea would have been entirely alien to Henry Ford.

Technology and Organizational Learning

Technology does not make the New Competition flexible; instead, the New Competitors make technology flexible. A study by Ramchandran Jaikumar (1986), which compares the application of flexible manufacturing systems by American and Japanese machine tool companies, illustrates the social embeddedness of technology. A flexible manufacturing system (FMS) is an integrated group of computer-numerically controlled and robotized workstations linked by automated material-handling systems. In principle, an FMS combines the specialist advantages of a job shop for small-batch production with the scale advantages of a flow line for high volume production. An FMS is flexible in that it functions as a general tool capable of producing a range of specialized products by simply changing the instructions.

In contrast, an automated mass production system is an integrated group of special purpose machines linked by rigid transfer mechanisms. The mass production automated line can do volume runs but lacks the flexibility to produce small batches economically. Once in place an automated mass production line can be operated by machine tenders with little training, but to change over from one product to another requires a team of process engineers, or at least highly trained machine setup personnel and a new configuration of transfer machines to carry the materials between machining processes. An FMS eliminates the barriers of rigid transfer machines and manual setups to combining the variety of a job shop with the volume of a mass production plant. Obviously the stand-alone general machines of a job shop offer more flexibility than an FMS, but they offer none of the scale advantages of long runs.

Jaikumar studied 35 flexible manufacturing sytems in the United States and 60 in Japan, a sample that represented roughly half of the installed capacity in each country. He concluded that:

> the flexible manufacturing systems installed in the United States show an astonishing lack of flexibility. . . . The average number of parts made by an FMS in the United States was 10; in Japan the average was 93. . . . The U.S. companies used the FMSs the wrong way – for high-volume production of a few parts rather than for high-variety production of many parts at low cost per unit. Thus the annual volume per part in the United States was 1,727; in Japan, only 258. Nor have U.S. installations exploited opportunities to introduce new products. For every new part introduced into a U.S. system, 22 parts were introduced in Japan. (Jaikumar, 1986, p. 69)

Jaikumar adds that the problem facing the United States cannot be solved solely by investing in more equipment: "It is how the equipment is used that is important. Success comes from achieving continuous process improvement through organizational learning and experimentation" (Jaikumar, 1986, p. 70). In Japan, "Operators on the shop floor make continual programming changes and are responsible for writing new programs for both parts and the system as a whole" (Jaikumar, 1986, p. 72). The key point here is first that the New Competition shifts competition from economies in running a plant to planning it, and second that only people who are also involved in operations can gain the experiential knowledge required to make the new technology perform to its full potential.

The American firms that separated planning from doing cannot generate the new knowledge required. Engineers that set up the FMS cannot be faulted; their job is to set the system up, not run it. At the same time the operators cannot be faulted; who could blame them for doing long runs rather than risk a malfunction in machinery that they had not set up and do not understand. The problem is that reliability and flexibility can only be developed in the process of operations; designing flexibility into the machines is only part of the job.

Using FMSs, like new product development, demands a redefinition of management tasks. In the words of Jaikumar: "the new role of management in manufacturing is to create and nurture the project teams whose intellectual capabilities produce competitive advantage. What gets managed is intellectual capital, not equipment" (Jaikumar, 1986, p. 75). Used properly, FMSs, unlike the specialist rigidly linked machines of mass production, will not require large production plants even in assembly. In Jaikumar's words, "The minimum efficient scale for FMS operations is a cell of roughly six machines and fewer than a half a dozen people. That's the new reality" (Jaikumar, 1986, p. 76).

Source Inspection versus Specialist Quality Control

In chapter 2 we examined the types of information that went into Taylor's scientific management for increasing the productivity of labor. The Japanese forsook Taylorist information for another type altogether, that of statistical quality control championed by W. Edwards Deming. The two systems of information represent two contradictory approaches to work organization. The purpose of Taylorist information is to minimize direct labor costs in the production of a standardized product. It is the heart of the mass production paradigm. The purpose of Deming's information is to provide a basis for continuous upgrading of production methods and product quality. Deming's message was that quality and productivity are positively related, contrary to the tradeoff presumed by orthodox economic theory and adherents to the mass production paradigm.

In 1960, Deming became the first American to be awarded the Second Order of the Sacred Treasure by the Japanese. The attached citation states that the Japanese attribute the rebirth of Japanese industry to Deming (Walton, 1986, p. 15). The year 1960 also marked the tenth annual contest for the Deming Prizes, one to an individual in statistical theory and the other to companies for accomplishments in statistical application. It is the most prestigious award a company can receive in Japan, or anywhere. Its status to Japanese industry can be compared with that of the Nobel Prize to scientists. The Deming Prize has served to concentrate the minds of much of Japanese industry on the ever advancing goal of excellence in quality.

How could this American, largely unknown to this day in his own country, have come to receive such high honor in Japan? The story begins with Deming's mentor, Walter A. Shewhart, a statistician at Bell

Telephone Laboratories. In 1931, Shewhart wrote a book entitled *The Economic Control of Quality of Manufactured Product*, in which he demonstrated procedures capable of bringing industrial processes into "statistical control". Statistical controls distinguish the common or systemic causes from special causes. The lack of statistical controls makes it easy for management to blame workers for defective parts when, in fact, the causes are rooted in systems beyond the influence of workers. The application of statistical control procedures is designed to identify targets for problem-solving efforts.

Shewhart was the orginator of statistical quality control (SQC) techniques. SQC was propagated by the War Department during the Second World War but was abandoned afterwards by American companies. At precisely the same time members of the newly formed Japanese Union of Scientists and Engineers (JUSE) saw potential in such methods for addressing the Japanese problem of low quality products. These same men also read about Deming, a statistician who had worked with Shewhart, and some knew him from a visit he had made to Japan in 1947 as a statistical sampling advisor to facilitate the 1951 Japanese census. In 1950, JUSE officials asked Deming to give a series of lectures on SQC.

Deming accepted, but with a proviso. He had learned a lesson about SQC implementation from his experiences with its short life in the United States. He had witnessed with dismay the postwar deepening of Taylor's scientific management in American industry and, in the process, the abandoning of SQC. It meant the establishment of top-down rule-bound corporate bureaucracies geared to meeting output quotas for which quality was considered an expensive luxury. Deming attributed the short life span of SQC in the United States to two factors: the postwar shortage of goods meant that firms could ignore quality, and, unlike many technical people, top management did not understand the virtues of SQC. But without the commitment of top management, the fundamental changes in work organization and production methods could not be made. Consequently, Deming stressed the need to meet with and convince top management. JUSE arranged the meetings. The rest is history, as the methods came to be adopted by virutally all of Japanese industry. The extraordinary result was that whereas in America accounting became the language of the elite in business, "[s]tatistical symbols and methods became in Japan a second language for everybody, including hourly workers" (Deming, 1982, p. 105). Perhaps nothing better captures the distinguishing substance of the two paradigms.

Deming, Joseph Juran, and A.G. Feigenbaum all carried the same message to Japan – they took statistical process control methods to everyone in the firm, including hourly workers, and to every activity in which the firm is involved, not only production but also market research, product design, and materials acquisition. Their point was not simply that quality should be the number one priority. Many American managers took quality seriously, but their instrument was to create specialized quality control departments, In Deming's words, "[t]hey took quality control away from everybody else, which was of course entirely wrong, as quality control is everybody's job" (Deming, 1982, p. 101). It is axiomatic to Deming that quality cannot be imposed; it must be built into the job, not inspected in. Building quality in means respecting the right of the workers' "pride of workmanship".

Statistical quality control is based on simple premises. One is that defective products are usually (Deming estimates 85 percent of the time) caused by poor systems and not workers. Thus firms need procedures for identifying systemic problems and not for disciplining workers. In fact, argues Deming, traditional labor relations in the West are counterproductive. The threat of being fired instills fear which inhibits learning and systemic improvement; furthermore, incentive, quota, and piecework systems of pay all foster competition rather than teamwork among workers and undermine morale because of their inherently arbitrary nature. The third is that improved quality leads to lower costs because of less rework, fewer mistakes, fewer delays and snags, and better use of machines and materials. But most of the costs of poor quality are hidden costs such as consumers that do not purchase again, the deterioration in a company's reputation, or workers that are not motivated to produce high quality products. Ironically, Deming stresses the priority of invisible numbers. The problem with "interchangeable managers", a common criticism Deming has of the footloose character of American management, is that all they know about is maximum profit and not excellence of product: "They know nothing of the invisible numbers. Who can put a price on a satisfied customer, and who can figure out the cost of a dissatisfied customer" (Halberstam, 1986, p. 314).

Accountants have no measure for the invisible numbers that promote or detract from the links between quality and competitive position. How does one measure the competitive advantage from a reputation for reliability, schedule dependability, learning effects of different work arrangements, the adaptiveness that comes from "driving fear out of the workplace", or product flexibility? Deming emphasizes that each can promote competitive position but none can be precisely measured. The concentration of American companies on measurable aggregates introduces a powerful bias towards output quotas and against product quality.

Deming's stress on purpose and worker self-respect both as a source of competitiveness for the firm and of motivation for the worker are manifestations of an implicit critique within the SQC movement of the theory of human nature common to conventional economics and scientific management. It is a similar critique that the "human relations" school has long made of American management philosophy and which has long roots in critical social theory. Deming is explicit: "[t]his obstacle by which the hourly worker is deprived of his right to do good work and to be proud of himself, may be the single most important contribution of management to poor quality and loss of market. . ." (Deming, 1982, p. 66).

The main theme of the critique is that people seek identity and meaning in work, and that work arrangements in which people have no input in decisionmaking undermine trust, teamwork, and the opportunities that work offers humans to develop their creative, problem-solving, and cooperative capabilities. Thus the learning firm is in accord with the pursuit of meaning in work.

The point is not that the specific purposes and values that give meaning to Japanese workers are beyond critique, or that they are sustainable. In-depth analysis of company loyalty may reveal cases of subtle forms of psychological regimentation. Or the very success of Japanese companies in achieving international leadership may undermine the meaning systems required to achieve the goal; or economic success may have been achieved at a high price in terms of family life – a price that new generations will not be willing to pay. The point is that Japanese companies have not been successful because of cultural characteristics peculiar to the Japanese but because of the organizational characteristics that have tapped human energies presumed, at least by scientific management, not to exist in working people.

Decentralized Supplier Networks

Most studies of Japanese industry focus on the kaisha, or lead manufacturers. But Japanese manufacturing is remarkable for its high proportion of small and medium-sized firms:[6] in 1982 they accounted for 99.4 percent of all manufacturing establishments, 81.4 percent of all employees, and 51.8 percent of all shipments (Murata, 1986, p. 221).

---

[6] Small and medium-sized enterprises in Japanese manufacturing are defined as having less than 300 employees and less than 100 million yen in capital. Very small manufacturing enterprises are defined as having less than 20 employees.

Changing Patterns

While small and medium-sized firms are a permanent feature of Japanese industrial organization, the relationships between parent and supplier firms have evolved with the competitive strategies of the parent companies. In the first postwar phase of economic growth, parent companies used subcontractors to economize on capital, as buffers against recession, and as sources of cheap labor and supervisory management. By 1965, economic growth had created labor shortages which spurred first rationalization processes, including the increased use of electronic machinery in both parent and supplier companies[7] and, second, enterprise spin-offs as skilled employees set up as subcontractors to the parent company. The slowdown years induced by the oil crisis in the mid-1970s stimulated product-led strategies of continuous improvement, superior quality, shorter product development times, and dependable delivery times. In the process, demands placed on suppliers became increasingly quality and time oriented as opposed to price oriented.

To advance the capabilities of suppliers, parent companies established *kyoryokukai* or formal associations of cooperative parts makers. *Kyoryokukai* are constituted by informal understandings, or "shared network norms" described by Imai et al. as follows:

> Written contracts are unheard of. But if the lead manufacturer delivers, a trusting relationship begins to develop. In the long run, this kind of relationship leads the subcontractors as a group to accept the lead manufacturer as the legitimate leader and establish a strong cooperative system in support of it. A set of "shared network norms" is established over time, laying out a basic understanding of how business should be conducted within the network. Such a norm may tolerate an unreasonable demand made by the lead manufacturer during times of competitive crisis. (Imai et al. 1985, p. 273)

Formal and informal associations between parent and supplier firms are means of transferring organizational innovations. JIT, zero quality defects, single-minute change of die, and *sashimi* product development methods all require consultative and sustained coordination across producing units. But the process is not without potential cost to the parent company. Increasing the technological sophistication and problem-solving capabilities of suppliers can reduce their dependence. By 1982, subcontractors had an average of 6.5 parent companies (Sato, 1983, p. 5).

[7] The ratio of numerically controlled machine tools to "old type" (non-numerically controlled) in Japan's metal processing industry increased from 2.3 in 1975 to 18.7 in 1983 (Ohta, 1987, p. 91).

their dependence. By 1982, subcontractors had an average of 6.5 parent companies (Sato, 1983, p. 5).

Even with these changes, large disparities in wages and working conditions between the parent and supplier firms have continued to exist. While the disparity in wages declined sharply between 1958 and 1968, it widened somewhat in the 1970s. Wages in firms with less than 29 employees were less than 60 percent of wages in large enterprises in 1983 (Murata, 1986, p. 237). One estimate of the disparity in working hours indicates that workers in small enterprises work 1.6 times as many hours as those in large enterprises (*White Paper on Small and Medium Enterprises, 1985*, pp. 122–3, cited in Murata, 1986, p. 237). The fact that these figures are averages over all small firms in Japan, many of which are highly dependent as well as those that are more independent, may hide trends that would be captured by a disaggregated analysis.

Clearly, Japanese small and medium-sized firms face competitive pressures from parent firms that have powerful bargaining leverage. But many have responded to the pressures from the parent companies that are pursuing product-led strategies in ways that can ultimately increase their independence. I will illustrate this tension by examining recent developments in parent–supplier relations in the Japanese automobile industry and contrasting them with the relations that comprise Big Business.

Buyer–Supplier Relations in Automobiles

The automobile is composed of perhaps 20,000 parts. The automobile industry is composed of a small number of automakers and a much greater number of parts makers. The relationships between the two vary between the United States and Japan in three ways. First, Japanese automakers are less vertically integrated: they make fewer parts and buy more. The average US automaker makes about 50 percent; the average Japanese makes about 30 percent.

Second, Japanese automakers deal directly with far fewer parts makers: in Japan the range is between 100 and 300 whereas General Motors deals with 3,500, not including materials suppliers. Toyota, for example, deals directly with 300 component suppliers, which, in turn, deal with 5,000 second-tier suppliers that, in turn, coordinate 20,000 third- and fourth-tier suppliers (*Business Week*, November 4, 1985, p. 44). At full capacity, the Nissan assembly plant in the United Kingdom will work directly with only 120 parts makers. The reason, according to Nissan officials, is that to go beyond 120 would risk undermining the personal knowledge required for high quality relations. They argue that it is crucial that production engineers at Nissan and the parts makers know one another personally and are able jointly to solve problems. This requires the nurturing of an open relationship and a common production "language" based on shared experience.

Third, the relations between Japanese automakers and parts makers is mediated by extensive *kyoryokukai* relations. With the exception of Honda, every Japanese automaker has a *kyoryokukai*, each of which includes between 100 and 300 parts makers.[8] It is estimated that 10 to 20 percent of the *kyoryokukai* are affiliated parts makers, defined as suppliers in which 20 percent or more of their stock is owned by an automaker. At the same time, most *kyoryokukai* members supply several automakers; thus the interrelationships suggest networking amongst firms rather than a single captive hierarchy.

Supplier Relations and Competitive Strategies

These cross-relationships between Japanese automakers and parts makers were initially established in the immediate postwar period more by accident than design. But the effect has been to enhance the capacity of the Japanese auto industry to compete on the basis of product innovation because it has increased the independent design capabilities of parts makers. To see why, we can distinguish three types of component design relationship between automakers and parts makers.

1 The automaker provides blueprint specifications to a range of potential parts makers, each of whom submits a price bid.
2 The automaker supplies blueprint specifications but expects the parts maker to suggest alterations in the development process.
3 The automaker does not provide blueprint specifications but only component performance requirements. Here the parts maker is expected to have an independent design capacity and be able to solve problems jointly with the automaker.

While each of these relationships is a market relationship in that an exchange takes place at a negotiated price, they carry very different possibilities for competitive strategy. The first, a price-led supplier relation, prevailed under the old competition; the second and third, design-led supplier relations, are representative of the New Competition.

American automakers' supplier relations were of the first type. Each automaker's engineers would prepare detailed specifications for component products and send them out to a list of subcontractors who would bid on the basis of price. The suppliers were not expected to

---

[8] Virtually all supplier firms are members of several *kyoryokukai* (Mitsubishi Research Institute).

make or suggest any modifications in design as the quality was "in the specifications". American automakers had so many suppliers that their engineers did not know their supplier firm counterparts personally and were not able to relate on a consultative basis in terms of design possibilities. A contract, enforceable in the courts, was the instrument to ensure that suppliers met the specifications as prescribed in the blueprints.

Japanese automaker–supplier relations are often of the second and third types. The automaker's engineers do not prepare detailed blueprint specifications for each component and send them to a list of subcontractors. Instead, they describe the function and the performance standards and ask a limited number of familiar suppliers to design the component. The supplier offers design ideas that are examined by the automaker's engineers and changes are suggested. A process of dialogue on the performance, quality, production characteristics, and costs ensues until a prototype and, eventually, product specifications are agreed. But instead of writing a price and quality standard into a contract in advance of its development, the automaker and parts maker agree a "target cost performance" and a "target quality performance". The task of the parts maker is then one of refining the product and production processes to meet the targets.

The first type of supplier relation works best for price-led competitive strategies but poorly for product-led strategies because the latter depend upon quality, organizational flexibility, or product innovation. The pure market type supplier relation offers no independent design capability as the specifications are described in advance by engineers that are detached from production. The second and third, or networked, types of supplier relation perceive of suppliers as offering independent design and joint problem-solving capabilities. The presupposition is that new ideas emerge in the process of making the component, particularly the first time, and that a consultative relationship is necessary to develop these ideas. The task of an automaker's engineers is not to design component specifications for the purposes of enforcing contracts but to foster consultative relations that can enhance the design capability of the automaker's productive system which includes parts makers.

The American system of coordination across the production chain by either hierarchy or market was developed along with the system of mass production. Ford sought to make virtually everything required for the production of cars. The strategy made sense at a time when few parts makers existed and when Ford's engineering success was based upon applying the assembly line concept to new production processes. But eventually the economies of expansion were overcome by the economies of specialization, and component suppliers emerged that could produce more economically than Ford's internal departments. This led to buying, but product and component design stayed lodged in Detroit. General Motors relied more upon buying but followed the Ford tradition of market- or price-led supplier relations.

The Japanese systems of the second or third type, or networked supplier relations, are especially suitable at a time of rapid technological change. Given the large number of parts, it is impossible for an automaker to stay on top of technological developments in every one.

Summary

Returning to the terms of chapter 4, we can conclude that the New Competition of Japan is Schumpeterian in that firms compete strategically by choosing the terrain of competition; firms may compete, for example, on the basis of price, product quality, technological process, or product innovation. It is Penrosian in that the firm is a learning organization that is continuously creating new productive services by teamwork and experience, and it is Richardsonian in that inter-firm relations can be cooperative or market oriented.

The New Competition can be better understood as conducive to industrial growth and restructuring as opposed to satisfying norms of allocative efficiency. Two powerful industrial restructuring institutions have been examined in this chapter, namely the kaisha and production chain networks. Both of these institutions have been shaped by and in turn have shaped a regulatory environment which is also distinctively geared to industrial growth and restructuring. I argue in the next chapter that the relationship between the economy and the government has been fundamentally altered to achieve compatability with the New Competition.

6
Industrial Policy and Antitrust in Japan

Industrial policy has not always been successful in Japan. In fact an international comparison of the growth capacity of industrial output during wartime mobilization indicates that Japan's economy was much less responsive to the directives of governmental authorities than that of the United Kingdom, the United States, or the USSR.[1]

The postwar economy has been different. To understand why we must suspend the conventional notions of the ideal terms of relation between the economy and the government that inspire academic and popular debates, for these debates are informed by theoretical perspectives which take for granted dichotomies between market and plan, private and public, competition and cooperation, and economy and polity.

Breaking with the plan–market dichotomy leads to a reconceptualization of both the market and the plan. A market is itself shaped, in part, by rules that enable and limit the actions of firms within it. These rules may be formal or informal, but they are subject to reconstitution by collective agreement amongst key groups, firms, or individuals within a sector, strategic action by a leading firm or government order. In this, markets are planned. Examples from chapter 3 include the planning of

---

[1] R.W. Goldsmith compared the volume of munitions production for the 1935–9 to 1944 period (in billion dollars at 1944 munition prices): Japan's munition expenditures increased from 0.4 to 6, the United Kingdom's from 0.5 to 11, Germany's from 2.4 to 17, the USSR's from 1.6 to 16 and the United States' from 0.3 to 42 (cited in Harrison, 1988, p. 172).

The 140-fold expansion of munition production in the United States dwarfs the 15-fold expansion of Japan. This suggests that the cultural explanations of postwar Japanese economic success based on the inherent "cooperation" of the Japanese people are unsatisfactory, for during the war years American labor, management, and government were far more cooperative than their Japanese counterparts in achieving production goals.

the market for ground transportation by General Motors and the creation of a market for auditors to underpin the securities markets by the Securities and Exchange Commission. The focus in this chapter is on industrial policy as a means of shaping (planning) markets to promote the international competitiveness of Japan's business enterprises.

The concept of industrial policy takes its meaning from the theoretical framework that informs it. From the free-market perspective industrial policy implies subsidization of inefficient enterprises, from the orthodox Keynesian perspective it is associated with market interference for stabilization purposes, from the mixed economy perspective it suggests correcting for market failure with public planning, and from the socialist economic perspective it means substituting planning for markets as a superior mechanism for coordinating resource allocation. But since these perspectives share the plan–market dichotomy, none adequately captures the role of industrial policy in postwar Japan. Here the purpose of industrial policy is to promote internationally competitive business enterprises in markets that are continuously being reconstituted by strategically aware competitors.

The argument is that, for Japan, the criterion of enterprise success is not allocative or productive efficiency but strategic advantage, and the criterion of economic success is not optimal resource allocation but a continuous reallocation towards higher value added production processes and sectoral compositions. The term "industrial policy" in this context presupposes that government economic policymaking is guided by a Schumpeterian accumulation (which presumes markets are instruments of growth) and not an allocative efficiency orientation (which presumes that market "interference" is bad).

The analysis of Japanese industrial policy that follows begins with the lessons learned from the failure of interwar Japanese economic planning followed by an analysis of the economic policy institutions created during the American occupation to foster competition and production. I turn next to sections on formal and informal post-occupation methods of industrial policy. The chapter concludes with sections on the political economic and macro-economic implications of Japanese industrial policy.

Interwar Japan: The Failure of Economic Planning

As an industrial follower, the issue of how the state can best promote the growth of production was an old one. Immediately after the Meiji Restoration in 1868, the government became an economic entrepreneur by establishing state-owned businesses. But by the 1880s, a century before Thatcherism, Japan had carried out a privatization program as a means of promoting an indigenous capitalist class. Since that time the ideology of private ownership of productive enterprises has prevailed. However, the issues of control over management decisions and the purpose of productive enterprises have been contested, particularly in the interwar period.

The advances in production methods that generated excess supply conditions in 1920s America and Western Europe meant, for Japan, a flood of low-priced imports, the undermining of domestic industry, a buildup of unemployment, and early onset of the emerging international depression. Keynesian demand management measures were hopeless in an open economy given the backwardness of Japanese production: instead of stimulating a domestic multiplier process, government deficit spending would merely absorb more imports and worsen the balance of payments. Japan turned to industrial policy measures to counter the emerging depression.

In 1925, the Japanese Ministry of Commerce and Industry (MCI) was created to promote production. The existing industrial structure was bifurcated between zaibatsu, large holding companies owned by powerful families, and small (5–30 employees) and medium-sized (30–100 employees) firms. The small firms were relatively dynamic and export oriented while the zaibatsu were conservative and domestically focused. MCI estimated that small and medium-sized firms employed an overwhelming majority of the labor force and generated between 50 and 65 percent of the exports, but they suffered from unequal terms of trade with the zaibatsu and many were losing money. The zaibatsu, in contrast, were lethargic holding companies that were run more like feudal domains than modern business enterprises. Nevertheless, they made money. But the MCI was convinced that much of their profit was made at the expense of the small and medium-sized firms.

With the onset of the depression in the early 1920s, the government attempted, largely unsuccessfully, to save failing small and medium-sized enterprises and lost a lot of money in the process. Thereafter, Japanese industrial policy agencies have rarely directly subsidized privately owned firms on an individual basis. Instead, they have emphasized classes of firms by sectoral, technological, size, or regional criteria, and they have coordinated industrial policy with banking institutions whose officials possess the financial expertise to assess individual cases.

At first, the MCI focused its attention on small and medium-sized enterprises, encouraging them to form unions or associations, particularly for purposes of exporting. In 1925, the Exporters Association Law was passed that authorized trade associations to form export unions which would market products cooperatively and control output, product quality, and the prices of exported products.

In 1927, the MCI created official deliberation councils composed of businessmen, industry experts, and ministry personnel as a means of promoting industrial modernization. The deliberation councils compiled statistics and gathered information on the status of foreign markets and competitive conditions. In the early days, the MCI loaned small amounts to small and medium-sized firms for the purpose of promoting exports. The enormous size of the task became evident with the increased awareness of the quantum leaps in productivity associated with large-scale industry, particularly in America and Germany.

The concept of "industrial rationalization" was refined to capture the idea that the expansion of industrial production depended upon adopting business organizational principles based upon Fordism in the United States, and the promotion of combines and cartels as in Germany. For industrial policy ideas, the MCI officials turned mainly to Germany. The management of foreign trade by tariffs and internal markets by cartels were key measures in German industrial rationalization efforts (see chapter 3).

After examination of the German cartels, the Japanese adopted the German notion of rationalization. Chalmers Johnson writes that in 1931 Nobusuke Kishi, who later became the Minister of Commerce and Industry and a postwar Prime Minister, spent seven months in Germany ". . . reporting on the industrial rationalization movement, and his reports directly influenced the path it took in Japan" (Johnson, 1982, p. 108).

The German notion of rationalization, that markets can be regulated by cartels to mobilize resources for production based upon international best-practice methods, provided the conceptual basis for the Temporary Industry Rationality Bureau established in 1930, and the Important Industries Control Law of 1931. The concept of control replaced that of competition as the vehicle for production modernization.

The theory behind cartels was that uncoordinated price competition was self-defeating over the business cycle. Price competition leads to overproduction, insufficient specialization, cutthroat competition, and bankruptcy in the inevitable business downturns. The result would be less investment as firms opted for financial liquidity for fear of bankruptcy during a downswing and less competition amongst survivor firms in the ensuing upswing. Control associations, or cartels, by facilitating cooperation amongst competitors on prices, output, and investment plans, could counter the tendency to cutthroat competition without sacrificing industrial dynamism. Higher prices to consumers in the short run would be counteracted by the lower prices resulting from long-term investments in the modernization of production in the long run.

The logic of cartel-regulated competition has been a central, if contested, feature of Japanese government policy toward business at least since the establishment of the MCI. A legal basis for cartels was first established with the Control Law of 1931 which gave the MCI the authority to organize "control associations", to enforce their terms on non-participants, and to receive and approve the investment plans of all firms. Control associations were organized in 26 designated "important industries".

The Control Law of 1931 was not intended to signal a turn by the MCI away from small and medium-sized industries. But by the late 1930s, the civilian orientation of products and the decentralized power structure of small and medium-sized firms were inconsistent with the military's goal of mobilizing a war economy. An Industrial Conversion Policy Department was established within the MCI to provide incentives for small and medium-sized firms to shift into munitions or exports and to merge into larger enterprises. The zaibatsu were willing participants in the economic centralization drives of the military.

But with the passage of the National General Mobilization Law of 1938 which "authorized the complete reorganization of the society along totalitarian lines" (Johnson, 1982, p. 138) and the creation of the Industrial Policy Bureau in the same year, the meaning of rationalization came to include the elimination of small and medium-sized enterprises. In 1941, a public corporation, the Industrial Facilities Corporation, was created to convert small and medium firms into large enterprises as part of the process of shifting production from domestic goods to munitions. The problem for the military was that small firms were able to avoid governmental controls and continue to supply civilian markets. Thereafter a licence from the MCI was required to start a business. Ironically, whereas the MCI had originally identified the zaibatsu as a major barrier to productive rationalization, the Control Law of 1931 and the military buildup reinforced the predominance of the zaibatsu at the expense of small and medium-sized firms.

The intention of the Control Law of 1931 and other centralization initiatives, including the promotion of cartels amongst large firms, was to increase production of civilian and military goods. The presupposition was that MCI officials could direct production by governing the control associations. But, as it turned out, the governance of the control associations was not a simple matter. From the early days of cartel formation the issue of control had been contested. In fact, converting formal into effective control of production was a difficult task. At first the Japanese followed the German model of cartel self-control by industry association with minimal governmental supervision. But self-control did not lead to increased production, which led MCI officials to seek new directions.

Faced with the power of the zaibatsu over the cartels and their lack of commitment to rationalization, ministry officials sought to gain industrial expertise and develop an independent capacity to establish sector strategies. Industry-specific, or vertical, bureaus were set up within the MCI to act as sector rationalizing agents. These vertical bureaus gained intimate knowledge of the sector domestically and secured information on the developments within the sector internationally. Without firsthand knowledge of the principles of production as well as the strengths and weaknesses of foreign competitors, a rationalization policy had little chance of success.

But while ministry sector experts may desire to parachute in a strategic plan for a sector, it cannot be implemented without acceptance by a critical mass of leading enterprises within the sector. All too often the zaibatsu were not willing to pursue rationalization strategies that MCI deemed necessary to modernize industry. The lesson was that a sector strategy, without consensus, is a purely scholastic exercise. Successful implementation of a sector strategy depends upon the active participation of enterprise management in its formulation not only because of the need for information, but also to gain their commitment to it. Thus once again the ministry officials were frustrated by the autonomous power of the zaibatsu families. No sector strategy could be agreed and implemented without their support, and they were not committed to rationalization.

Next, the MCI resorted to passing laws as a means of gaining control over production. A series of industry-specific laws were passed to rationalize key sectors including electric power, steel, machine tools, shipbuilding, and light metals. In the case of the Electric Power Control Law of 1938 ministerial supervision was accompanied by public ownership. The law ". . . forcibly merged 33 generating companies and 70 distribution companies into 9 public utilities under the control and supervision of the Electric Power Bureau of the Ministry of Communications" (Johnson, 1982, p. 126).[2]

In most cases, however, the ministry officials sought to supervise without ownership. Industrial rationalization, as in Germany, did not lead to widespread state ownership. An important reason was that the political power of the zaibatsu precluded nationalization as a viable

---

[2] Johnson adds that the nine companies still exist, although in the postwar period they are privately owned and supervised by the Ministry of International Trade and Industry (MITI).

option. When the zaibatsu were threatened by a Japanese version of national socialism, in which management would be taken over by the state with ownership left in private hands, the zaibatsu had the political power to force the military government's Cabinet Planning Board to back down in the form of the passage of the Important Industries Association Ordinance in 1941 which was designed to settle the control issue. A "control association" would be created for each industry. All enterprises in the industry would be members of the control association which would be given powers to allocate materials, set production levels, and control distribution. The head of each control association would be the chief executive officer of the largest firm in the industry.

This governance structure lasted until 1943 when the failure of the zaibatsu to reach production targets led the Diet to pass the Munition Company Law, which finally separated management from ownership. The 1943 Act empowered the Ministry of Munitions to turn the directors of the control associations into quasi-ministerial officials whose orders had the force of law. The officials were appointed by the ministry and the control associations were constituted as public corporations in which all capital was subscribed by the government. The Law authorized the stationing of "munitions supervisors" in the factories and made them responsible for production targets (Johnson, 1982, p. 168).

As a result of the failure to resolve the power struggle between the industrial policymakers and the zaibatsu, the issue of control over the cartels was never resolved. Consequently, even during the Second World War, the MCI and its successor, the Ministry of Munitions, were unable to administer an effective industrial policy. Economic performance was poor. Throughout the war production lagged behind what government leaders were convinced was possible, but they were powerless to push up productivity either by state ownership or supervision.

One lesson from Japanese wartime economic history was that in the face of a political stalemate, economic growth could not be dictated by government agency, even a government agency with all of the controls of the Japanese wartime government. In this case the stalemate was the result of two contending centers of economic management, the zaibatsu and the government planning authorities. Ironically, as we shall see, governmental power to influence enterprise decisions was greatly enhanced by the postwar occupying forces. They broke the back of the political stalemate in Japanese industrial policymaking by resolving the power struggle between the zaibatsu and a reconstituted Ministry of Commerce and Industry.

The American Legacy: Antitrust versus Industrial Policy

The first major industrial policy act of the General Headquarters of the Supreme Commander for Allied Powers (SCAP) was the dissolution of the zaibatsu which, because of their holding company organizational form, was straightforward. Over 80 holding companies were broken up during 1946 and 1947; Mitsui, the largest, was divided into about 200 companies and Mitsubishi into 139 companies. Zaibatsu shares were confiscated from the zaibatsu families and sold to the public (Aida, 1979, p. 5).

The breakup of the zaibatsu was accompanied by the first Antitrust Act in 1947. Modelled on US antitrust law, the Japanese Antitrust Act of 1947 had the following provisions (Aida, 1979, pp. 5–6):

1 Private monopoly and unfair transactions were prohibited.
2 Joint actions, such as output, price, and marketing cartels, were prohibited except where their effects on competition were negligible. Exclusive buying or selling by any association of enterprises was prohibited. International investments were prohibited if they included joint action.
3 The following business organizational activities were prohibited: holding companies, cross-company share ownership, more than 5 percent holding of a finance company in any other company, interlocking directorship amongst competitors, and mergers without permission of the Fair Trade Commission (FTC).

The Anti-Trust Act of 1947 reflects the intention of SCAP to decentralize the Japanese economy and reconstruct it according to the theoretical vision of perfect competition that guided American antitrust policy. To this end SCAP passed the Law Relating to the Prohibition of Private Monopoly and to Methods of Preserving Fair Trade, referred to as the Antimonopoly Law, and created the FTC, modelled on the US Federal Trade Commission, to administer antitrust laws.

However, unlike American antitrust, in which inter-firm price agreements are a per se violation of the law, the Antimonopoly Law has never been open to the charge that it fostered a concentration of enforcement officer energies on price-fixing agreements amongst small firms. In fact, the Antimonopoly Law did not stop the Ministry of Munitions from establishing, in 1948, a Medium and Smaller Enterprises Agency to act, in effect, as a cartel headquarters for small business within the Ministry. But this act of the Ministry of Munitions, shortly before it was converted into the Ministry of International Trade and Industry, was symbolic of a tension between the FTC, as the enforcement agency for antitrust legislation, and the Ministry as an administrator of industrial policy. Awareness of this tension is central to an understanding of the success of postwar Japanese economic policymaking, a theme to which I will return.

But the Antitrust Act of 1947 was no sooner enacted than SCAP abruptly reversed its policy towards the industrial structure of the economy. The altered outlook was a consequence of the success of the communist movement in China. SCAP's concern with the power of the prewar Zaibatsu vanished once Japan's potential role as an ally in a war against China was considered. This meant mobilization of the productive power of the Japanese economy. In the new context, the decentralization provisions within the Antitrust Act not only thwarted the re-emergence of Japanese Big Business, but limited the role of foreign investment in Japan by large American firms. The Pentagon procurement system, like all war planning agencies, is simplified by contracting with large rather than small businesses. Abruptly the SCAP industrial decentralization ideal was replaced by the imperatives of military procurement.

A revised Antitrust Act came into effect in July 1949. Each of the anti-holding-company provisions of the 1947 Act was relaxed. Companies could freely hold shares in other companies provided that the effect was not to reduce competition substantially. In fact a company was permitted to hold more than 10 percent of the shares of a competitor if it notified the FTC (Aida, 1979, pp. 7–8). The early revision of the Antitrust Act paved the way for the eventual re-establishment of zaibatsu-type enterprise groups organized around banks and holding companies.

At the same time that the Antitrust Act was being revised, the General Headquarters of SCAP resurrected the prewar industrial policy agency: in May 1949, the wartime Ministry of Munitions, which had replaced the prewar Ministry of Commerce and Industry, was reconstituted as the Ministry of International Trade and Industry (MITI). The FTC, created earlier to promote economic decentralization, now had a powerful competitor committed to an entirely different vision for reconstructing business and industrial organization in Japan.

Whereas the emerging Cold War had profound effects on the industrial restructuring policies of SCAP, the massive Korean war expenditures in Japan by the US military fostered industrial investment and economic growth. The contours of a distinctly new industrial order were emerging. The institutional arrangements bequeathed by SCAP formed the foundations for a novel set of industrial policy institutions that would facilitate the rise of Japanese Big Business to international leadership in the space of two decades.

The halcyon days of state power to shape, implement, and enforce sector strategies on individual firms were not during the war, but during the foreign occupation following the war. By breaking up the zaibatsu, SCAP created a power vacuum, and with it an opening that the Ministry of Munitions never had even under the wartime National General Mobilization Law. In effect, SCAP gave power to the ministry that it had not been able to wrest from the zaibatsu on its own: control over the inter-firm associations. The fact that new cartel formation was illegal became irrelevant with revisions to, and "flexible administration" of, the antitrust laws. The result was a radical alteration in the distribution of power between the business and state sectors.

SCAP not only eliminated the major source of opposition to MITI's predecessors in industrial policymaking, it also gave MITI instruments that had been controlled previously by a rival within the state, the Ministry of Finance – namely, controls over foreign exchange and capital flows. The passage of the Foreign Exchange and Foreign Trade Control Law of 1949 gave discretionary power to MITI to control imports and foreign exchange. Business enterprises were beholden to MITI for import licenses and access to foreign exchange (even of foreign currency generated by their own sales abroad). The 1949 Act was not a new policy; during the depression the Capital Flight Prevention Law of 1932 and the Foreign Exchange Control Law of 1933 had made all international transactions subject to the approval of the Ministry of Finance. But MCI (MITI's predecessor) never had such powers.

The Ministry of Finance maintained ultimate control of the money supply, but MITI also gained considerable influence over the conditions of credit as a result of structural changes in the financial system established by SCAP. SCAP ordered the creation of six government banks including the Japanese Development Bank (JDB) and the Export Bank, both of which have played a major role in channelling finance away from free-market priorities towards long-term industrial investments, often with very low short-term returns.[3] The JDB has purposefully segmented the capital "market", financing new industries that would probably never have been started in a "free" capital market such as the stock markets of America and Britain.

The JDB provides investment funds to industry by rationing personal savings deposited in the postal savings account system, a government institution with more assets than any private bank in the world. In the early postwar years MITI used its authority to screen all loan applications to the JDB to target credit to designated sectors and firms.

Taking these measures together, a potentially powerful and centralized

---

[3] For an analysis of why low rates of return do not deter Japanese firms from productive investments see Abegglen and Stalk (1985, chapter 7).

industrial policymaking agency emerged during the occupation of Japan. By the early 1950s MITI's formal industrial policymaking instruments included access to foreign exchange, foreign capital, imports, technology, and licenses, access to domestic credit and selective tax measures and authorization to form cartels. These instruments were crucial in establishing MITI as a catalyst for economic restructuring and development.

Japan was perhaps fortunate that the ideology of free markets was not imposed. Instead, after a brief period of promoting free markets, SCAP turned to the creation of a series of political and economic institutions that were designed to mobilize resources under the tutelage of a visible hand – MITI. In this, US economic policymakers were remarkably successful in overseeing the development of a governmental agency for economic restructuring and enterprise rationalization. It has never been so successful in Third World countries when the same role has been assigned to the invisible hand of the free market.

Formal Inter-firm Cooperation

Industrial Policy Cartels

Foreign occupation and the Korean War both ended in 1952. A recession followed. Faced with excess production, MITI created a series of cartels to prevent "overcompetition" and enforced them by control over the instruments listed above.

While cartels amongst large companies were in violation of the Antitrust Act, the FTC chose not to prosecute in cases in which agreements had been achieved in consultation with MITI (Aida, 1979, p. 15). But pressure from small firms hurt by cartels amongst emerging Big Business coalitions led to the passage of the Act of Provisional Measures for Stabilizing Selected Small and Medium Enterprises in August 1952. This Act was the first in a series that relaxed the anti-cartel provisions of the Antitrust Act of 1947. The new pro-cartel Act provided that "if more than half of the qualified enterprises in an area agree to be members and two-thirds of the members are small and medium sized enterprises", they could form a cartel. Furthermore, MITI could order outsiders to join after obtaining consent from the FTC.

The Act excluding small and medium-sized firms from antitrust legislation was followed by the Export Trade Act and a series of Acts by other ministries for the exemption of client industries. Examples include the Ministry of Posts and Telecommunications and the telecommunications industry including Nippon T & T, the Ministry of Transport and railroad equipment producers and operating companies, and the

178   *The New Competition*

Ministry of Health and Welfare and the pharmaceuticals industry (Magaziner and Hout, 1980, p. 33). The justification for exemption was cutthroat competition, a concept that has no theoretical content in free-market theory, the imported theoretical underpinning of Japanese antitrust legislation, but is meaningful to Schumpeterian economics which, as already noted, is the implicit theory that guides Japanese industrial policy.

In 1953 a revised Antitrust Act was passed which attempted to save the idea of antitrust policy by establishing cartel guidelines. The Revised Antitrust Act gave the FTC authority to approve cartels and mergers and judge them in terms of their consistency with a weakened competitiveness criterion.

In this new round of cartel creation the economic justification shifted from the pernicious effect of cutthroat competition during recession to that of price competition during the early stages of long-term investment in new plant and equipment. Firms making long-term investments would eventually generate economies of scale but were vulnerable to non-investing competitors in the short term. Cartels could now be justified on one of two grounds, cutthroat competition (recession cartels) and infant industry (rationalization cartels). Both were defended on the grounds of increasing future competitiveness.

MITI sought to expand its statutory power to regulate competition by a proposed amendment to the Antitrust Act in 1958 which would have made rationalization and recession cartels effective simply by notifying the FTC as opposed to receiving permission. The amendment would have relaxed the conditions for large-scale mergers. The proposed amendment faced a barrage of criticism in the Diet and did not pass. With the failure of the amendment MITI has relied upon "flexible administration" of the revised Act of 1953. In 1971, over 800 cartels were registered with the FTC as shown in table 4.

But MITI's influence over inter-firm cooperation has never been limited to formal cartels. MITI's sector bureaus depend upon and promote active trade associations as a conduit for shaping and implementing sector strategies which, in turn, can have considerable influence in the shaping of the business plans of individual firms. The number of trade associations that had filed with the FTC before 1982 exceeds 23,000, a figure that does not include about 77,000 small-business cooperative associations registered under various statutes (Okumura, 1984, p. 75).

Table 4 Laws authorizing cartels and number of cartels authorized under each, March 1971

Law	Number of cartels
Rationalization cartels	13
Machine Tool Industry Emergency Act	17
Electronics Industry Promotion Act	2
Fertilizer Industry Price Stabilization Act	4
Sake and related industries	7
Marine Products Export Promotion Law	8
Marine Products Adjustment Act	7
Services Industry Sanitation Law	123
Domestic Sea Transportation Act	21
Export–Import Trading Act	195
Small and Medium Enterprise Law	439

Source: Fair Trade Commission, 1971; cited in Yamamura, 1982, p. 82.

Enterprise Groups

At the same time that MITI was attempting to increase its statutory powers to promote cartels, the Japanese industrial structure was being reconcentrated with the reincarnation of the outlawed zaibatsu as enterprise groups, underpinned by the postwar kaisha described in the last chapter. The three largest zaibatsu, Mitsubishi, Mitsui, and Sumitomo, led the "zaibatsu revival" of the mid-1950s. The organizational structure was altered: instead of a pyramidal holding company owned and managed by a single family as in the zaibatsu, the enterprise group is a network of crossed stock-holdings with a bank and a trading company at the center. Besides regular meetings of the chief executives, the core bank and trading company coordinate activities amongst the member firms and promote the collective marketing and financial interests of the group.

The enterprise groups are joint owned in that each member commonly owns 1–2 percent of the equity of each other member; together 20–30 percent of the shares of each corporation are held by group members (Okumura, 1984, p. 172). By 1981, six enterprise groups (the above three plus Fuji, Daiichi, and Sanwa) owned about 25 percent of the total assets, realized 15 percent of the sales, earned 20 percent of the profit, and employed 5 percent of the employees of all incorporated enterprises (Okumura, 1984, p. 175).

The "zaibatsu revival" indicated the lack of power of the FTC. At the same time, the failure of MITI to push the proposed antitrust amendment through the Diet signalled a changed economic and political environment and hence a reverse shift in power within the state away from MITI and toward FTC. But the FTC has never enjoyed intellectual support within Japan similar to that offered by the American economics profession for its United States counterpart, the Federal Trade Commission. One reason is that, even with the reconcentration of the Japanese economy, competition has remained intense. It has not been the form of competition celebrated by free-market theory, but Schumpeterian competition over new products, processes, and organizational forms. Competition has been particularly intense over the early establishment of market share for new products and whole new sectors amongst enterprise groups. Often six new firms, each backed by an enterprise group, emerge with each new sector (Johnson, 1982, p. 206). The new firms are often joint ventures amongst firms within each enterprise group.

Against the background of the "zaibatsu revival", cartels have maintained intellectual credibility. While cartels are presumed to be anticompetitive by conventional economic theory and antitrust legislation, they have not undermined the Schumpeterian competitiveness of Japanese firms. Cartels amongst small and medium-sized firms can counter the power of enterprise groups and foster Penrosian interstitial competition. Foreign trade cartels can generate exports by sharing marketing and distribution expenses. Recession cartels can apportion reduced demand amongst firms as opposed to bankruptcy amongst the weakest firms, with the consequence that in the upswing more competitors would be around to ensure competition.

It is safe to conclude that whether cartels will facilitate or retard economic progress cannot be decided by theory. It depends upon the ever-changing mixture amongst forces, both private and public, that both enhance and diminish competition, and the form it takes, in an economy.

Administrative Guidance: Sector Restructuring

MITI's influence has not depended on statutory powers. Surprisingly, governmental regulatory agencies in the United States have statutory powers that do not exist in Japan. For example, the contempt power of US courts and the investigatory power of US administrative agencies are either absent or nowhere near as effective in Japan (Haley, 1986, p. 116). Perhaps more significant, MITI does not have the legal power to limit entry to the degree that many regulatory commissions in the United States can. Lacking formal enforcement powers, MITI has not been able to control entry in many crucial sectors. For example, Honda, Sony, Kawasaki, Matsushita and Kobe Steel have all successfully entered industries despite efforts by MITI to block them. The power that the Civil Aviation Board had to regulate the entry of companies into the airline industry would be the envy of MITI officials.

MITI turned its statutory weakness into a strength with the refinement of administrative guidance, a term for the non-statutory informal institutional processes whereby MITI and other administrative agencies exert influence over business enterprises to promote their international competitiveness. The formulation of sector strategies is fundamental to administrative guidance.

Sector Strategies

As noted above, in the inter-war period MITI's predecessors, the MCI and the Ministry of Munitions, established "vertical bureaus" or sector planning departments for carrying out sector-specific rationalization plans. MITI continued and expanded the idea of vertical bureaus and sector-specific "deliberation councils" composed of private and public officials who met on a permanent basis.

The success of vertical bureaus depended on forging a joint private–public consensus around a sector development plan; it was not to be left to industry associations or unilaterally imposed by MITI experts. MITI's influence during the 1950s was substantial because of the following range of instruments that it could use to mold a consensus:

1 tariffs and quotas;
2 control of foreign exchange;
3 influence over credit allocation in public and private banks;
4 technology import licenses;
5 accelerated depreciation allowances;
6 land subsidization;
7 influence over cartel legalization with the FTC;
8 creation of a joint private–public company.

Clearly, many of MITI's early industry policy measures involved market restraints which by 1960 put the Japanese government under pressure from foreign governments and international agencies such as the International Monetary Fund (IMF), the office of the General Agreement on Trade and Tariffs, the EEC, and the Office of Economic and Cultural Development. Access to foreign markets meant that Japan had to submit plans for the removal of restraints on imported commodities, foreign exchange, and capital flows. The loss of direct controls in each of these markets reduced MITI's power to influence enterprise decisionmaking. At the same time the increasing profitability of many Japanese firms was reducing their dependence on bank loans and thereby on MITI's indirect influence over credit allocation.

To compensate for the loss of market controls, MITI urged enactment of the Provisional Act for Promoting Selected Industries in 1963 and 1964. The object of the Bill was to give MITI statutory authority to promote concentration, merger, and cartels amongst firms in industries threatened by trade liberalization. But, as in the case of the 1958 effort to revise the Antitrust Act, MITI lacked the political muscle to get the proposed Act through the Diet. MITI was caught between, on the one hand, the pressures of the kaisha for "voluntary adjustments" administered by private industrial associations as opposed to joint public–private cooperation, and on the other hand, the combined pressures of anti-Big Business interests and rival governmental agencies, particularly the Ministry of Finance and the FTC (Aida, 1979, p. 32).

Faced with the challenge of loss of market controls to impose development plans on sectors, MITI responded by providing firms with sector strategic analyses. The development plans of the inter-war vertical bureaus were not based upon a strategic analysis of the threats to and opportunities for specific sectors in the international market. In contrast, MITI's vertical bureaus developed sector strategies as criteria to justify formal cartels and monitor their progress in terms of promoting the underlying rationalization of the sector; however, where formal cartels were not legal, sector strategies formed the conceptual core for rationalization quasi-cartels. What distinguishes postwar Japanese industrial policy is not the idea of sector planning but of sector *strategic* planning.

Never enamored of free-market theory and having learned the limits of government planning from the inter-war experience, MITI sought to integrate the two creatively in ways that redefine both concepts: instead of markets we find market forces and instead of planning we find strategic visions. Market liberalization, by forcing MITI to look to alternatives to market controls as means of promoting rationalization, contributed to the institutionalization of the process of establishing sector strategies.

Market forces are simply competitor firms. As such, market forces are continuously being reshaped as firms adjust strategies and develop productive capacities. Government planning is not about creating masterplans for directing business activities to avoid the market, but about fostering strategic planning within business enterprises so that they will become market forces with which other forms have to reckon. The first step in fostering strategic planning is the articulation of a long-range vision suggesting the future sectoral contours on a world scale; the second is to suggest the potential place of Japan's firms within that broader picture; the third is to shape the strategies of individual business enterprises to make the transition from the present organizational capabilities to those required by the sector strategy and thereby convert Japanese firms into international market forces.

The basis of competitive success in the international economy depends upon strategic awareness. Japanese firms have been most successful in sectors in which foreign competitors have lacked strategic sophistication. Famous examples include the motorcycle, electrical appliances, steel, and automobile industries. As noted in chapter 5, American and British firms retreated to low volume up-market products when faced with the invasion of the Japanese-made motorcycles at the high volume lower end of the market. But Japanese success at the bottom end was used to finance moving up a segment which led to further retreat by the traditional producers. The process of segment retreat continued until Japanese firms were using scale economies to produce at costs that could only be achieved by focused production (Abegglen and Stalk, 1985, p. 89). In the case of consumer electrical products, US competitors chose to produce overseas rather than modernize their production facilities at home. But losing control of production has turned out to be one step towards losing control of the market.

These cases illustrate again the crucial importance of strategy in international competition. All too often, Western competitors have been slow to respond to strategic initiatives from Japanese firms and, even when they became aware of the threat, they lacked the production flexibility to respond.

The idea of sector strategy, however, is more than the promotion of effective strategies within individual firms. It implies that the strategies of firms within a sector are interdependent. A strategy of price competition, for example, can create irresistible pressures for firms to cut margins and compete on the basis of lowest cost and thereby undermine the long-term investments required for rationalization. The purpose of a sector strategy is to negotiate the form that competition takes to ensure the long-term development of the sector. It does not mean eliminating competition, but shaping its terms. The task is to create the right mix of competition and cooperation, a mix that is continuously shifting.

MITI's success in industrial policy derives from the effective joint public–private articulation and coordination of long-term strategic analysis at the sector level. Sector strategic analysis is a public good in that it costs no more to provide it freely to all than it costs to provide it to one consumer. Unlike private consultancies, which depend upon the provision of private products, MITI supplies the information for forming strategic orientations within all cooperating firms in a sector. But in the process the strategies of individual firms are shaped within a context of accounting for the long-term effects on the international competitiveness of the sector. In this MITI serves to demystify and, ironically, to decentralize strategic planning within the individual enterprise.

At the same time, promoting cooperation enhances the potential of firms in a sector to insulate themselves from market forces and extract monopoly profits. Here the task of MITI is to keep firms honest. Milestones built into a sector strategy for establishing and maintaining international competitiveness provide a standard for assessing an enterprise's performance.

Successful strategic planning does not come from having a secret strategy but the right strategy, in terms of both competitors and the culture and organization of the enterprise. A theme of the last chapter was that strategy implementation in a business enterprise, unlike in the military, is improved by strategic thinking at every level of the organization. Here the theme is that strategic planning is too important, and its effects too pervasive, for its formulation to be left to the private sector.

Of course, the public articulation of sector strategies is anathema to many business managers in the West, where confidentiality is considered a competitive necessity. As a result Western firms often lack an institutional means of testing strategies before implementation or of refining strategies over time. One way to test a strategy adjustment is to try it out on industry experts. MITI, as a non-profit-making strategic planning agency, provides a testing board for strategic discussions. MITI is aware, like perhaps no other single agency anywhere, of the competitive strategies and production capabilities of leading firms everywhere in the world. But the value of MITI is not simply that it is sensitive to global business dynamics, but that its deliberation councils have a capacity for dispassionate analysis of strategies that it is impossible for firms to supply to themselves. Involvement of trade associations, academics, ministry personnel, and other firms precludes confidentiality, but by not having pecuniary involvement of its own, or of client firms, MITI is well situated for such discussions. At its best, MITI's strategic analysis to the firm is like psychoanalysis to the individual: it digs beneath the surface to find the hidden sources of anxiety – sources that the subject's own defense mechanisms have hidden from conscious perception.

Technology Transfer and Diffusion

One of the elements in the success of Japanese firms has been the capacity to absorb and refine technological developments that originated elsewhere. MITI has played an active role in promoting technology transfer and diffusion as part of its production rationalization campaigns.

The Japanese Productivity Center was set up in 1955, financed by the US government, Japanese businesses, and the Japanese government, to carry out a productivity campaign of "joint public and private efforts". The productivity campaign stressed the need to introduce technologies from advanced capitalist nations. The most rapid means was to promote generic or sector-wide technology transfers that would benefit all the firms in a given sector.

Rationalization cartels were created, in part, as efforts to diffuse technology. To the extent that they were successful, such cartels promoted long-run competition by increasing the number of firms that had access to the new technologies. However, market provision of technology transfer could be used by individual firms to erect barriers to entry. Cartels or sector strategies, overseen by MITI, could ensure that technology transfers were used for the purpose of developing the sector and not merely individual firms in it.

Between 1951 and 1984, Japanese companies and agencies entered into nearly 42,000 contracts for importing technology at a total cost of about $17 billion (Abegglen and Stalk, 1985, p. 127). The negotiations for most of these contracts were overseen by MITI officials to ensure favorable terms and rapid diffusion. The Louisiana Purchase is an analogous bargain in the wholesale purchase of productive resources by one nation from another.

The Ministry of International Trade and Industry and the Automobile Industry

The automobile industry provides an example of MITI intervention. MITI had few doubts about the strategic advantage of car production to building an independent industrial base, or about the use of trade controls. Quotas, in effect from 1950 to 1965, limited passenger car imports to under 10,000 per year and tariffs lasted until the spring of 1978.

For MITI, the purpose of cartels, tariffs, and other market controls is to promote production rationalization. In the case of Nissan, MITI encouraged and supervised a seven-year tie-up with Austin, beginning in 1952, first to assemble and then to produce Austin A40 cars in Japan.

Austin agreed to provide the technical assistance as well as the designs to enable Nissan to shift gradually to locally made components over a three-year period. As a percentage of Nissan car sales, the A40 declined from 44 percent in 1953 to 13 percent in 1959 (Cusumano, 1985, p. 92). Nissan used the tie-up to develop the production capacity for its own Datsun and, when the joint venture was completed in 1959, to produce the Cedric, a clone of the Austin A40.

But just as tariffs can promote rationalization, so can tariff removal in other circumstances. MITI's decision to remove import quotas in 1965 was bitterly opposed by the automakers. But from the viewpoint of Naohiro Amaya, the MITI vice-minister, "The timing was quite important and was probably the greatest single contribution made by the ministry to the industry's development" (Jim Smith, *Automotive News*, March 9, 1987). Amaya argues that to have removed the quotas five years sooner or later would have been equally damaging to the industry's development.

At the same time, removing import quotas reduced MITI's influence over the industry. In 1966, MITI arranged a merger between Nissan and Prince Motor Company and was aggressively pursuing a strategy of reorganizing the entire industry around the two leaders, Toyota and Nissan. The strategy involved promoting a merger between Mitsubishi and Isuzu Motors against the wishes of Mitsubishi. To the embarrassment of MITI, Mitsubishi countered by establishing a joint venture with the Chrysler Corporation. MITI was opposed to American automaker investments in Japan. Izusu followed with a General Motors joint venture and Ford acquired an equity holding in what was to become Mazda Motor Corporation (*Automotive News*, March, 1987). MITI believed that the Japanese automobile industry had too many producers and would be overwhelmed by the more advanced American companies. Here MITI was wrong.

By 1980, Japan led the world in car production with an annual output of 11 million vehicles; the United States produced 8 million and Britain produced 1.3 million. By 1983 Nissan-Japan overcame Ford-USA to become the third-largest automaker behind General Motors and Toyota (Cusumano, 1985, pp. 2–3). By now the threat to the Japanese automobile industry was not that of direct foreign competition, but protective legislation by foreign governments faced with structurally depressed regions that had historically depended upon car production.

MITI's influence was quickly reasserted in the new conditions. Anticipating protectionist legislation in the United States, MITI placed a ceiling on passenger car exports to the United States in spring 1981 as part of the 1981 Voluntary Restraint Agreement with the Reagan administration. Japanese automakers objected, but sat down and negotiated the relative shares with MITI. MITI's power, in this case, was assisted with a cabinet "order" to facilitate implementation. But the automakers were aware that MITI was effective in defending them against a worse outcome: the passage of a protectionist trade Bill by the US Congress.

Administrative Guidance: Intersector Restructuring

Competitive for Comparative Advantage

MITI's vertical bureaus focus on individual sectors. It is the task of the Industrial Structure Division and its joint private–public deliberation council to coordinate the vertical bureaus and establish guidelines for long-term investments which shape the future sectoral compositions. These guidelines prioritize sectors for the purposes of signalling to business enterprises and officials in charge of credit allocation, research funding, and educational planning.

MITI cannot impose sector guidelines on to the investment plans of individual enterprises. But MITI's sector guidelines, built up from the strategic analyses of the vertical bureaus, provide bankers with a basis for both choosing amongst and coordinating long-term investment projects. In the real world future enterprise success depends upon long-term financial commitments to irreversible developmental investments in specific processes, organization, and individuals.

Developmental investments have opportunity costs; developing steel capacity, for example, means not developing enterprises with the physical resources, skills, teamwork, and experience required to compete against enterprises that have made such developmental investments. The task of choosing which sectors offer the greatest development potential is as difficult as it is necessary. Intersector strategic planning depends upon a criterion for making these choices.

The neoclassical theory of comparative advantage, as modified by Hecksher–Ohlin, offers the simplest criterion for signalling the desired composition of sectors: relative factor endowments.[4] Comparative

---

[4] For a critique of static comparative advantage theory and an appeal to replace it with a dynamic theory of comparative advantage see Scott (1984). Elsewhere, the "new international economics" has altered the assumption of decreasing returns to scale and established the result that returns to scale can be as important as comparative advantage to explaining trade. The case for non-interference by governments in markets has shifted. For the theory of comparative advantage the case against government interference was economic: growth would suffer. For the "new international economics" the case against government interference is political: in theory it could lead to higher growth, but

advantage theory recommends that a region specialize according to relative costs of production, and the Hecksher–Ohlin amendment posits that relative costs are a function of a region's endowment of resources. For postwar Japan, which lacked both natural resources and capital, labor was the cheap resource, relative to other nations, which meant that Japan would maximize national income by producing and exporting labor-intensive products. The virtue of free markets, according to neoclassical trade theory, is that businessmen responding spontaneously to market prices would shift toward those products that utilized the comparatively abundant resource. Government interference with free markets, according to the theory, could only lead a country away from the income-maximizing allocation of resources.

For MITI, the problem with passively accepting the composition of industries that are generated by the "market" is that the market, left alone, can reinforce productive backwardness. The reason is that production begets Penrosian economies of organization and learning which can be self-reinforcing under conditions of free trade. From the early days, MITI officials argued that Japanese productive services would suffer, consumers would seek foreign products, and Japan would become a permanent follower in production capabilities. Japanese firms would remain a victim of market forces rather than becoming market forces themselves.

The problem with comparative advantage theory is that it suffers from the same weakness as the neoclassical theory of the firm: it is taken as given that markets are opposed to institutions that can be shaped by strategic actions. If integrating market theory with Schumpeterian competition breathed life into the theory of the firm, integrating industrial policy with Schumpeterian competition breathes life into the theory of comparative advantage and alters its meaning. It is no longer about static resource endowments and abstract optimality criteria. The theory of comparative advantage becomes a theory of competitive advantage.

The idea of competitive advantage gives explanatory power to strategy and organization. The success of firms in the market depends upon the organization of work, firm, and sector and their interrelationships. Japanese economic policymakers did not choose to specialize according to measures of comparative resource endowments. They sought instead to maximize growth by specializing in those sectors where a competitive advantage could be established by developing organizational superiority.

---

governments cannot be trusted. Ajit Singh has made this point to me. For a review of the "new international economics" see Krugman (1987).

This required information that was not embodied in resource prices. It meant articulating competitive strategies based upon a comparison of the organizational strengths and weaknesses of foreign firms, sector by sector.

Japanese economic policymakers gambled that organization, the intermediary variable between the cost of resources and the value of output, could be the basis of competitive advantage, and that organization is a non-marketable input. Unlike natural resources, but like teamwork and experience, organization could not be sold and purchased in the market. Therefore competitive advantage based upon organizational superiority, once established, would be both difficult and time consuming for competitors to match, even from countries with relatively abundant resource endowments.

At the same time that organization can be considered as a basis for competitive advantage, it is not sufficient for such an advantage. For example, the best organized shipbuilding sector in the world will not be competitive against a less well organized sector elsewhere that pays a fraction of the Japanese wages. For this reason, maintaining a competitive industrial sector depends upon getting industrial organization right in two senses: firm and inter-firm organization, and sector composition. The right sector composition depends upon the developments in firm and inter-firm organization elsewhere.

Japanese industrial policy involves sequential targeting of sectors to maintain industrial competitiveness. As shown in figure 3, it started with low-skilled labor-intensive products, but with the intention of moving first to medium-skilled medium-capital-using products, second to skilled-labor raw-material-intensive sectors, and third to knowledge-intensive sectors. The process of moving through such a hierarchy of sectors is depicted in figure 3 as a reshaping diamond. As resources were shifted from unskilled-labor intensive sectors through raw-material- and skilled-labor-intensive sectors and eventually to knowledge-intensive sectors the diamond shifted from the lower to the upper quadrants. Sectoral restructuring meant increasing the value added of existing resources as Japan established competitive predominance in more organizationally complex processes and developed more highly skilled labor and experienced enterprises. Clearly, most nations seek to make such a transition across sectors; Japanese industrial policy has been more successful than others in integrating this shifting sectoral pattern with the competitive strategies and organizational capacities of individual business enterprises.

The idea of allocating resources according to the notion of establishing competitive advantage does not ensure success. In fact, the history of industrial policy in Western Europe has made one lesson clear:

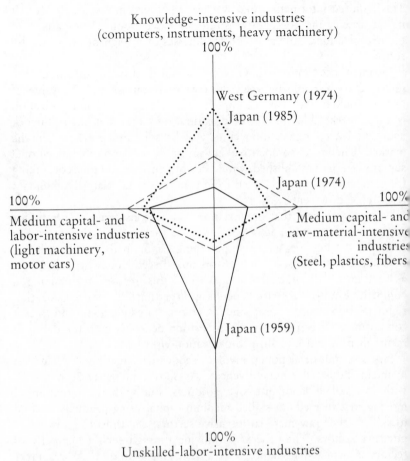

Figure 3 Evolution of Japanese industrial structure.
Source: Japan Economic Survey, Economic Planning Agency, 1974–5; cited in Magaziner and Hout, 1980, p. 7.

government officials do not possess a crystal ball for predicting which firms, or even sectors, will be leaders in the future. Who would have predicted, for example, that the "mature" television industry or the radio industry offered the opportunities for growth that were achieved by Sony? The challenge is to anticipate the relative rates of growth and decline in individual sectors even though no formula for making such choices exists. MITI's Industrial Structure Division employs multiple criteria to negotiate sectoral investment guidelines across competing vertical bureaus.

The starting point is a comparative assessment of the actual and potential competitiveness of a sector in international markets. One factor affecting competitiveness is natural resource intensity and availability. Sectors depending, for example, on raw material inputs that are lacking in Japan but which are presently supplied by Third World countries will likely have a shorter period of competitiveness; eventually, the Third World countries will process the same resources domestically. However, industrial activities that depend upon complex production processes using highly skilled labor will have greater potential for growth in Japan. The newly industrializing countries cannot easily move to such products by purchasing turnkey production processes and utilizing unskilled labor.

However, projections of the desired sectoral composition of industry are not based on estimates of contribution to income growth in the short run. Sectors are assessed in terms of their capacity to generate foreign exchange, highly skilled jobs, technological advance, and regional balance. Comparing the existing with the desired future industrial composition highlights the sectors that are likely to become structurally depressed and those for which growth opportunities can be expected.

The task guiding allocatory decisionmaking across sectors would be simplified if products followed a life cycle. If they did every product could be assumed to have an infant, growth, mature, and declining stage. Since they do not, every product is subject to redefinition and, with it, sectors can suddenly be revitalized by material, process, and product innovations, as the textile industry was transformed by synthetic fibers and the typewriter industry was transformed by the miniaturization of electronic components. Thus an inherent goal of industrial policy is to counter the logic of sector maturity by anticipating new materials and technologies that lead to redefinitions of old sectors. The choice between betting on new technologies for old industries versus betting on new industries is not simple but it is inescapable. MITI's Industrial Structure Deliberation Council ensures only that such bets are informed ones.

The strategic analysis of each sector is pivotal to success of the firms; it also affects the role that MITI plays in a sector at any given time. The role will depend upon the changing relationship between Japanese firms and their competitors in the rest of the world.

In the early or high growth stages of the development of a new Japanese sector for which powerful competitors already exist, both the firms involved and MITI have the same goal: modernization (or creation) of productive plant as quickly as possible. The firms are likely to welcome MITI protection initiatives, including the formation of rationalization cartels where agreed by the FTC, or to agree to sector initiatives proposed by MITI officials under administrative guidance.

If the sector becomes successful in the international economy, MITI's influence wanes. The firms are well situated to carry out strategic analysis, to generate long-term finance on their own, and to pursue technology agreements and even joint ventures with foreign firms. They have little interest in having their policies examined by MITI. But even here MITI often continues to play a role. In the automobile industry, as noted, individual companies are ill suited to negotiate quota arrangements with the US government. The car companies depend upon MITI to make the best possible case and negotiate through MITI with each other over quota shares.

Over time, success in any sector will eventually be followed by tendencies to excess production and structural depression in the industry. MITI seeks to anticipate these developments and negotiate a planned reduction in the growth of Japanese capacity and eventual shift of resources to emerging sectors, many of which will likely be offshoots of the declining sector. Here again, firms are more receptive to MITI initiatives, formal and informal. Nevertheless, consensus is still problematic. In the car industry, for example, MITI believes that the present nine domestic competitors should be reduced to three or four. The car companies do not agree. But where excess production eventually leads to chronic excess capacity, cooperation with MITI can bring considerable relief in the efforts of firms to run down plants in a planned manner. The effectiveness of worker retraining and relocation programs is greatly improved if it is part of a long-term strategy. In the next two sections I will examine the cases of structurally depressed and knowledge-intensive industries.

Structurally Depressed Industries

By the 1970s a number of major Japanese industries were becoming "structurally depressed" or non-competitive in world markets because of soaring energy and raw material costs, increasing wages, and expanding world production capacity in raw material processing and non-complex manufacturing processes. Examples included steel, petrochemicals, pulp and paper, aluminum smelting, shipbuilding, and artificial fibers. As a result in 1978 a Structurally Depressed Industries Law was passed enabling MITI to administer a planned reduction in production capacity for depressed industries and a regional adjustment program for depressed areas. Fourteen structurally depressed industries and 30 depressed areas were identified. Cartels, loan guarantees, unemployment compensation, and priority allocations of public works could be targeted by MITI on each industry and area.

Under the 1978 law, depressed industry cartels can be established only if two-thirds of the firms in a sector petition MITI. This condition puts pressure on the firms within the industry to establish the outlines of a planned reduction in capacity by discussion amongst themselves before MITI becomes involved. The process then is more one of firms negotiating concessions amongst themselves, in contrast with MITI negotiating with each firm individually.

Perhaps the most significant aspect of the Structurally Depressed Industries Law is not the specific measures that MITI can deploy but the refinement of the dynamic concept of industrial policy that is implied. The presupposition is that Schumpeterian competition, by inducing new products and processes, also generates pressures for sectoral change. Sectors are not constant but evolving. The domestic furniture industry, for example, is evolving into the interior design and furnishing industry, or the machine tool industry becomes part of the electronics industry with the development of computer numerically controlled machine tools. The implication is that firms and regions must prepare for economic change to avoid becoming victims of market forces and collapses in sales, margins, investments, tax revenues, and public investments followed by community demoralization. Preparation involves several elements.

1 Anticipation: firms and regions that are monitoring competitive developments are in a position to define the problem earlier. Crucial to anticipation is the existence of an ongoing forum or deliberation council made up of managers and workers rather than the sudden creation of such a forum at the onset of a crisis.
2 Objective analysis: it is crucial that the problem is properly defined. If firms are losing market share because of innovations in organizations in competitor firms then wage reductions will not address the problem.
3 Rationalization strategy: any cartel that simply affects output and price will not work. Reductions in output must be part of a long-term plan to develop internationally competitive firms. This may require radical firm and inter-firm organizational measures. If the products of local firms are inferior in quality or design, for example, the problems could be in the organization of work. This means that any rationalization strategy that is not based upon a consensus and plan about work reorganization is likely to fail.
4 Regional employment program: the best solution to structurally depressed industries is expansion of growth industries. For knowledge-intensive products this implies an educated labor force. In any case the openness of channels to new opportunities is the best way to ensure that the costs of transformation are not displaced to the least powerful. Even this group has a capacity to block change.

Knowledge-Intensive Industries

By the 1970s Japan was entering the club of the most advanced industrialized nations. Nevertheless, MITI feared that, unless the composition of Japan's industrial structure continued to evolve, the Japanese economy could become trapped between industrial followers exploiting low wages and industrial leaders, particularly the United States and West Germany, dominating the new high technology industries. Continued high growth for Japan depended upon gaining a share of the new industries. MITI's fear was that the West's leadership in scientific research was a major advantage for Western enterprises for potential domination of the emerging "knowledge-intensive" sectors. That potential would likely be realized if the industrial composition was left to the market.

MITI's long-range planning documents continue to stress the priority of knowledge-intensive industries to Japan's future. To realize the opportunities in knowledge-intensive industries, MITI is empowered to shape markets by promoting the development of a limited number of strong competitors. The shaping of markets involves promoting cooperation amongst the competitors, particularly at the process developmental stages.

A new market becomes most attractive once the basic technology has been developed. Until that time, an individual firm prefers to wait rather than pay the development costs alone or risk becoming committed to the wrong technology. The industrial policy task becomes one of facilitating the development of the general production technology; private companies will develop its application for specific products. Until recently, MITI has not encouraged the development of new technology concepts; the focus has been on completing and refining technologies for which the basic research has been undertaken elsewhere. MITI's research priorities have stressed the development of generic production processes that enable firms to convert the emerging technologies into a low cost, high volume output.

The recent period has seen a shift from this highly successful development orientation to one of research. MITI is not the only arm of Japanese government turning to industrial research. The Science and Technology Agency (STA) guides Japanese space and nuclear fusion research by funding three specialist public corporations staffed by non-civil servants. In addition, STA partially funds the Japan Research and Development Corporation which transfers research results from university and government laboratories to private companies. The main body responsible for industrial research and development (R&D) is the

Agency of Industrial Science and Technology (AIST), a branch of MITI. AIST includes a staff of 3,500 scientists and runs 16 national laboratories. Finally, various functional ministries, including transport, construction, education, health, and telecommunications, sponsor R&D in their areas and compete with both STA and AIST.

Since 1971, AIST has sponsored a series of technology development projects with the creation of fixed-lifetime agencies. The agencies are funded jointly by MITI and the participating firms. They do research on production-related technologies that will be of use to each of the participants. While most projects are limited to 5–15 firms, chosen by MITI, all firms have access to any results (*National Technology*, August, 1985, p. 28).

Two high priority areas for MITI in the late 1980s are superconductivity and biotechnology. Forty-four Japanese companies are taking part in the MITI-sponsored International Superconductivity Technology Center which opened in 1988. The center will examine markets, applications, and resources for the new materials which carry electricity with practically no resistance. The center will include a MITI-funded superconductivity laboratory. If successful, the new material could result in superfast computers, rapid trains, and cheap energy. The cost for a participating company ranges from $16,000 for an associate membership (which entitles the company to survey findings but not the detailed laboratory results) to $800,000 for full participation. Foreign firms can join; the only one to do so is the Italian chemical and engineering company, Montedison S.p.A. (*Wall Street Journal*, December 30, 1987, p. 14). MITI has mounted a similar campaign in biotechnology. Since 1984, 12 R&D associations have been formed amongst 49 companies. Here the possibility is for a revolution in food processing and drug treatments that could rival the effects of microelectronics in industrial processes (*Wall Street Journal*, December 17, 1987, p. 1).

MITI seeks to integrate knowledge-intensive sector development with a regional policy. In 1983, legislation was passed to effect the location of new industries. "Technopolis policy" is "a plan to form new cities integrating industry, education, and housing near existing focal cities and utilizing existing social resources to create regional centers for industrial development focusing on high technology" (Imai, 1986, p. 153). Fourteen such regional centers and their targeted sectoral concentrations are shown in table 5.

Table 5 Features of the technopolis development plans

Technopolis region			
Prefecture	Name of region	Principal universities	Targeted industrial sectors
Hokkaido	Hakodate	Hokkaido University	Marine-related industries and those making use of natural resources (electronics, mechatronics, biotechnology, etc.)
Akita	Akita	Akita University	Electronics, mechatronics, new materials, natural resources, energy, biotechnology
Niigata	Nagaoka	Nagaoka College of Science and Technology	Higher systems industries, urban industries (design, fashion), industries using local natural resources
Tochigi	Utsunomiya	Utsunomiya University	Electronics, mechatronics, fine chemicals, new materials, software
Shizuoka	Hamamatsu	Shizuoka University Hamamatsu College of Medicine	Optoelectronics industries, advanced mechatronics, home sound culture (electronic musical instruments), etc.
Toyama	Toyama	Toyama University Toyama College of Medicine and Pharmacology Others	Mechatronics, new materials, biotechnology (medical etc.), information industries

Okayama	Kibikogen	Okayama University, Okayama College of Science	Biotechnology, electronics, mechatronics (medical and pharmaceutical industries), etc.
Hiroshima	Hiroshima Chuo	Hiroshima University	Electronics, mechatronics, new materials, biotechnology, etc.
Yamaguchi	Ube	Yamaguchi University	Electronics, mechatronics, new materials, ocean development, biotechnology, etc.
Fukuoka-Saga	Kurume-Tosu	Kurume College of Engineering, Kurume University	Mechatronics, fine chemicals, fashion, next generation (bio)industries, etc.
Oita	Kenhoku-Kunizaki	Oita University, Oita College of Medicine, Others	Electronics, mechatronics, bioindustry, software
Kumamota	Kumamota	Kumamoto University, Kumamoto College of Engineering, Others	Applied machinery industry, biotechnology, electronic equipment, information systems industry
Miyazaki	Miyazaki	Miyazaki University, Miyazaki College of Medicine	Local-oriented (bio), introduction-oriented (electronics etc.), and urban-oriented (urban systems) industries
Kagoshima	Kokubu-Hayato	Kagoshima University, Kyushu Gakuin University	Electronics, mechatronics, new materials, biotechnology, etc.

Source: MITI, "The technopolis plan: recent developments", *MITI News*, NO. 289, March 6, 1984; cited in Imai, 1986, pp. 156–7.

Industrial Policy: Economic Flexibility versus Political Accountability

MITI has been able to convert the statutory weakness of administrative guidance into a strength for two reasons. First, administrative guidance depends upon shaping a consensus with respect to the challenges and opportunities facing a sector. Since MITI does not have the power to impose strategies, it forces MITI officials to maintain close contact with people in the sectors. This ongoing dialogue has been a vehicle for hammering out effective sector strategies and emphasizing the structural changes in production required to implement them.

Since the first requirement of a sector strategy is an assessment of the challenges facing firms in the sector, one of MITI's functions has been to puncture illusions with which corporate executives elsewhere protect themselves from discomforting facts and maintain comforting practices. Profitable firms, for example, do not have to pay millions of dollars in annual salaries to top executives or reduce costs by shedding labor during market downturns. Second, administrative guidance is always provisional and thereby subject to revision and abandonment as conditions change. Unlike statutory agencies whose time has passed, MITI officials cannot appeal to legislative enactments to prolong their existence and must seek new ways to maintain their credibility and effectiveness with their customers.

Informal regulation is not peculiar to Japanese economic policymaking. It has close affinities with the advance notice philosophy of regulation in the United States described in chapter 3. While outwardly adversarial regulatory methods predominate in the United States, informal regulatory mechanisms can be identified in certain agencies. The self-regulation procedures of public disclosure and professional auditing in the Securities and Exchange Commission, for example, serve to promote as well as police the industry (McCraw, 1984, chapter 5). But examples of regulatory agencies developing sector strategies that account for the strengths and weaknesses of domestic firms and their competitors on a world scale are not common in the United States.

One reason is the economic philosophy that informs regulatory policy. The ideal of perfect competition has no space for the concept of strategy or Schumpeterian competition. What makes for the success of administrative guidance is less the means of informal enforcement than the economic analysis which underlies it, namely the goal of promoting Schumpeterian competition on an international scale. Quite inadvertently, the tension between administrative guidance by MITI and antitrust by the FTC has had just this effect. MITI without the FTC would likely have clung to more formal, less strategic, and less flexible instruments of industrial policy and the FTC without MITI could have attempted to impose the same theoretical model of price competition on business enterprises that has made US antitrust policy so contradictory.

The end result has been successful economic management. Both industrial policy and antitrust policy in Japan have promoted industrial enterprises and rationalization. Cartels have aided small businesses, unlike in the United States, by promoting non-price competition; recession cartels have kept firms alive during recessions which has reduced the incentive to cutthroat competition amongst firms and the fear of job loss amongst employees. Together these measures for managing markets have facilitated the notion of firm as community, so important to the idea of the entrepreneurial firm, without suppressing entry and Penrosian interstitial competition. Thus the god of competition has dominated the devil.

But the strength of administrative guidance as an informal means of enforcement is also its weakness: judicial and political review are both absent. For this reason the FTC has urged that guidelines be established for the implementation and accountability of administrative guidance in line with antitrust laws. Not surprisingly MITI has been less than open about the purposes and substance of administrative guidance. The tension between industrial policy measures and decentralized economic powers is unabated. While who holds the upper hand between MITI and the FTC oscillates over time, each frames its activities and policies in the light of the other.

At another level, the ongoing tug of war between MITI and the FTC is over means more than ends. Both agencies are committed to the same goal: increasing the competitiveness of Japanese industry. Neither is held responsible for the social costs of the single-minded pursuit of economic competitiveness. The very informality of industrial policy instruments makes them less accountable to elected officials, just as the lack of industry-based unions makes corporate executives less accountable to an independent workforce power base.

Macro Economics and Industrial Policy

The postwar Japanese industrial experience has been one of extraordinary creativity in institution building. In chapter 5 the business enterprise and supplier networks were examined. In this chapter the supporting industrial policy institutions have been analyzed. The fourth leg of the new stool is macro policy. The main thesis is that the culmination of Schumpeterian competition on an international scale has undermined the institutional presuppositions of both Keynesian and monetarist demand management economics. One of those presuppositions is that domestic production can be regulated by demand management. To explain I will make a brief and schematic comparison of demand management in the United States and the United Kingdom during the Reagan and Thatcher years.

In the United States of the 1980s, the interest rate has been used to squeeze out inflation while the government has run large fiscal deficits: high interest rates attracted foreign short-term capital which drove up the exchange rate. The rising exchange rate curbed inflation by lowering import prices which limited domestic price rises. The only difference in the United Kingdom over the same years was that the government did not run a deficit. It curbed inflationary pressures by both deflationary fiscal policy from 1979 to 1981, when nearly 20 percent of Britain's industrial firms went into bankruptcy, and an appreciating currency driven up by high interest rates and North Sea oil.

Both governments appeal to the virtues of free markets determining the price of credit and foreign exchange, but at the same time, along with taxes and spending, these are the major instruments of "demand management". The purpose of demand management was not to regulate production, but to regulate demand for purposes of stabilization policy. The long-run effects on production are largely ignored in the process.

In fact, American and British governments go a step further: they tend to define economic problems in terms that are manageable by the instruments of monetary and fiscal policy. Thus unemployment is caused by insufficient spending or inflation is caused by too much money. Defining the problems in terms of the remedies at hand may be soothing in the short run, but it only obscures the deeper structural problems. If the analysis in this book is correct, it has intensified them, for the high interest and overvalued exchange rates of the Reagan and Thatcher years have curbed inflation but undermined the long-term productive base of both economies in the process. Both countries have enjoyed a consumption-led boom but the productive capabilities have been built up elsewhere.

Not surprisingly, postwar Japanese fiscal, monetary, exchange rate, and financial policies have reflected an industrial policy orientation. In the early postwar period the exchange rate was consistently undervalued to favor exports. Business enterprises could count not only on favorable interest and exchange rates for long-term investments, but on stable rates over time. In recent years the exchange rate has appreciated dramatically but only after Japanese firms have become world leaders. The appreciating yen has had the opposite effects on the New Competitors: it has led to even greater competitiveness to maintain market share. Thus the markets for credit and foreign exchange have been regulated by the Japanese government with the object of promoting the competitiveness of industry.

The contrast in the allocation of long-term industrial finance is particularly striking. Whereas long-term industrial finance in Japan is deeply influenced by the public–private administrative interplay described in this chapter, in the United States and the United Kingdom the stock market plays a leading role. Here prices fluctuate freely as anonymous investors gamble on the value of companies which, in turn, adjust with every speculator's purchase or sale.

In the name of revitalizing the private sector and reducing the role of government, the high interest rate policies of the Thatcher and Reagan governments have crowded out domestic industrial investments at precisely the time when domestic firms were being challenged by the New Competition. The short-term result has been a production boom for countries in which the entrepreneurial firms are established and a consumption boom in America and Britain. The long-term results of eroding industrial bases will take years or a severe recession (or, in the case of Britain, a fall off in oil revenues) to be felt.

Why has the economics profession been so slow to emphasize the inconsistency between short-run macro-economic policies and the promotion of long-term strategic industrial investments? A part of the answer is the micro foundations of neoclassical macro-economic theory. Those foundations presume perfect competition and the passive firm. Replacing them with Schumpeterian competition and the entrepreneurial firm would go some distance to illuminating the consequences for industrial enterprises of demand management macro-economic policies. But it is crucial to integrate a concept of industrial policy into a redrawn micro and macro economics. Here again a comparison with Japan is instructive. United States industrial regulatory policy had presumed the ideal of perfect markets and defined inter-firm cooperation as collusion against the public interest.[5] Japanese industrial policy, in contrast, has been based on the presupposition that a mix of inter-firm competition and cooperation can promote international competitiveness.

---

[5] While antitrust policies in the United States and the United Kingdom both take the perfect competition ideal for granted, following the passage of the 1976 *Restrictive Practices Act*, UK law allows certain restrictive agreements amongst firms. To be exempted from the laws against restrictive agreements, the agreement must pass through one or more of eight escape clauses or "gateways" stipulated in the 1976 Act. For details see Cable (1982, p. 220).

Summary

The history of postwar Japanese industrial policy is one of evolution of extra-firm institutions for promoting the competitiveness of business enterprises. While some of these institutions are purely private, such as consultative supplier relations, industrial groups, and private inter-firm associations, others are a mixture of public and private, such as the cartels, sector strategies, public corporations, and the R&D agencies of Japan's technology policy. Each case denies the dichotomies of market and plan, private and public, economic and political, that characterize the theories and policies of both the United States and the United Kingdom.

The claim that the underlying market versus plan dichotomy obscures more than it illuminates with respect to industrial policy should not be surprising. It is the same claim made earlier with respect to understanding the business enterprise in the economy. There I argued that the adoption of the ideal of perfect competition to meet the requirements of a formal theory of price limited the concept of the firm to a passive entity bearing no relationship to the strategic enterprise of the real world. Here the appeal of the perfect competition ideal is the implication that the economy and the polity are autonomous self-regulating spheres. Again, even though debate may rage over the proper role of government in the economy it presumes the dichotomy. The result is that the academic and popular idea of industrial policy is no more relevant to actual practices than the notion of the firm in conventional economic theory.

The implication is not that other countries must copy Japanese industrial policy institutions to be successful. In fact, the tenuous relationship between democratic institutions and industrial policymaking in Japan calls out for careful examination and critique. But neither can the potential effectiveness of such institutional arrangements be ignored in theory or practice.

7

The Third Italy: Regional Cooperation and International Competition

Introduction

The Japanese story of economic growth is one of large firms seeking a dominant domestic market share and international competitiveness, and a powerful central government pursuing an industrial policy geared to establishing the competitive advantage of national firms over foreign rivals. It is being imitated successfully by Korea, Taiwan, Hong Kong, and Singapore where kaisha-type global corporations and central government are combining to integrate firm, sector, and intersectoral competitive strategies. The competitive success of leading Japanese firms suggests a series of questions. Is there a new irrefutable logic of production economics that must be obeyed by all firms that hope to compete in the international marketplace? Must a citizenry that seeks economic growth adapt its government policies and political institutions to promoting kaisha-type enterprises? Must employees and unions accept the inevitability of Japanese-style work practices?

The success of a rapidly growing region of Italy suggests that the New Competition does not entail a single institutional configuration. The "Third Italy", located in the North Central part of Italy (as distinct from the northern industrial heartland of Milan–Turin–Genoa and the agricultural south), is based on groups of small firms. Its industrial organization has more in common with the industrial districts of the Connecticut River Valley and the Birmingham small arms manufacturing region examined in chapter 1 than with the mass production enterprises examined in chapter 2. But its enterprises, like the kaisha, are entrepreneurial firms which pursue a strategy of continuous innovation, deploy flexible production methods, and integrate planning and doing in work. The Third Italy raises an issue buried by the economic success of Japan: is it possible to have a high standard of living without corporate giants?

A Small Firm Economy Success Story

Between the early 1970s and the mid-1980s Italy enjoyed the fastest rate of growth of the big four European economies and passed Britain and France to become the fourth-largest capitalist economy in terms of gross national output. But growth was not associated with a shift from small to large firms. In fact the share of national output produced by firms employing between 20 and 100 workers increased from 31 to 34 percent between 1972 and 1980. Nor are Italian small firms backward in terms of rates of investment. Over the same eight-year period the fixed investment per employee ratio of small firms went from 3 percent less to 16 percent greater than that of firms with over 500 employees (Schiattarella, cited in Storey and Johnson, 1987, p. 145). But aggregate figures for the nation conceal substantial differences amongst firms in both the small and large categories and across regions. The focus here will be on one particular province within one region which has grown rapidly and is populated by small firms.

Of Italy's 20 regions, the fastest growing in recent years has been Emilia-Romagna, which has become the highest per capita income region in Italy. In 1980 Emilia-Romagna had a population of 3.9 million, an economically active population of 1.7 million, and 325,000 registered firms, i.e. an average of about five workers per firm. Ninety percent of the manufacturing firms employed under 99 persons and accounted for 58 percent of the total workforce. Over a third of the workforce is self-employed.[1]

The manufacturing center of Emilia-Romagna is the province of Modena, with a population of around 600,000. Per capita income in the province of Modena has increased from seventeenth place in Italy in 1970 to second place in 1979 (Brusco, 1982, p. 168). Between 1951 and 1971, the share of labor employed in agriculture dropped from 56 percent to 19 percent and the share in industry increased from 25 percent to 51 percent; by 1986, 9 percent of the workforce was employed in agriculture and 45 percent in industry.[2] Unemployment in Modena in

---

[1] Data in this paragraph from Hatch (1986).
[2] Data in this and the next sentence are from *Modena in Cifre*, Camera di Commercio di Modena, June 1985.

1987 was about 5.5 percent compared with the national average of 12 percent.

The number of registered industrial firms in the province of Modena increased from 12,500 in 1971 to nearly 22,000 in 1981, and the number of employed people, artisans (craftsman–owners), and employees increased from 100,000 to over 140,000 for an average of 6.4 per firm. Large firms are rare in Modena: only 14 employ more than 500, 119 employ between 101 and 500, and 180 employ between 51 and 100 (Associazione Industriali). The province is famous for racing cars (Ferrari and Maserati), ceramics (40 percent of the world's ceramic tiles are produced around Sassuolo), and textiles and clothing. The largest manufacturing sectors are metalworking and machine making with over 43,000 employees, ceramics with 26,000, and textiles and clothing with 18,000 (*Modena in Cifre*, p. 48).

The region of Emilia-Romagna accounts for approximately 10 percent of Italy's exports and 4 percent of imports which, in 1983, meant an international trade surplus of $5 billion. Modena is the number one Italian province in per capita exports and enjoys a ratio of exports to imports of roughly 4:1 with a surplus of $2 billion (*Modena in Cifre*, p. 59). A quarter of Modena's exports are transport vehicles, followed by ceramics, clothing, and machine and metalworking products (*Modena in Cifre*, p. 59).

The prevalence of small firms linked to large exporting firms in Japan demonstrates that small manufacturing firms are compatible with the New Competition. But the Third Italy also demonstrates that small firms can be independently export oriented. Whereas in Japan small firms whose products are exported are suppliers of the kaisha, in the Third Italy, large companies are few. To understand how the small-firm-based economy of the Third Italy works we examine first the organization of the small firm itself and relations amongst small firms, and second extra-firm institutions which play functional roles comparable with the managerial hierarchies of Big Business.

The Industrial District as Collective Entrepreneur

Three types of small firms can be distinguished. The first are traditional small firms that produce non-tradeables for the local market. Bakers and butchers, for example, can compete by offering superior quality products as their Big Business competitors must use preservatives or freezing techniques to centralize production. The second are design-dependent firms that subcontract for lead firms which shape product design and control a critical phase in the production chain such as assembly or retailing. The lead firm interfaces with a regional, national, or international market; the subcontractor competes with other subcontractors on the basis of price and lacks independent design and marketing capabilities. The third are design-independent suppliers that have the capacity to refine designs and thereby shape products and markets. They may not produce own-brands, but they are not tied to the designs of assembly or retailing firms.[3]

By drawing these distinctions we can distinguish between industrial districts in terms of their collective capacity to engage in Schumpeterian competition over product, process, materials, and organization. At one end of the spectrum are groups of firms that are dominated by lead firms, external to the district, that control one of the final phases in the production chain, such as assembly, distribution, or retailing, and dictate product design. Further along the spectrum are industrial districts that have a mix of subcontractors and design-independent firms. The greater is the independent design capacity, the greater is the power of an industrial district to collectively shape, rather than react to, markets. Market-shaping power, in turn, can be turned into leverage over profit margins.

While indices of the degree of design independence or interdependence within a district are not readily available, a number of studies of industrial districts within the Third Italy are suggestive. Brusco discovered, for example, that, for the clothing industry, roughly 50 percent of the small firms in Modena "produce on their own account" whereas the figure is only 8 percent in Ferrara. He also refers to studies which suggest that, whereas in Modena and Reggio Emilia 60 percent of metalworking small firms had more than 20 clients per year, the same figure for Bassano was only 30 percent (Brusco, 1986, p. 190).

A more fully entrepreneurial industrial district is one in which associations of firms along the production chain can collectively and simultaneously redesign products. This requires close consultation along the production chain. A fully developed industrial district would behave like a collective entrepreneur: it would possess the capacity to redesign process and organization as well as product. This is the area of greatest challenge facing industrial districts since the rise of the kaisha.

But Schumpeterian competition is not limited to product design. A

---

[3] This small-firm typology is similar to that of Brusco and Sabel (1981). It differs, however, in emphasizing the crucial role of design. A large assembler, for example, may be a dependent subcontractor to a retailer, as is commonly the case in the United Kingdom. Brusco and Sabel's categories, which are based on the Italian case of decentralized retailing, imply that a firm that interfaces directly with a retailer is not a dependent subcontractor.

second challenge to the industrial district is the capacity to restructure without managerial hierarchy. For if small firms are to do more than fill Penrosian "interstices" created by large firms they must be able to reorganize collectively to seize new opportunities. Otherwise, the Third Italy could be today's equivalent to the Connecticut River Valley metalworking district described in chapter 1: a prelude to the creation of a managerial hierarchy. For as we saw, the managerial hierarchy was created in the United States largely to rationalize production according to the new principles of the day, namely mass production. In the case of the United States the small family-owned firms were no match for the emerging central office, functionally departmentalized managerial hierarchies which were able to remove the impediments to productive rationalization.

The challenge, then, is one of restructuring without hierarchy. Crucial to the restructuring process is the capacity of the district as a whole to permanently promote specialization as technologies develop so that operations with a high minimum efficient scale of production can continue to be centralized and distinctive competences can continue to be developed in each phase of production. One index of the health of an industrial district is the rate of creation of new firms, particularly spin-off firms that emerge in response to Penrosian interstices within the district.

One form of spin-off is the satellite firm which is established with the aid of an existing firm. The aid may come in the form of equity or debt finance, loan of machinery, sharing of orders, or long-term contracts. In each case the spin-off is created in response to an existing need and by an individual with experience in the same or a related phase of production. In most cases within Emilia-Romagna the new firm will be headed by a family member or trusted previous employee who wishes to establish an independent firm. Together such firms form a socially integrated system (Brusco, 1982). Finally, spin-offs increase the flexibility of an industrial district without risking whole production chains. In this they resemble the process of "chunking" identified by Peters and Waterman (1982) as a characteristic of "excellent" companies in the United States.[4]

If each of these conditions is met, an industrial district is like a collective entrepreneur. In Brusco's terms it combines productive decentralization and social integration. But it adds the capacity to engage

---

[4] Chunking involves the creation of a small group of people with different functional skills to tackle a problem over a specified time period. The group has access to top management but is not responsible to line chains of command (Peters and Waterman, 1982, p. 126).

in Schumpeterian competition without the creation of managerial hierarchy. While we cannot foretell the future, we can identify a large number of cooperative institutions within the Third Italy that serve as functional equivalents to managerial hierarchy. To the extent that they contribute to the development of the industrial district as collective entrepreneur they are establishing an alternative to the Japanese institutional complex as a form of the New Competition. I will return to these issues in the next chapter, after examining various forms of economic cooperation in the Third Italy.

A Politics of Economic Cooperation

The history of institution building that sustains the small-firm world of the Third Italy begins with politics and political alliances which, as in Japan, were profoundly altered following the defeat of fascism.

Since the end of the Second World War the municipality of Modena has been governed by the Italian Communist Party. At the end of the war roughly 60 percent of the population was engaged in agricultural production (most were sharecroppers), and of the 25 percent in industry, many were employees of large firms, the largest being FIAT tractor. The political power of most large landowners and industrialists had been broken by the defeat of fascism. The political parties of the left were defeated at the national level but successful at the local level. Since the doctrines of communist theorists dealt with seizing state power at the national level, the newly elected communist politicians had little to guide them as to how to construct a socialist *local* economy. Fortunately, as it turned out, they were ignored by both hostile and friendly foreign governments.

With hindsight, two principles that guided municipal Communist Party practice can be discerned. The first was to distinguish between monopoly capital (or Big Business) and artisan capital (or small business) run by craftsmen. The Italian Communist Party attributed the success of fascism in Italy to the success of Mussolini in attracting small business people even though Italian corporatism did not accommodate their economic interests. Thus, for political reasons, the Italian left sought to join forces with the small-business community. It is not inconsistent in the Third Italy to be a banker and a communist.

Second, the communist-governed municipalities sought to govern by consensus. Thus communist local governments invoked democratic processes, which had not previously existed in Italy or communist countries, and an alliance with small businesses, a group excluded from communist theory and practice. The possibility of a communist government at the local level, particularly one based upon notions of alliance with business groups and of consensus, was created by the popular role that the Communist Party played in the antifascist underground. But in Modena, at least, the Communist Party was more a political party of the community than a party based upon doctrinaire principles of communist political theory and Marxist economics.

In localities governed by the Italian Communist Party the notion of free enterprise has taken on a new meaning. For nowhere is small business more ably attended to by government than in Communist Party governed provinces such as Modena. At the same time the government has not become dominated by economic imperatives or become a lobbying arena where private interest groups vie for special privileges; the idea of government as a place where private interests can be transcended in pursuit of the common good has not been ignored. Local government has been able to pursue an aggressive economic program and retain a degree of insulation from interest group politics by creating a range of extra- and inter-firm institutions. Their purpose is to promote the development of small firms within a democratically accountable political environment. One of the first of such postwar inter-firm institutions was the National Conferation of Artisans.

Inter-firm Productive Associations

The Confederazione Nazionale dell' Artigianato (CNA) was created at a national conference of artisans in Rome in 1946. The CNA became, and remains, the biggest business association in Italy with 340,000 member firms, a staff of 7,000 and 2,300 offices throughout the country (Hatch, 1986, p. 14). By statute, every CNA chapter must be managed by elected directors (who must be artisans), an executive committee, and a council. At least 60 percent of the executive committees and the councils must be artisans who are actively engaged in business. The CNA is organized vertically into trade federations representing 27 sectors of the economy.

The CNA was largely the creation of the communist and socialist parties in Italy and, at least in regions such as Emilia-Romagna, continues to be associated with the political Left. The category of artisan does not easily translate into English because it denotes an economic category that has much less significance and certainly less infrastructural support in the form of associations of artisans or governmental facilities. An artisan implies a craftsman in English, but the same term in Italy is used for a firm that is owned and worked in by a craftsman or a partnership of craftsmen. Of the 22,000 artisanal firms in the province of Modena, about 7,400 have employees (Associazione Industriali). Thus it is common in Italy, unlike America or Great Britain, for a worker to develop craft skills with the aspiration of establishing his/her own firm in which he/she will continue to practice those skills. The building trades industry offers the closest counterpart to an artisan in America and Britain. Here skilled craftsmen may become contractors one year and return to waged labor the next without loss in status.

The CNA is the largest of four national confederations of artisanal firms. The Associazione Industriali is the largest confederation of industrial, as distinct from artisanal, firms. The distinction between an artisanal and an industrial firm is not definitive, but attempts are being made to make it so in Italian business law. To qualify as an artisanal firm in 1986, a firm must not have enjoyed limited liability, the owner must have been a working manager by engaging in the production process, and at least one other member of the firm must have been from the same family. By law, an artisanal firm cannot employ more than 18 people, family members and trainees excepted. Beyond these rules the law permits firms to choose between registering as an artisanal or industrial firm. In practice artisanal firms are smaller, with an average of three employees, and are associated with the communist or socialist parties; industrial firms are larger with an average of 25 employees and their owners tend not to be associated with political parties of the Left.

Firms enjoy certain benefits by registering as an artisanal as opposed to an industrial firm. An artisanal firm can apply to a national government fund to subsidize a portion of interest charges on borrowed money and is not forced to disclose a balance sheet. But the greatest advantage is the services that an established artisanal association, particularly the CNA, can offer. These services extend beyond those of an ordinary trade association found in other countries. In fact, the artisanal associations are a blend of trade association and governmental agency.

The province of Modena chapter of the CNA has 14,000 member firms, representing 39,000 persons (artisans and "dependents"). The 14,000 firms are grouped into 11 sector federations, the largest of which are the federations of metalworking, clothing, construction, transport, barbieri misti, woodworking, newspaper, food, and traditional artists, plus a category of non-classified. The CNA has 60 locations within the province for supplying administrative services to artisan firms including the following.

1 Accounting services: the CNA routinely provides bookkeeping, income statements, tax returns, and payslips. The CNA in Modena, for example, prepares 15,000 payslips each month for a fee of under $20 per year per payslip.

2 Financial services: the CNA helps to organize financial cooperatives such as the Financial Consortium of Modena, described below, which is a vehicle for collectively guaranteeing loans to individual artisans based upon an assessment of their business ideas.

3 Assistance in the development of property facilities: the CNA in Modena, in association with the municipal and provincial governments, has participated in the creation of industrial parks as described below.

4 Assistance in the creation of business service centers in industrial districts: in cooperation with ERVET, a regional government development agency, and municipal governments, the CNA has aided in the creation of nine sector-specific real-resource centers. Real resources, as distinct from financial resources, include marketing and technological information and training facilities such as the Textile Information Center of Emilia-Romagna described below.

5 Assistance in establishing cooperatives to solve general problems for a group of firms, such as quality control or bulk purchasing of raw materials or export marketing. For example, the CNA in Modena aided a group of ten metalworking companies to form an export cooperative to market products in Germany.

In sum, the CNA is a confederation of trade associations that does more than lobby the government: it provides business services to member firms, particularly those services for which substantial economies of scale exist. While member companies pay an annual fee for membership of the CNA, as well as a fee for specific services, the relation between member firms and the CNA is neither a market nor a bureaucratic relation. Artisan firms do not seek the lowest cost provider of such services on the market nor do they find themselves in a subordinate relation to CNA officials as in a managerial enterprise. The relation is better described as a cooperative relationship in which information flows laterally, as opposed to a hierarchical relationship in which information flows vertically from the apex to the base of a pyramid and vice versa.

Membership of the CNA allows member firms to cooperate in the provision of collective services while remaining autonomous in areas of decisionmaking and finances. But the CNA can operate most effectively in partnership with other extra-firm agencies such as governments, trade unions, and universities.

Industrial Parks: Planning "External" Economies

The mid-1950s was a time of intense political struggle within the Italian workplace (Sabel, 1982, chapter 4). Mass firings in the early 1950s at Modena's largest employer, FIAT's agricultural equipment division, added to the already high unemployment in the province following the Second World War. As an unemployment-reducing effort the municipality established its first industrial park by purchasing an area of land on the periphery of the city. Industrial parks in Modena have evolved through three phases.

In the first phase, the municipality paid the market price for agricultural property and sold it in small lots to unemployed artisans. By acting as an agent for a large group of artisans and by removing the speculative element in land prices, the municipality was able to reduce substantially the price of land to individual artisans. In addition, the municipality delivered the conventional common infrastructural services. Within three to four years 74 firms, mainly metalworking, were established in a self-financing project.

The success of the first experiment led to a second initiative involving 178 companies beginning in 1962, and a third for 124 firms in 1969. Together the three industrial parks housed 376 firms and employed 3,000 employees. It has been calculated that the purchase of such property at agricultural prices and converting it to industrial purposes saved artisans an average of 80 million lira (roughly $70,000 in 1986 dollars) per firm (Benatti, 1988, p. 11).

The second phase of innovations in governmental land use policies to promote small-firm development followed the passage of national legislation granting the power to municipal authorities to expropriate large areas of land for industrial parks. Modena, together with ten adjoining municipalities, formed the District Plan which set up five new industrial parks encompassing 252 hectares for larger companies (those with over ten employees and more than 3,000 m² of land). The goal was to consolidate the polycentric character of industrial specialization and thereby spread the employment-generating effects throughout the province. An inter-municipal consortium was established in 1974 to manage the five industrial parks. The consortium used a flexible pricing system to promote inter-municipal relocation in line with sectoral specialization by the municipality without subsidization.

The District Plan called for municipal management of industrial parks for smaller companies. The Plan for Small Firms Areas, established by the municipality of Modena in 1974, called for the development of artisanal consortia to assist in the creation of industrial parks for firms seeking areas of less than 1,000 m², which had been the lower limit in the first three industrial parks of Modena. The idea was again to locate firms with complementary and similar productive activities in the same parks.

In the second phase the municipality was not only acting as a market coordinator for a group of firms seeking property but, in collaboration with artisans and small-industry associations, as a market maker organizing demand by industrial sector. By organizing firms according to productive activity the municipality was able to customize the building construction and achieve economies of scale in the provision of collective services. For example, woodworking firms require sawdust extraction systems; the collective provision of such systems reduces the cost per firm and the minimum efficient scale of production, and increases the effective demand for industrial space.

Firms were encouraged by pricing policies to organize into sectoral consortia to facilitate the creation of targeted business services. The main instrument was control of land prices which was made possible by the elimination of the speculative element, as noted above. By statute, the municipality could sell a maximum of 50 percent of the lots obtained within industrial estates and had to offer the other half as surface right leases for a minimum of 60 years while retaining ownership. A firm can receive the benefits of the industrial park by leasing surface rights. But once the surface rights lease is given up it cannot be sold on the open market but is returned to the municipality to be leased at the original price to another firm. By the control of leases the municipality retains a voice in the use of the industrial parks.

The third phase of the municipal land management program began in 1978 with the development of "covenanted building programs". Under these arrangements artisans purchased both the land and a portion of a finished building. These were originally designed for small artisan shops requiring 150–450 m², and the municipality, in conjunction with the artisans' associations, invited bids from building companies to construct customizable layouts that could be rearranged over time to meet user needs flexibly. The building constructors had to submit an acceptable plan for construction and come up with a list of users, and in return it acquired surface rights to the land. Management of the construction and operation of the industrial park was then turned over to the building construction company. The municipality retained influence with clauses in the contract including the proviso that the construction company sell exclusively to purchasers approved by the municipal authorities.

Municipal planning authorities estimate that the final price of phase three property, including buildings, is about half the price of equivalent buildings on the private market. Purchasers are able to avoid the price markups of land speculation and real estate agents as well as obtain the economies of scale of custom buildings and shared land purchases.

By organizing end users and the building industry, the municipal authorities have been able to promote the development of small firms located in specialized facilities but without the burdens of operating the industrial parks themselves. The unitary management of land purchasing, architecture, building, and infrastructural services has made it possible for small firms to thrive without subsidization. Since 1951, the municipality of Modena has grown by 62 percent in population and over 500 percent in urban land area. But partly as a result of public management of business and residential property construction, Modena has remained an attractive and remarkably uncrowded city.

Consortia

The structure of consortia is fixed by law. They are non-profit-seeking associations of enterprises which must be registered. Registration includes a description of their primary aim and administrative structure. By statute a consortium must be accountable to its members, general assemblies must be held periodically, and a board of directors must be elected from amongst members at general assembly meetings. The total number of registered consortia in Italy increased from 48,000 in 1970 to 79,000 in 1979 (Economists Advisory Group, 1983, p. 157). The primary aims of consortia vary; two of the most common are the provision of finance and marketing activities.

Financial Consortia: Loan Assessment and Guarantee by Peers

Banks everywhere prefer to secure loans with property. Banks in early postwar Emilia-Romagna, if anything, were even more hesitant to make unsecured loans to industrial firms than elsewhere. For local banks had their historical roots in the agricultural sector which dominated prewar Emilia-Romagna and local bankers had little experience or expertise in assessing the capacity of artisanal enterprises to repay loans. Bank lending did not involve making assessment of potential competitiveness; it meant assessing financial statements, particularly the sales value of property.

Bank lending to artisanal enterprises demands detailed market information and subtle judgments on entrepreneurial potential. But sector studies, competitor analyses, and market research are extremely costly and often misleading. The type of intimate knowledge required is alien to industry outsiders and is always suspect to the accountant in pursuit of codifiable information. Financial criteria, in contrast, offer the banker an unambiguous means for assessment. Past accomplishments and property can be measured with precision, unlike entrepreneurial capacity in a competitive environment. The problem for bankers is that the information they need for measuring entrepreneurial capacity is not economically supplied in the market. The benefit-to-cost ratio for developing such information is prohibitively low in the case of artisan firms. An alternative to market coordination between bankers and firms was required if small firms were to be entrepreneurial in the sense of investing in new products and processes, i.e. in the Schumpeterian sense.

The challenge of economical provision of entrepreneurial information was met in the Third Italy by institution building. The information existed, but the market was (and is) inherently inefficient in providing the one ingredient required to obtain it, namely trust. Bankers can offer a price for information but they cannot purchase honesty, and without honesty the information is suspect. The best source of honest information is peer review backed by the personal integrity of people of established character. To this end the institution of the financial consortium was established.

The financial consortium is an association of producers which supplies three elements required for small firms to gain entrepreneurial credit from banks: an objective insider's assessment of entrepreneurial ideas at low cost, a strong incentive to pay back loans, and a means of recovering loan defaults. The Loan Guarantee Consortium of Modena has 3,500 members, a board of 18 members composed of artisans and CNA officials, and a small staff. Each member pays a membership fee, which is combined with contributions from the municipal, regional, and national governments to make up a loan guarantee fund. Any member enterprise that desires a loan must go to the local branch of the CNA and obtain a report prepared and assessed by fellow businesspeople. Only their peers have the intimate knowledge of the individual and the industry. The report is forwarded to the board of directors of the financial consortium and referred to a subcommittee. If accepted by both the subcommittee and the board the application is sent to the bank with a loan guarantee.

The credit cooperative of Modena has opened the market for credit to artisanal firms. The loan guarantees cover between 50 and 70 percent of the banks loans. The success and strength of the credit cooperative in negotiating with banks has reduced the interest cost to members to 1.5–2 percent below that of non-members. But most importantly it has changed the attitude and practices of banks with respect to artisan enterprises. It is now possible to seek loans on the basis of ideas, innovations, and community standing as well as traditional collateral.

The initial response of the banks to the establishment of the financial consortium in Modena was hesitant. Bankers considered it an interference with traditional practices, but over time they have changed their views. Out of a total of over $40 million in loan guarantees between 1975 and 1985, only $70,000 were unrecoverable without recourse to the guarantee. The reason, according to Sebastiano Brusco, is ". . . the person who receives a loan from the cooperative will stay up at night thinking of ways of repaying his loan; whereas the person who receives a bank loan will stay up at night thinking of ways of not repaying his loan" (Brusco, 1985, p. 25). Bankers have found that working with the financial cooperative has brought them depositors. They have also become aware that banking in the age of the New Competition depends upon developing means of assessing intellectual property. It is demanded by depositors seeking higher returns.

Marketing Consorzi: *Productive Decentralization and Shared Overheads*

One example of a cooperative marketing venture is the *Consorzio Poggibonsi*, an association of furniture firms established in the neighboring region of Tuscany in 1965. In 1983 it had a staff of six and 85 member firms which together employed about 2,000 people. Total turnover of the consortium was about $150 million with 30 percent coming from exports (Economists Advisory Group, 1983, p. 159). Sixty-three of the member firms were in furniture, with the other 22 distributed across a broad range of ancillary products and services including interior decoration, lamps and lighting fixtures, doors and windows, glassware, marble, shipping, paints and varnishes, metallurgical products, printing and graphic arts, building construction, woodworking machines, and ceiling tiles. Membership of the consortium costs about $6,000 per year. The services provided include the following:

- export promotion;
- trade fair and exhibit organization;
- sales missions to foreign markets;
- contacts with governmental bodies that promote trade;
- market research;
- an export office with translation facilities in Florence;
- domestic and export catalogs;
- files on financial soundness of existing and potential clients;
- bulk buying and warehousing of raw materials;
- a range of business services including computer and telex facilities, advice on compiling budgets and tax returns, a weekly newsletter, job advertisements, and information on exchange rate movements;
- training facilities.

A second example is the *Consorzio Cabiate Produce* in the region of Lombardy. The *Consorzio Cabiate* is an export consortium of 15 artisanal firms with total foreign sales of $4 million in 1987. The average number of employees per firm is ten. Cabiate is a furniture making town of 6,000 inhabitants with about 3,000 people employed in over 500 furniture firms (some employees do not live in Cabiate). Because it is in an industrial district the *Consorzio Cabiate* can stay small and still enjoy the external economies that come from sharing activities with high minimum efficient scale such as the *Scuolo de Arte Cabiate*, a technical school that has taught many generations of cabinetmakers, specialist finishing machinery such as curtain coaters, and local distributors for accessories and raw materials. The *Consorzio Cabiate* permanently employs four people in a central office and two in a showroom/ warehouse, and periodically employs freelance architects for design purposes. The task of the *Consorzio Cabiate* is to handle everything to do with marketing and delivering the furniture of its members for the export market alone.

A third example is the *Consorzio Esposizione Mobile* (CEM) of Cantu, Lombardy. CEM, established in 1949, operates a four-storey 600 m² showroom for 120 member artisan firms. It employs ten people, more than any of the member firms. Unlike export consortia, CEM does not sell directly but acts as a broker between, on the one hand, architects, interior designers, and final consumers throughout the region (including Germany, Switzerland, France, and Holland) and, on the other hand, the artisanal firms. A committee of the CEM establishes and monitors quality standards in order to maintain its reputation for highest quality. In Cantu, as throughout the region, artisanal firms specialize in individual phases in the production chain and thereby generate external economies of scale for the rest of the members of the industrial district.

National and regional governments subsidize up to 50 percent of the running costs of consortia. By law, the consortia cannot make profits; any net revenue must be reinvested and cannot be returned to member firms. The concept is to reward private collective action as opposed to subsidizing individual firms.

Marketing is crucial to international competitiveness. Undoubtedly marketing economies of scale are one pressure for firm expansion, or to link up to big firms that do have large international marketing capabilities. What is remarkable about the Third Italy is the development of specialization in marketing through alternatives to either increasing size or subordinate relations to giant enterprises. Joint marketing is one way. It is not ideal, but it does offer an alternative to both subcontracting and building marketing departments that is particularly important in the age of the New Competition.

Subcontracting risks losing product design capability and direct experience in marketing; direct marketing, in contrast, involves scale economies that will put pressure on the firm to expand in size and thereby risk the "defenses in depth" that come from specialization.

While marketing consortia do not offer the degree of control in marketing that any firm would prefer in an ideal world, they offer a greater opportunity than subcontracting for maintaining product design independence. The challenge in establishing an effective marketing consortium is one of promoting inter-firm production specialization without undermining product quality and production performance. Here again the goal of promoting cooperation in certain areas and competition in others involves organizational skills akin to the art of political negotiation that is required to establish common ground amongst potentially contradictory interests. Not unexpectedly, the political in the economic is as important to competitive success as the economic in the political.

But the coordination of marketing is not a sufficient condition for success in the New Competition. For marketing supplies information; the way that information is used to orient and reorient production is crucial. Here again the public sector is playing a leading role in the Third Italy.

Collective Service Centers in Emilia-Romagna

The municipality of Modena did not attempt to do everything at once. Chronologically, the industrial park came first followed by the financial consortium. By the late 1970s, the most pressing challenge facing many small and medium-sized firms was no longer property or finance, but intensifying competition in export markets, particularly in the standardized product, lower quality segments with the emergence of mass production capacity in the newly industrializing countries.

The small firms of the Third Italy were, and remain, ill equipped to compete on the basis of price with mass producers. The strength of the Third Italy is in the flexibility and innovation that come from decentralized and autonomous design capabilities. But competing on the basis of product design, quality, or customization depends upon integrating marketing capabilities and competitor analysis with production flexibility which, in turn, depends upon staying abreast of technological developments. Here again small firms are faced with the need to undertake activities characterized by substantial economies of scale.

Government economic policymakers in Emilia-Romagna are aware that small and medium-sized firms must have access to economies of scale in the provision of both marketing and technological information if they are to remain competitive with vertically integrated firms. A novel response has been to create industrial district centers that offer collective services particularly in informational activities. The idea that information is a public good that will generally be undersupplied in the market is not a new one. But information is much more important in the era of the New Competition.

Three ideas guided the creation of these centers: first, that they be sector specific since the challenges and opportunities of each sector are different; second, centers would be located in the municipality where industrial districts were already located; third, centers would provide information to enable firms to develop their independent design-making capacities as opposed to the provision of firm-specific resources. The fundamental notion was that firms must maintain and nurture design and entrepreneurial independence and not become dependent upon external sources of creativity or become clients of public agencies. Thus the collective services centers would provide information; the application of the information would be up to the companies themselves.

In 1976, ERVET (a quasi-public economic development agency of the regional government of Emilia-Romagna) opened the first collective services center, for the textile industry. It failed, in part because the proposed center's office was located near ERVET's office in Bologna as opposed to a geographical center of the textile and clothing industry. At the same time ERVET was sponsoring a training project in Carpi for artisans who sought to upgrade the quality of their products. A number of courses were prepared for fashion, styling, productive organization, marketing, and technology. The courses were attended by 200 people every year for four years. Professors from local universities, consultants, and technicians who worked for firms throughout Europe discussed the changing contours of the industry. Out of these discussions the concept of a collective services center was modified.

Centro Informazione Tessile dell'Emilia Romagna (CITER) is a textile and clothing industry information center for Emilia-Romagna that was founded in 1980 as a limited liability consortium. The founding members were ERVET, three artisanal associations including CNA, and two industrial associations. Today, of 500 member companies, 51 percent are in knitwear and 49 percent in clothing, 60 percent are artisan companies and 40 percent industrial companies, and 80 percent produce proprietorial products (as distinct from being subcontractors). CITER is governed by member companies which annually elect a 19-member board of directors made up of representatives of companies, government, and productive associations. It is managed by a president's office of three and a staff of 14. Staff members can call upon over 40 consultants for specific projects. CITER provides three types of support services to firms: fashion, marketing, and technology. Each will be examined.

The most distinctive feature of the clothing industry is the sensitivity of orders to fashion. Even small firms that choose to counter the mainstream have to be aware of fashion trends in order to differentiate their products. In the "planned" market segment, fashion trends are set between 12 and 15 months before the season in which they are marketed. This means making choices in theme, material, color, style, shape, cut, and trim. Consequently the first service of CITER is in collecting and disseminating fashion information. CITER's staff act as a fashion information center for the entire industrial district by maintaining close contact with the international fashion-creating centers. This involves attendance at exhibitions and fashion shows, discussions with purchasers, designers, researchers, and material producers, and awareness of media uses and construction of cultural symbols. Fashion information is made available to companies by meetings, publications, video presentations, and consultation.

The second service of CITER is marketing, which includes the tracking of competitor developments around the world. The development of worldwide excess supply has led CITER to assist firms to drive down the 12–15 month lead time between the presentation of collections or samples and deliveries to outlets typical of the "planned" system of production. The result is the development of "semi-planned" production methods which have reduced the 12–15 month period to between two and three months. Not surprisingly, this means radically altering supplier relations.

Under the semi-planned system, companies rely upon fewer suppliers with whom they have more intimate relations. Reducing lead times can quickly escalate costs, for it is expensive to requisition and produce the right button, buckle, or yarn on the spot. Thus the semi-planned approach reduces the risk of guessing wrong on fashion but increases the costs and reduces the ranges that can be offered.

A third strategy, "ready fashion", is emerging which can deliver orders in 15–23 working days by introducing five or six new pieces each week to a limited distributional network. But even more than with the semi-planned system, the range of clothing is limited to inputs that can be produced to short order.

The microelectronics revolution is impacting on the viability of competitive strategies. CITER, in cooperation with ENEA (the Italian Atomic and Alternative Energy Agency which maintains considerable expertise in high technology), has developed a computer-aided design (CAD) system that can substantially reduce the time and cost of preparing samples (clothing firms provide samples from which retailers and wholesalers order for upcoming seasons). Over 50,000 entries have been entered into a computer memory including colors, drawings, sketches, stitches, images, and materials. These entries become data from which a computer program can generate a virtually infinite variety of color and pattern blends. Collections can then be created on the screen and printed on high resolution graphic paper, as opposed to being made up in the actual materials. It becomes possible to experiment with styles and combinations that would have been prohibitively expensive before. CITER staff members estimate that the cost of the CAD system will be under $50,000. But member firms may choose to pay a fee for using the system at CITER as opposed to buying one themselves.

The example of CITER illustrates the unusual characteristics of the clothing industry and the entrepreneurial role that government can play in institution building for the provision of collective services within an industrial district. Collective service centers with the same governance structure have been developed in Emilia-Romagna in each of the following sectors: earth-moving equipment, metalworking, agricultural machinery, shoes, clothing subcontracting, construction, and ceramics. Each has identified specific collective services that are the key to the success of the industrial district they serve. CITER is the first and the most advanced to date.

Labor Unions in Modena

The province of Modena has the highest proportion of unionized workers in Italy, which suggests that unions and small firms are not incompatible. Officials of the largest union in Modena, the Communist Party affiliated General Confederation of Italian Labor (CGIL), claim that the degree of unionization cannot be explained by the size of the firm. They cite comparisons with Turin, a nearby center of mass production, as evidence. Whereas 30–40 percent of employees in artisan companies in Modena are union members, in Turin only 2–3 percent of the artisan firms are unionized. The contrast holds for large firms as well, as illustrated by FIAT, the largest employer in the municipality. FIAT tractor, located in Modena, is 50–60 percent unionized; FIAT cars, located in Turin, is under 20 percent unionized.

These discrepancies suggest that union strategies can be more important in affecting the degree of unionization than the size of the firm. Unions in Modena have played a role in shaping the consensus which forms the political background for the industrial policies of the municipality of Modena. The CGIL has also developed different strategies for organizing small and large firms. Each of these will be examined below.

Small Firms

Strong unions in small firms depend upon strong associations amongst small companies. While the CNA is present in all regions it is strongest in Modena. In Emilia-Romagna, 80 percent of the artisanal companies are in either the CNA or the CGIA, its Christian Democratic counterpart, whereas in certain regions in the south less than 40 percent are in artisanal associations.

The agreement reached between the CNA, as a representative of small firms, and the CGIL, as the representative of workers in artisanal firms, began a tradition in 1974 in which settlements reached in Modena became a standard for wage bargaining at the national level. This is not to imply that wages in small firms are the same throughout Italy – they clearly are not – but that a national standard is established in the region where small firms are most effective. A national agreement for artisanal companies is negotiated every three years for salary, working hours, and working conditions; the actual settlements are adjusted up and down from this agreement beginning at the regional level, then at the provincial level, and finally at the firm level.

The existence of national associations of artisans and national unions exerts pressure on artisanal firms to compete on the basis of innovation and quality as opposed to wages. The fact that a standard wage for small firms is public information shifts the burden of argument in low wage companies: managers must explain why wages are lower than the standard. Equally important is the pressure that high wages put on artisanal companies to adjust productivity upwards rather than the pressure in a competitive wage environment to adjust wages downwards to match low productivity levels.

In Modena unions have benefited from strong artisan associations with which they could bargain. But in order to be effective the unions had to have ways of uniting workers in small firms around their common interests. One means that has enhanced this process was the creation of multi-firm canteens. Whereas large firms were required to establish canteens by law, this was clearly uneconomical for small firms. Consequently, the unions, in conjunction with the municipalities and the artisanal associations, established "social canteens". The municipality paid for the land, cooperatives were formed to run the canteens, and the costs were equally divided between companies and the workers. The first such cooperative, established in 1973, has become one of the largest firms in the province with 400 employees. It prepares 22,000 meals per day in canteens located in areas throughout the province.

The protean character of firms and the high skill levels of the Modenese worker combine to create an economic force for high wages and ease of union organizing. A craft laborer has the option of becoming an independent artisan, which puts pressure upon the company owner to maintain attractive work conditions or risk simultaneously losing a valued employee *and* creating a competitor. Obviously, however, this pressure works with different degrees of force in different settings and time periods. Employers everywhere seek the power to dismiss workers in bad times, and the Third Italy is no exception. The CGIL provides, in part, an insurance policy for workers to guard against future hard times.

The pressure for innovation created by high wages and the career trajectory of artisans in small firms is important for union organizing; it is also crucial to the long-term viability of small firms. In Modena, where wages are about the same in both small and large firms, small firms have to seek means of increasing productivity to match productivity gains in large firms. In the south, where wage discrepancies between small and large firms are substantial, small firms are generally fragmented, slow to innovate, and fit the traditional image of backward enterprises. Here the case for the traditional focus of unions on large firms cannot be denied.

The challenge for unions in the small sector in Modena is to match the safeguards, particularly against firing, that workers enjoy in large firms in Italy. To date the issue has been less serious than in small-firm districts elsewhere because of the large numbers of artisan company owners who were and are themselves craftsmen raised in the union culture of large firms. But the reorganizational efforts in large firms in Emilia-Romagna are now making employment in these firms attractive to younger workers who, until recently, preferred small firms for the greater opportunities for learning, including gaining knowledge of how to run a small company.

Large Firms

Whereas union success in organizing small-firm employees in Emilia-Romagna has involved political activities outside the firm as much as inside it, success in organizing large-firm employees requires political activity inside the firm, but of a new type. Successful organizing within large firms, just as in small, depends upon the development of a strategy that is appropriate to the altered pressures facing managers in the age of the New Competition.

In the Third Italy, managers of large firms were at a disadvantage in hiring younger workers between the mid-1970s and mid-1980s because of the greater opportunities for skill development and the aspiration of workers to establish a firm of their own one day. Recently, however, the advantages have been diminishing because the sharp division between skilled and unskilled jobs within the large plant is disappearing. Many large firms have increased the outsourcing of unskilled repetitive activities and focused on higher value added stages which require more skilled workers. The result has been a simultaneous increase in small-firm subcontracting activity of lower skilled work and an increase in the variety of tasks and learning opportunities within the large firm.

Behind these shifts in the demand for labor in the large firms are the shifting competitive pressures facing managers. Not unexpectedly, managers of large firms have been forced to upgrade their innovation and performance capabilities which, in turn, exerts pressure on existing organizational structures. Reducing product development times or increasing product quality, for example, require greater production flexibility. The traditional pyramidal organization in which information flowed up and down a managerial hierarchy is too cumbersome compared with organizational forms that promote lateral flows of information. As noted in previous chapters, the New Competition is less about increased productivity of labor and capital than about streamlined organization. But radical organizational changes are impossible without changes in power relationships as well. It is here that the unions face their greatest challenge and their greatest opportunity.

The task of management under the New Competition is less one of coordinating, monitoring, and disciplining detail laborers and more one of facilitating teamwork amongst skilled workers with intimate knowledge of production processes. The Taylorist compartmentalization of people into categories of worker, technician, and manager upon which mass production was based is a model of organization that is giving way to alternatives in which the three functions blend into one. Product innovation and product quality depend upon workers having greater knowledge and decisionmaking power. The task for unions in the Third Italy is to develop a new vision of work organization which redefines both the relations between worker and manager and the role of the union in ways that are consistent with the strategies of the New Competition and the aspirations of workers. More than ever before the union must become an active force in redesigning production in large firms as well as small. The problems facing managers of large firms are the starting point for defining a new vision.

The problem for management is that the imperatives of the New Competition are inconsistent with top-down control systems: management control and labor creativity are contradictory. To be creative, people must be responsible; to be responsible, people must be given autonomy, and autonomy implies independence and power. The difficulty lies in both negotiating autonomy of workers and achieving production goals. Unions offer an alternative to paternalistic relations between managers and workers: the acceptance of unions as a bargaining agent for defining productive roles and setting production targets is a means of granting autonomy in return for the acceptance of collective performance responsibility by workers.

Whether or not unions will play a formative role in shaping production in the age of the New Competition depends upon their capacity to develop an analysis that both makes sense to workers and provides a basis for negotiation with managers. Obviously, the outcome cannot be stated with certainty at this early stage. It does seem clear, however, that unless unions break with the mindset and the strategies formed in the struggle within the mass production organization in which they originally flourished, they will waste a historic opportunity. Nostalgia for the old days of rigidly defined job categories associated with scientific management and the emphasis on economistic demands will direct unions to organizing efforts in firms with little chance of long-term viability. The opportunity for unions is that financial viability, given the New Competition, is enhanced by mutual respect between workers and managers and a blurring of roles between workers, technicians, and managers.

Conclusion

The Third Italy provides an interesting contrast to Japan. Both areas have achieved high rates of economic growth in recent years. But, unlike Japan, the Third Italy is led by internationally competitive independent small firms, strong unions, leftist political parties, and an active citizenry at the local level. It is clear that the New Competition does not come in only one form. But it is associated with institution building which blurs a number of classic boundaries and suggests new concepts.

The concept of an inter-firm association with governmental-like powers blurs dichotomies of economy or polity and market or plan. In chapter 4, the term cooperation was used to suggest the existence of a range of activities that defy such bifurcations. By cooperating in the provision of services with substantial economies of scale, small firms can maintain their independence in production without being reduced to subcontractors for products designed in the central office of a giant firm. The idea of inter-firm cooperation presumes an administrative governmental structure which does not base decisionmaking authority on ownership. In the next chapter I examine the idea of the industrial district as a mode of regulation amongst networked groups of small firms. But an industrial district is more than a collection of firms. In this chapter a variety of partly private, partly public institutions were explored that are crucial to the idea of an industrial district. The generic term quasi-public can be used to capture the idea of a range of such institutions.

A quasi-public is a non-profit-seeking economic development agency which is accountable to public officials but not managed by civil servants. Quasi-publics are often partially financed by public monies, and their budgets are overseen and their activities monitored by democratically accountable officials. The board of directors will include civil servants or appointees of elected officials, and the charter or at least the legal structure will be established by legislative enactment. Finally, a quasi-public is usually created for a single purpose.

The Japanese Ministry of International Trade and Industry is an administrative agency of the government and not a quasi-public. A trade association that lobbies government for its members is a private association and not a quasi-public. However, the industrial property development agency of Modena described above is a quasi-public. Its goal is to establish industrial parks which, in turn, enable small and medium-sized firms access to property and plant by a pricing formula that cuts out land speculation.

Finally, the New Competition denies another traditional dichotomy, that between manager and worker within the firm. The artisan of the Third Italy is both a manager or entrepreneur and a skilled worker. The task for unions in large firms is to develop concepts of the artisan that break down the boundary between the two there as well. For only then will unions become an active force in the redesign of production in large firms as well as small.

8
The Industrial District and Sector Regulation

The Third Italy and postwar Japan illustrate two widely divergent but growth-generating productive systems. The concept of a "productive system" signifies a group of interrelated institutions by which goods and services are created. The term "system" emphasizes that the institutional features of a firm cannot be examined in isolation from institutions that interact with firms, for example, supplier and buyer relations, inter-firm associations, worker organizations, financial institutions, and governmental agencies.

The idea of the New Competition is of productive systems oriented to continuous improvement in product and process, whereas the Old Competition is a productive system geared to minimize cost for a given product and process. An economic analysis of the New Competition must account for the capacity for collective action to reshape production-related institutions as new challenges and opportunities develop.

Inter-firm cooperation goes some way to explaining the success of networked groups of small firms in the Third Italy; it also implies that market coordination can undermine the competitiveness of small firms. The implications are far reaching for economic theory and policy. To date, most industrial policy in the United States and the United Kingdom has been based upon the presupposition that the government's task is to promote price competition. But if inter-firm cooperation is a condition of small-firm success, then policymaking based upon the competitive market ideal may actually contribute to industrial decline.

I illustrate this thesis with a comparison of two groups of furniture firms, one coordinated by prices in the market and the other by a combination of market and associational institutions. With this example in mind, I then extend the Marshallian concept of the industrial district as a mode of inter-firm regulation and as a model for regional industrial policy. Finally, I return to Japan for an examination of the role of central government in the promotion of small and medium-sized firms in that country.

A Tale of Two Furniture Sectors: North London versus the Third Italy

North London

Table 6 lists 25 North London furniture firms that existed in the early 1970s. By the mid-1980s only two remained. The North London furniture industry demonstrates how rapidly a sector can collapse. By 1986, the two surviving firms, Nathan and Stonehill, employed roughly 550 people in a furniture district that had employed over 16,000 in the 1960s. What happened?

The British furniture market had been insulated from foreign trade by tariff and non-tariff barriers. The major barrier was the cost of transporting bulky items. But container ships and flatpack techniques greatly reduced the cost of transportation, and entry into the European Economic Community (EEC) lessened the artificial trade restrictions. By the mid-1970s the British market had become a target for European furniture manufacturers.

Faced with slackening demand in the mid-1970s, the North London furniture manufacturers perceived the problem in terms of excessive wages and competition from their neighbors in the same or nearby industrial estates. They reacted to the seemingly excessive wage rates by hiring less skilled workers, increasing the intensity of work, and substituting machines for labor (Best, 1985, p. 107). Furthermore, they reacted against their apparent competitors by cutting prices in order to drive them out of business, after which they hoped to pick up their order books. In fact, both responses left the North London firms less able to respond to the real problem.

The real problem was neither high wages nor their local competitors, but the emergence of foreign competitors benefiting from strategically oriented and cooperatively organized industrial districts. Consequently, each round of cost reductions and bankruptcies in North London did not result in the expected expansion in orders. Instead it merely sealed the fate of the survivors as it had the losers in the previous round. The eventual winners were, first, firms, mainly foreign, who were offering higher quality and better designed furniture, and, second, discount retail chains that were orchestrating price wars amongst manufacturers by sourcing internationally to offer ever cheaper and lower quality furniture.

Unfortunately, this response was not limited to North London furniture firms. Everywhere, the fragmented British furniture manufacturers were cutting costs and seeking volume sales by bidding amongst themselves for orders from discount chains. Meanwhile, import penetration rose from 3.5 percent in 1968 to 7 percent in 1973, 15 percent in 1978, 30 percent in 1982 and 35 percent in 1986 (Best, 1985, p. 98). Between 1980 and 1986 imports nearly tripled from £280 million to £760 million while British furniture production increased by less than 40 percent from £1 billion to nearly £1.4 billion. Most of the increased imports were from high wage Western European countries, particularly Italy, Germany, and Sweden.

The notion of furniture manufacturers adopting a collective approach to counter the margin-squeezing power of mass retailers and to promote productive restructuring by developing distinctive competences in complementary activities was alien to a group of producers who had always sought individualistic solutions. Nor did furniture manufacturers react strategically to the rise of the retailing chains by developing independent marketing capabilities or flexible production systems. It was easier to blame the industry's decline on the bogey men of immoral retailers and obstreperous labor.

The Third Italy

Between 1973 and 1981, Italian furniture exports increased fivefold, from less than a half to more than double those of Germany, the other major furniture exporter of the world. By 1980, Italy enjoyed a $1.8 billion furniture trade surplus (Politi, 1986, p. 7).

The increase in international competitiveness of the Italian furniture industry was not associated with large firms. In 1981 over 86 percent of Italian furniture firms employed less than ten workers and only two employed more than 500 (Silvestrelli, 1985). The employment share of furniture firms with between one and nine employees did drop sharply from over 50 percent in 1961 to 36 percent in 1981, but the shift of employment has never been to firms with more than 100 employees. In fact, firms with between ten and 49 employees increased their share from 28 percent in 1961 to 38 percent in 1981 (Silvestrelli, 1985).

As shown in table 7, between 1967 and 1981, value added per employee, fixed investment per employee, and pay all increased by roughly ten times in money terms for furniture firms with over 20 employees (Silvestrelli, 1985) (similar data do not exist for firms with less than 20 employees as they are not required to report such information). Using 1967 as a base year, the Italian consumer price index stood at 472 in 1981 (*Economic Report of the President*, 1988). This suggests that output per employee more than tripled and value

Table 6 Losers and survivors in the North London furniture industry

Firms closing down before 1983	Workforce	Firms closing down, 1983–6	Workforce		Survivors	Workforce	
			1970	1984		1970	1986
Angel Colony							
Great Eastern Cabinet Co.	300	Carasell	130	30	B. & I. Nathan	400	150
Sparrow & Simmons	130						
Coller	200						
Supasuite	200						
Beautility	1,000						
Ely's Estate							
Homeworthy	500	Howard	130	100	Stonehill	900	400
Cabinet Industry	1,000	Welsell	300	130			
Wrighton	500	Uniflex	400	100			
John Citizen	100						

Lea Bridge			
Berrys	100		
Henry Wilkes	100		
Grant	100		
Liden (Whitewood)	300		
Bluestone		300	150
Austin		500	200
Others in North London			
Lebus	3,010		
Eyelock	400		
Summers	300		
Schreiber (Harlow)	1,000		
	13,430		
Job losses:			
Plant closings		710	
Shrinkage		1,050	750
Jobs remaining (1986)			550

Source: Michael H. Best, interviews with North London furniture manufacturers and workers.

Table 7 Growth indices of the Italian furniture industry, 1967–1981[a]

Year	Output per employee	Value added per employee	Fixed investment per employee	Pay per employee
1967	100	100	100	100
1981 (current $)	1,675	1,178	914	1,089
1981 (deflated $)	355	250	194	231

[a]For firms employing more than 20 employees.
Source: adapted from Silvestrelli, 1985.

added per employee, fixed investment per employee, and pay all roughly doubled in real terms over the period.

The important implication to draw from these empirical details is that the enormous growth and improvement in competitiveness of the Italian furniture industry was not associated with an emergence of large firms. The increase in productive efficiency came primarily from increased specialization which, in turn, was a consequence of consultative inter-firm relations with elements of both competition and cooperation.

Because British furniture firms were too small to develop international marketing capacities individually, they did not market internationally. Italian furniture firms, in contrast, reacted to the same problem by forming joint marketing associations such as the three described in chapter 7. The perpetuation of purely market relationships with retailers kept North London furniture manufacturers in a divided and subordinate relationship from which they were unable to escape.

Upstream inter-firm relations were also mediated by price. Furniture manufacturers treated component and machinery suppliers in the same way that they themselves were treated by retailers: prices, and prices alone, did the talking. The result was lower prices but lack of long-term investment by supplier firms followed by an atrophy of domestic sources. In a comparative study of British and German kitchen-making firms, Hilary Steedman and Karin Wagner note the remarkable extent to which today's British furniture-making industry imports from abroad. Virtually all high quality plastic laminated chipboard, specialized veneers, carcase fronts made from high grade materials, spring door hinges, door handles, and various fittings are imported. The same is true for machinery: "in Germany, even in small firms (20 employees), highly sophisticated – usually computer numerically controlled (CNC) – woodworking machinery was generally installed" in contrast with Britain where computer numerically controlled machinery is rarely seen in furniture companies (Steedman and Wagner, 1987, p. 87).

What explains the stability of systems of small firms in the Third Italy and elsewhere? Why have successful firms not gone the way of vertical integration and Big Business as described in chapter 2? The answer lies in recognizing that the Marshallian industrial district is an alternative to the large company as a means of organizing production.

The (Static) Industrial District: External Economies of Scale

Chandler's theory of business evolution does not preclude the possibility of the permanence of small firms in peripheral, as distinct from core, sectors. But it implies that such vertically specialized sectors will be technologically backward. Clothing and furniture are sectors in which vertical integration failed and which continued to be dominated by small firms coordinated by the market. Such sectors will not benefit from the economies of high throughput.

Marshall, however, suggested a basis for both industrial development and stability of small firms in terms of industrial districts. In his words,

> (T)he economic use of expensive machinery can sometimes be attained in a very high degree in a district in which there is a large aggregate production of the same kind, even though no individual capital employed in the trade be very large. For subsidiary industries devoting themselves each to one small branch of the process of production, and working it for a great many of their neighbours, are able to keep in constant use machinery of the most highly specialized character, and to make it pay its expenses, though its original cost may have been high, and its rate of depreciation very rapid. (Marshall, 1920, p. 271)

The idea of an industrial district suggests a group of geographically concentrated firms specializing along the lines of the Richardsonian distinction between similar and complementary activities and developing Penrosian experiential knowledge. For the group the end result is greater skill and productive knowledge. For each firm the result is external economies of scale over time.

The North London furniture sector was not an industrial district. Instead of external economies of scale derived from localized inter-firm specialization, each firm produced the same product and competed on the basis of minimum costs. But costs were minimized given the non-specialized structure of inter-firm relations. The market coordination that prevailed in the North London furniture industry left firms with limited options to compete against European firms that were members of industrial districts.

Several efforts by North London furniture manufacturers to integrate vertically, merge, and establish dominant market share failed. Lebus, Schreiber, Austin, and Bowater are all examples of efforts to rationalize the industry by establishing internal economies of scale. None succeeded (Best, 1985, pp. 108–9).

The emerging furniture industrial districts in Italy and Germany gave furniture firms a range of specialist machinery makers and component suppliers which supplied both inputs and ideas. Consequently it was not an accident that German kitchen manufacturers developed the capacity to provide high quality cabinets with a range of accessories that could not be matched by British manufacturers, or that the Italian furniture makers could offer a range of new designs to British retailers that were beyond the capacity of the British furniture manufacturer. The German and Italian furniture-making firms could rely upon a circle of specialist component suppliers and retailers with which long-term consultative relations facilitated the flow of knowledge and, with it, product and process innovation.

Explaining the emergence of successful industrial districts shifts the emphasis from issues of distribution and labor productivity to those of organization, internal and external. The task of inter-firm institution building comes to the forefront, as spontaneous market coordination will suffer from the "tyranny of small decisions" when a collective decisionmaking process is required. It also means that a historical analysis is required to explain the geographical location of industry; simply examining the relative abundance of factors of production ignores the central role of organization.

The Marshallian notion of the industrial district goes some way to describing a productive system of small firms. But the source of stability of small firms in the Third Italy is based on more than specialization and external economies of scale. Successful industrial districts are in a state of continuous restructuring as firms seek to remain competitive in a world of rapid technological change and intense international competition. For the competitive edge of firms in an industrial district comes from the combination of, first, high quality based on distinctive competences that result from specialization by phase within the production chain and, second, flexibility that results from the capacity for reconstitution of the micro production units along the production chain as technology advances and market conditions change. To capture these opportunities an industrial district must be collectively entrepreneurial.

The Industrial District and Mutual Adjustment

The Marshallian industrial district, like Marshallian price theory, is static: firms, like pieces of a puzzle, each form distinctive elements of a fixed whole. But a static conception of an industrial district does not capture the major strength of the Third Italy: the institutional capacity to continuously learn, adjust, and improve in economic performance. The North London furniture industry was not outcompeted on price but on product performance (Best, 1985). The continental European competitors were innovative in product, process, and marketing, while the British industry was stagnant.

Successful European furniture firms were often located within an industrial district. But success across industrial districts depended upon a capacity to innovate. An innovative industrial district can be described as a dynamic constellation of mutually adjusting firms. The constellation is dynamic in that the responses to new challenges and opportunities involve a continuous redefinition of the inter-firm networks and external boundaries of the district. Adjustments are mutual in that initiatives from one firm intersect with others and modify the production capabilities and opportunities for each firm. Finally the image is of an engendering industrial district in that something new is emerging perpetually out of the old.

Coordination in a dynamic industrial district is not planned in that the initiatives, responses, networks, and aggregated constellation cannot be specified in advance, but instead are developed in processes of mutual adjustment in unforeseeable ways. But the quasi-spontaneous coordination is not market coordination for two reasons. First, the media of exchange are not only money and goods but ideas, particularly solutions to problems. Money and goods can be measured and the basis of exchange can be defined in prices. Knowledge, in contrast, is not a private good. Unlike private goods, knowledge can be shared, and even expanded, but not exchanged in social intercourse. The sale of information, unlike the sale of private goods, does not result in a decrease in supply to the seller.

The public good aspect of information is less important in explaining industrial districts than the process by which production-relevant information is created. To the extent that product and process innovation is based upon new ideas and that the creation of ideas is a social process involving discussion, then geographical proximity is important in innovation. The idea of coordination by cooperation as distinct from coordination by market is that the purpose of coordination is not simply efficiency in terms of the lowest price, but innovation in terms of how to improve productive performance by altering the way it is done. Marshall did not ignore the role of consultation and the development of ideas in industrial districts:

> Good work is rightly appreciated, inventions and improvements in machinery, in processes and the general organization of the business have their merits promptly discussed: if one man starts a new idea, it is taken up by others and combined with suggestions of their own; and thus it becomes the source of further new ideas. (Marshall, 1920, p. 271)

The idea of market coordination obscures a second feature of a dynamic industrial district: unlike the process of market exchange which leaves the totality of resources unchanged, the process of mutual adjustment in a dynamic district creates new possibilities which forever alter the constellation of firms – their experiences and capabilities in the Penrosian learning sense. Thus the idea of opportunities forgone is not simply that of the use of resources in one way rather than another. Instead, it has an element of permanent irreversibility. Pursuing a particular production process alters the capabilities of resource services and of the constellation of firms. Choosing one path irrevocably closes another. The implication is that any constellation of firms is not organic but contingent. Happenstances play a role in shaping a particular constellation of firms; firms develop in response to opportunities which were created by the previous mutual adjustments.

This implies that an industrial district in which participants do not have a concept to describe it is vulnerable to being undermined. Perhaps one of the essential features of a dynamic industrial district is a means of comparing alternative development paths. That means can be formal or informal. In the case of the Third Italy, common political or religious affiliations create a bedrock of community that sustains a collective identity and with it a notion of "we" as well as "I".

Industrial Districts and Collective Identity

Creating a successful industrial district involves establishing links of cooperation amongst firms so that they have the confidence to specialize – a prerequisite to increased productive efficiency in small firms. These links of cooperation are sustained by social norms that inhibit price and wage competition within the sector and channel competition toward product innovation, design leadership, and specialty niches.

The social ties that bind these firms together have similarities with those at Toyota described in chapter 5. Knowledge and ideas are shared across individual firms and each specializes cognizant of the business plans of associated firms. In this case the inter-firm relations are based on neither market contracts nor a pyramidal network overseen by a lead manufacturer or retailer. But in another way the supplier networks are very different.

The ideal of a dynamic industrial district is networking without hierarchy. The notion of a community of producers, in which a single firm is at the apex of a captive hierarchy, is replaced with the idea of intersecting networks with multiple apexes in which no single firm is permanently at the head of any hierarchy. Without the possibility of shifting networks, a dependency relationship will emerge between the lead firm and permanent subcontractors. The criticism of hierarchy is not simply that non-hierarchical forms promote an egalitarian society. The protean feature of a non-hierarchical dynamic industrial district may enhance the capacity for learning. Supplier firms that have multiple relations with firms in other sectors are also firms that are exposed to new ideas.

Efficiency is also improved if a firm can concentrate on new production ideas and technology in a limited range of activities yet count on other firms to be developing new technologies in related activities. Thus an industrial district composed of firms specializing in complementary activities and in which each firm concentrates its attention on a narrow technological field is likely to be more innovative than a district in which production is not specialized.

Clearly the norms that sustain cooperation are subject to erosion if they are not reinforced by community – a shared vision of a just society which presumes a mutual awareness of unwritten norms of what it means to be a respected member of the community. One of those norms is that cooperation towards another member of the community today will be reciprocated by yet another tomorrow. In Big Business, as already noted, a task of top leadership is to establish a sense of community by articulating a vision that gives purpose to the organization with which members can identify. That workers are motivated by more than the calculus of interests is understood by effective top management who strive to gain commitment and loyalty from their workforce. In chapter 5, the role of company leaders in imparting a distinctive cultural identity to each kaisha was described. Local governments can also nurture a collective identity, but one that appeals to more ennobling aspirations than inter-firm rivalry for market share or "beating America".

A carefully nurtured collective identity can potentially provide the social fabric which sustains cooperation in an industrial district as in a corporation. Here again, the role of geographically concentrated small firms is important for an industrial district. For geographical proximity makes it possible for individuals to interact socially and politically as well as economically. In the case of Modena, the commune, or town, has a long illustrious history which is objectified in the buildings in which official town activities take place.

Since an industrial district is a looser organizational entity than a corporate hierarchy, local government and inter-firm associations face a formidable challenge in establishing a shared vision. The organization of the CNA by industrial sector and the development of collective resource centers by local and provincial government are means of establishing such forums to facilitate organizational cohesion. In this they are performing functions not unlike the central office in the Pennsylvania Railroad in the 1850s or General Motors in the 1920s, namely centralized coordination with decentralized responsibility. In the case of Modena, political economists have played a role similar to that of Edgar Thomson, Alfred Sloan, and Donaldson Brown in developing concepts to understand and thereby deepen the institutions that enable joint action without a top–down hierarchy that stifles operational autonomy at the local level.

In summary, the vision of an internationally vibrant sector that emerges is one with a capability to adjust to change. A key ingredient is a heterogeneous complex of mutually interdependent firms that both cooperate and compete. Instead of one ideal business organization or one perfect strategy, we find a variety of forms and a mix of strategies. Long-term viability requires that the sector as a whole has the capacity for both minimum cost production and product innovation. It is possible for a single firm to internalize each of the required functions but it cannot specialize in each. It is possible for a sector but not a single firm simultaneously to pursue distinct strategies. The result is that firms are mutually interdependent in that each depends upon the existence of others. But it is also important that the sector has an institutional basis for establishing a collective identity or concept of itself as a mutually interdependent set of firms. Only then can it sustain the coordination required to develop the specialization and skills required to adapt continuously to new challenges.

Community as a Medium for Joint Action

The Third Italy is a goldmine for studying institutions by which individuals can achieve the benefits of joint action that are beyond the reach of individual action. For example, an individual cannot supply the requisite trust to a banker to obtain working capital, but a financial consortium can. Similarly, an individual firm cannot maintain distinctive competences in a number of activities required to produce a complex product, but a network of specialist producers can.

The reason that these institutions are not prevalent elsewhere is explained by the parable of the "tragedy of the commons": the advantages of joint action depend upon norms of mutual responsibility which are subject to erosion by the opportunistic actions of "free-riders", individuals who enjoy the benefits of the joint action but without observing the rules required to sustain joint action. In the "tragedy of the commons" parable the common is a public resource that is destroyed by the opportunistic pursuit of self-interest by abusers of the grazing rights. While it is in the enlightened self-interest of individual members of the community surrounding the common not to overgraze it, good citizens who do not allow their sheep to overgraze will be victimized by bad citizens who do allow overgrazing. The existence of bad citizens seeking to take advantage of the fact that good citizens have refrained from grazing their sheep will, in the end, turn all citizens into bad ones. The common will be overgrazed and destroyed as a public resource because each citizen will pre-emptively graze his/her sheep rather than risk being a victim of the free riders.

The financial consortium and the network of specialist producers described above are both types of public resource and as such both are subject to the "tragedy of the commons" if individual responsibility is eroded. For example, if a group of artisans were to politicize the CNA by making side deals that involved misrepresenting assessments of character for purposes of obtaining loans, the financial consortium would be subverted and a return to the bankers demand for marketable collateral to back loans would ensue.

The conventional wisdom in economic analysis holds that a "tragedy of the commons" can be averted by either private ownership of the resources involved or state provision. Two drawbacks to market provision can be cited. First, a market does not exist for the key ingredient in the transaction: trust. A firm, for example, could not sell the same information that a financial consortium can give to a banker because the seller of financial information has a pecuniary interest in making a sale, unlike the financial consortium. Thus there is no way of knowing that one has the genuine article. Second, monitoring activity will be highly costly. As noted, borrowers from the consortium are under the additional pressure of peer condemnation if they fail to repay their loans. Government provision, in contrast, does not ensure the degree of attention that comes from those with a financial or professional stake in the outcome.

The Third Italy offers a third response to the inherent problem of the free rider that is built into joint provision of public resources, namely community-based institutions that are part public and part private. This approach does not suggest that people will "naturally" take the common good into consideration. Instead, it suggests that development of community institutions can lead to the economical supply of collective goods by creating safeguards against the erosion of individual responsibility. These institutions depend upon enforcement mechanisms to deter the free rider and thereby diminish the tendency to pre-emptive opportunistic actions. One such safeguard is the capacity of a community to withdraw the respect and honor bestowed upon an individual. From this perspective it is the erosion of community that causes the "tragedy of the commons".

In short, what the institutions of community supply is an efficient monitoring system. Individuals observe norms of reciprocity because they are enforced by other individuals in the community. What distinguishes the Third Italy is not that institutions are created to achieve the benefits of joint action, but the form of such institutions. Whereas in Japan the kaisha engenders individual responsibility to the collectivity, the Third Italy obtains similar results without a top–down hierarchy and the more oppressive social structure that accompanies it.

Inter-firm Cooperation Amongst Small and Medium Enterprises in Japan

We are now in a position to return to the industrial organization of Japan armed with the concept of inter-firm association as an alternative to hierarchy. The first remarkable feature with respect to Japanese industrial organization has already been noted: namely the prevalence of small firms, which can be observed in table 8. In 1981, small and medium-size enterprises in non-primary industries accounted for 99.4 percent of Japanese firms and 81.4 percent of employment; in manufacturing, small and medium-size enterprises accounted for 51.8 percent of shipments.[1] It is estimated that small and medium enterprises hold a 40 percent share of exports of manufactured goods, if both direct and indirect exports are taken into account (*Outline of the Small and Medium Enterprise Policies of the Japanese Government* (hereafter *Outline*), p. 41).

---

[1] Small and medium-size enterprises in manufacturing and related industries are defined as having 300 or less employees and 100 million yen or less in capital. Small enterprises in manufacturing are those with 20 or less employees and 10 million yen or less in capital (*Outline of the Small and Medium Enterprise Policies of the Japanese Government*, p. 1).

Table 8 Size distribution of industrial enterprises

Size of enterprise	Distribution (%)				
	China 1982	South Korea 1981	Japan 1972	Yugoslavia 1981	Hungary 1981
5–33 employees	59.2	70.6	80.2	6.6	2.2
33–75 employees	19.5	14.4	10.7	15.8	4.8
75–189 employees	12.2	9.2	6.1	32.1	18.7
189–243 employees	8.5	1.5	0.8	12.0	9.2
More than 243 employees	0.6	4.3	2.2	33.5	65.1

Source: World Bank; cited in *Economist*, August, 1987, p. 10

The Small and Medium Enterprise Modernization Promotion Law

The second remarkable feature is the range of organizational infrastructure, particularly in the form of government agencies. Much of this infrastructure emanates from the first of a series of laws beginning with the Small and Medium Enterprise Modernization Promotion Law passed in 1963. The concept of modernization that informs the Law is defined as follows:

> The modernization of small and medium enterprises implies a concept of a very comprehensive nature. It covers not only the modernization of management and facilities of individual small and medium businesses, but also extends to the modernization of a small and medium enterprise *sector as an entire system*, which includes modernization of relationship between individual enterprises as well as different industries. (*Outline*, p. 8, my emphasis)

The focus on sectors and extra-firm organization as opposed to individual firms evokes comparison with the concept of rationalization as developed by German industrial policy in the late 1920s (see chapter 3). But the new twist is the attention to small and medium-sized enterprises.

By 1985, 65 sectors had qualified for modernization plans under the 1963 Law, 44 of which were designated as in need of structural improvement. The carrot for a sector to be designated as in need of structural improvement is a series of low interest loans and tax incentives that extend beyond those enjoyed by firms in sectors that qualify for modernization plans. The stick is that small firms cannot appeal for the benefits as individual firms; they must formulate structural improvement plans in cooperation with other firms in the sector. The structural improvement plans are developed in consultation with the ministry with jurisdiction over the designated industry.[2] The ministry with jurisdiction is not a rubber stamp for structural improvement plans; the ministry official conducts an independent survey of the industry and consults with the Small and Medium Enterprise Modernization Council (created by the 1963 Law) in order to judge whether the plan is consistent with the "sound development of the national economy or the maintenance of social stability" (*Outline*, p. 8).

The Law on Cooperatives of Small and Medium Enterprises and Other Parties

The formation of inter-firm cooperatives is not restricted to sectors for which structural improvement plans have been agreed. Since the Law on Cooperatives of Small and Medium Enterprises and Other Parties was passed in 1949, and upgraded with the Law on the Organization of Small Business Associations of 1957, inter-firm cooperatives have been an instrument for the improvement of management and the advancement of productivity in and amongst small firms. Forms of cooperation include the following:

> 1 Common facility cooperatives [which] conduct joint economic activities including joint production, processing and sales with the aim of improving the management of member companies and the terms and conditions of their business transactions. Member companies maintain independent management. (*Outline*, p. 34)
>
> 2 Commercial and industrial cooperatives, organized for each industry, [which] conduct research and studies, guidance and training in order to improve and develop the industry *as a whole*. They also adjust *excessive competition* and form cartels to stabilize the management of small and medium enterprises during recessions. (*Outline*, p. 34, my emphasis)

At least four enterprises are required for the establishment of inter-firm cooperatives of the common facilities type; half or more enterprises of the "specified industry in the district" are required to form the second, commercial and industrial, type of cooperative (*Outline*, p. 36). Guidance

---

[2] As of 1985, MITI had jurisdiction over structural improvement plans in 35 industries, the Ministry of Agriculture, Forestry and Fisheries over 19, the Ministry of Transport over four, the Ministry of Construction over 11, and several other ministries had one each (*Outline*, pp. 10–12).

on the establishment of inter-firm cooperatives is provided by the Federation of Small Business Associations (one in each prefecture), and the National Federation of Small Business Associations (*Outline*, p. 34).

The Law on Extraordinary Measures for Regional Small and Medium Enterprises

This law provides tax incentives in 198 designated production areas for promotion and rationalization plans approved by the prefectural governor (*Outline*, p. 54). The Small Business Finance Corporation and the National Finance Corporation both allocate sizeable amounts of finance to help small and medium enterprises in designated production areas to do the following:

> (i) raise their capacity to develop new products, (ii) develop new markets, (iii) improve the quality of management, and (iv) achieve large scale production and sales. (*Outline*, p. 54)

The Law on the Prevention of Delay in the Payment of Subcontracting Charges and Related Matters

The Small and Medium Firm Enterprise Agency (established in 1948) and the Fair Trade Commission are both in charge of implementing the Law on the Prevention of Delay in the Payment of Subcontracting Charges and Related Matters, passed in 1956. The purpose of the Law is to establish "measures to adjust the business activities of large enterprises in order to secure equitable business opportunities for small businesses" (*Outline*, p. 58). The Law describes a number of duties of parent firms to subcontracting enterprises, such as the payment date which must be no more than 60 days from the date of delivery of the ordered item. A record of the actions taken by both the Fair Trade Commission and the Small and Medium Enterprise Agency in support of the Law is given in table 9.

Table 10 provides a summary of the governmental and quasi-governmental agencies (and the number of officials involved) that are charged with the task of guidance of small and medium enterprises.

Figure 4 summarizes the whole range of extra-firm institutions that promote small and medium-sized businesses in Japan. Many of these extra-firm functions are the same as those provided by middle management of Big Business. Without such services small and medium-sized firms in Japan would be under more pressure to provide such services for themselves which, in turn, would lead to larger firms and hierarchical organizations. Seen from this angle, Big Business was, in

Table 9   Enforcement of the Law on the Prevention of Delay in the Payment of Subcontracting Charges and Related Matters

Item	FY 81	FY 82	FY 83	FY 84
Actions taken by the Fair Trade Commission				
No. of business establishments examined (on document)	31,759	36,558	39,484	50,319
No. of business establishments where violations were suspected	1,175	1,354	1,441	1,482
No. of cases where action was taken[a]				
Advice	1	4	0	0
Administrative guidance	932	1,014	1,119	1,224
No violation proved	252	271	317	693
Total	1,185	1,289	1,436	1,917
Actions taken by the Small and Medium Enterprise Agency				
No. of business establishments examined (on document)	44,000	48,000	51,000	56,625
No. of business establishments where violations were suspected	6,666	8,487	7,080	8,204
No. of cases where action was taken				
No. of on-the-spot investigations	1,462	1,620	1,664	1,745
No. of investigations by summons	544	533	417	522
No. of investigations on document	2,206	4,443	2,379	3,086
Total	4,212	6,596	4,460	5,353
Results of investigations on the spot or by summons				
Administrative guidance for improvement (reported back within 3 months after guidance)	1,979	2,124	2,066	2,821
Administrative guidance for improvement (reported back within 6 months after guidance)	19	15	12	27
Requests made to the Fair Trade Commission for further action	8	14	3	0

[a]*The number of cases where action was taken includes those carried forward from the preceding year.*
Source: *Outline*, p. 60.

Table 10 Small and medium enterprise guidance organizations

Organizations	Activities	Officers in charge	Number of officers FY 1985
Small and Medium Enterprise Agency			
Guidance Division	Coordination in guidance activities	Analysis officers	2
Small Enterprise Counselling Office	Counselling for small enterprise	Small enterprise guidance officers	5
Trade and Wholesale Division	Counselling, arbitration, and mediation concerning conflicts concerning areas of business between large and small and medium enterprises	Small enterprise mediation officers	2
Regional Bureaus of the Ministry of International Trade and Industry			
Commerce and Industry Department, Small and Medium Enterprise Division	Interprefectural consultation, etc.	Small and medium enterprise analysis officers	16
	Counselling for small enterprises	Small and medium enterprise analysis officers	17
	Counselling, arbitration and mediation concerning conflicts between large and small and medium enterprises	Small and medium enterprise mediation officers	10

Organizations	Activities	Officers in charge	Number of officers FY 1985
Prefectural and major municipal governments			
Comprehensive Guidance Centers for small and medium enterprises	(1) Management analysis and guidance activities	Analysis and guidance personnel	1,178
	(2) Management counselling (score system)[a]	Small and medium enterprise management committee members	255
Public testing and Research Institutes	(1) Technological guidance	Technological guidance personal	5,405
	(2) Technological advisory activities	Technological advisors	
Regional Information Center	Gathering and disseminating information		846
Japan Small Business Corporation (JSBC)	Analysis and guidance		
Small Business Information Centers	Gathering and disseminating information, overseas investment advisory service	Overseas investment advisors	457
Office Automation (OA) System Center	Advisory service on introduction of computers	Office automation system advisors	4
Institutes	Training		

Cont'd

Federation of Small Business Associations			
(National Federation)	Guidance for establishing and managing cooperatives	Travelling guidance personnel	949
(Prefectural Federations)	Guidance for establishing and managing cooperatives	Labor relations guidance personnel	8
		Shopping district guidance personnel	
Japan Chamber of Commerce and Industry	Guidance for management of Chambers of Commerce and Industry	Central guidance personnel	21
Central Federation of Boards of Commerce and Industry	Guidance for management of Boards of Commerce and Industry, and Prefectural Federation of Boards of Commerce and Industry	Central guidance personnel	
Prefectural Federations of Boards of Commerce and Industry	(1) Management of Boards of Commerce and Industry, and small enterprise management improvement dissemination activities	Boards of Commerce and Industry guidance personnel	425
		Management guidance personnel	337
	(2) Special counselling activities for prevention of bankruptcy (certain Chambers of Commerce and Industry also conduct this)	Commercial and industrial arbitrator	568

Cont'd

Organizations	Activities	Officers in charge	Number of officers FY 1985
Chambers of Commerce and Industry and Boards of Commerce and Industry	Small enterprises management improvement activities	Management guidance personnel Chief bookkeeping guidance personnel Bookkeeping guidance personnel	8,636 3,980 5,589
National Association for Subcontracting Enterprises Promotion	Guidance for management of Prefectural Associations for Subcontracting Enterprises Promotion	Guidance personnel Guidance assistants	7 1
Prefectural Associations for Subcontracting Enterprises Promotion	Counselling, arbitration, and mediation concerning subcontracting	Guidance personnel Guidance assistants	218 93
(Small and Medium Enterprise Consultants Association)[b]	Cooperation with prefectural governments in analysis and guidance activities	Small and medium enterprise consultants	9,691 (as of April 1, 1985)
Total			38,720

[a]Score system refers to a system offering managerial advice and guidance derived from actual experiences. Under this system, retired businessmen, who until recently held active roles in top management, are appointed as small and medium enterprise management committee members. They offer advice and guidance on management policies for small and medium enterprises.

[b]The Minister of International Trade and Industry approves the establishment and supervises the activities of the Consultant Association. The said Minister has jurisdiction over the certification of the qualification of the small and medium enterprise consultants, and conducts the necessary examinations, training, and screening.

Source: *Outline*, pp. 18–19.

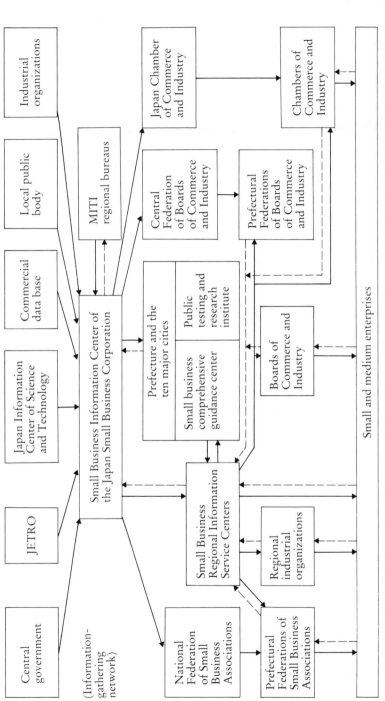

Figure 4 Information-gathering and dissemination system for Japanese small and medium enterprises.
Source: Outline, p. 26.

part, an effort to exploit the economies of information gathering and, having done so, to preclude its widespread dissemination. The advantages of the governmental provision is that officials have no incentive to exclude any firms, existing or new.

Conclusion

The Third Italy and Japan offer two approaches to the promotion of small and medium-size enterprises; both depend upon a combination of cooperation and competition. The Third Italy approach is rooted in the institutions of community established at the level of the municipality; the Japanese approached is anchored in Laws passed by the Diet, or national congress, and carried out by a plethora of central government industrial policy agencies. A common prerequisite for cooperation is trust, and industrial policy in both Japan and the Third Italy is geared to promoting trust by collective incentives. Instead of focusing on individual firms, both approaches seek to develop sector strategies which encourage firms to learn to cooperate. Only then can the specialization by activity be developed that meets the requirements of the New Competition.

A third approach is exemplified in this chapter by the North London furniture district; it was exemplified in chapter 3 by the principles that guide American antitrust policies. The tendency of Big Business to overwhelm small business enterprises in both America and Britain was perceived as evidence of the inherent superiority of large business enterprises. This lesson was also absorbed into the industrial policy activities of socialist states. It is an inference that must be drastically modified in the light of the New Competition.

9

The New Competition:
Interpretations and Challenges

From Big Business to the New Competition: Transcending the Taylorist Legacy

The old competition is about Big Business, which means managerial hierarchy, scientific management, and either vertical integration or "arm's length" market-oriented supplier relations. Permanency is the guiding spirit of Big Business. In Chandler's words (his fourth proposition), ". . . once a managerial hierarchy had been formed and had successfully carried out its function of administrative coordination, the hierarchy itself became a source of permanence, power, and continued growth" (Chandler, 1977, p. 8). Not only the hierarchy, but the production process is designed with permanency in mind. Just as the hierarchy is established to regulate and replace markets, the assembly line is set up to stabilize production runs.

In Big Business, the tasks of workers are minutely classified and occupations are contractually codified in order to govern impersonally. In the beginning the purpose of the rule-governed procedures was defended in "scientific" terms: namely, the pursuit of order and predictability.[1] What could be predicted could be controlled, and

---

[1] The quotation marks around the word "scientific" are meant to imply that the term is being used in the positivist sense, in which the purpose of science is to discover laws that regulate actions, such as the law of gravity. The presumption is that the same methodology is appropriate to the study of both natural and social phenomena. The purpose of "science" (or the discovery of laws), in this positivist sense, is prediction. One problem in applying a positivist methodology to social activities is that positivism denies reflexivity between thought and action. If, however, the objects of the theory are potentially self-conscious (they have the capacity to comprehend the theory that is being used to describe their actions), they have the capacity to refute, deny, undermine, or

controls took the form of bureaucratic rules to minimize human error and eliminate the unexpected.[2]

Once mass production and the managerial hierarchy were in place, the task became one of guiding consumption to match productive capacity. Multiple stabilizing institutions emerged: business hierarchy (to coordinate complementary production activities and administer quasi-cartel activities), collective bargaining (to match worker buying power and productive capacity), the welfare state (to guard against business recessions being reinforced by underconsumption). Keynesian demand management (the use of tax, government spending, and credit instruments to equate aggregate expenditures with productive capacity), sector-specific governmental regulatory institutions (to guide production within a sector), and international monetary institutions (to balance foreign trade and capital flows). Each of these institutions was shaped by, and in turn reinforced, the drive to promote economic stability in the wake of Big Business. The prerequisite was to regulate markets in ways that balanced mass consumption with mass production.

The New Competition is attacking the base of this whole superstructure: the production unit, its organization, and internal governance structure. The organization of the production unit is affected by technology, but also by the choice of competitive strategy and the form of regulatory institutions. Strategies can be price or product led, and regulatory institutions include the means of adjusting first coordination (market, plan, or network) across production units, second the mix of competition and cooperation at the sector level, and third the balance of industrial policy and demand management policy (the fiscal, monetary, and exchange rate activities that preoccupy national economic policymaking in the United Kingdom and the United States).

The New Competition is about business enterprises that pursue strategies of continuous improvement in product and process within a regulatory framework that encourages industrial restructuring. One claim of this book is that the American business enterprise and regulatory framework tend to be organized according to, or derived from, the principles of Big Business. The task is to make a transition to business enterprises and regulatory institutions organized in terms of the New Competition.

The message that we are living in a time of economic transformation is not lost on managers and workers. Nevertheless progress is slow.

otherwise counter it. Given such a reflexivity between subject and theory, the possibility of a science of prediction in the social sciences is seriously challenged. For more on this critique of positivist methodology see Charles Taylor (1971).

[2] For more on the relation between predictability and control see Brian Fay (1975).

The biggest barrier is social: transforming a way of industrial life organized around the principles of scientific management. The gains in competitiveness that a firm can achieve by a committed workforce are apparent today. Most Big Business enterprises in America and Britain have experimented with "quality of worklife", "employee involvement", or related programs to advance worker commitment to the goals of the firm. But the experiments are usually abandoned after a few months. Both workers and management become disillusioned and business as usual returns.

The question is: why do such efforts generally fail in the United States and Britain? The answer is because they are imposed within a context of a Taylorist work organization, an alien form to the integration of thinking and doing. Breaking with Taylorism is a task that requires a new definition of the role of both workers and managers, and the old definition is rooted in the culture of Big Business. Furthermore, it has a historical legacy that must be addressed directly if industrial revitalization is to succeed.

The legacy derives from the manner in which each country resolved the class struggle between workers and owners – managers during the formative stages of establishing industrial enterprises. The terms of that resolution had a crucial impact on the organization of the business enterprise for decades to follow. In the United States the struggle between organized workers and enterprise owners over the implementation of mass production technologies, as described in chapter 2, was resolved by the development of managerial hierarchies and scientific management. In the inter-war period the organization of Big Business was solidified with the development of collective bargaining and the welfare state. Thereafter, the Taylorist division of the workplace was accepted as a fact of industrial life by the workforce in exchange for collective bargaining and the welfare state.

In Britain, the existence of a powerful trade union movement prior to the establishment of Big Business limited the power of management to reorganize work according to the principles of mass production (Lewchuck, 1986). The British system of industrial relations tended to rely not upon mechanization and tight supervision, but upon incentive systems accompanied by delegating considerable responsibility to shop stewards for achieving output goals (Tolliday and Zeitlin, 1986). The political power of the trade union movement spread to the political arena and was manifest in the Labour Party's commitment to nationalization as a means of modernizing British industry. British industrial management, caught between the short-term international commerce orientation of a centralized banking system and a powerful trade union movement was ill prepared to counter the competitiveness of industrial enterprises based elsewhere.

In Japan, intense class struggles took place at the emerging automobile companies in the early postwar period (Cusumano, 1985, chapter 3; Ichiyo, 1984). The resolution was the establishment of welfare capitalism within the firm: the company relinquished the right to fire workers in exchange for a company union and no resistance to organizational change. In the Third Italy, the combined effects of the strategy of Big Business to break the leftist unions and subcontract, on the one hand, and the active small business promotion policies of the local governments, on the other, led to the emergence of dynamic industrial districts.

The form of the resolution of the class struggle in these critical stages in the development of industrial capitalism had a powerful effect both on the definition of manager and worker and on the terms of relation between the firms and the government. A career ladder for a worker in a Japanese factory can progress from group leader, to production supervisor, up to production manager. The occupational pinnacle for a blue collar worker in America and Britain is foreman or front line supervisor; the ranks of management are closed. Not only does a sharp class divide exist within productive enterprises, but individuals begin and end their careers in the same class. Teamwork across the class divide is not sustainable, nor is the commitment to the goals of the enterprise of those forever lodged on the bottom. This is an unstated reality of life in Big Business.

In the United States the welfare state picked up responsibility for workers displaced by economic change; in Japan the state became a promoter of an active industrial policy to guide firms in the restructuring processes. In the Third Italy the local government took over the role of providing both physical and economic infrastructure for the support of groups of small firms. In each of these case studies, the resulting institutional configuration limited the enterprise strategies that could be pursued. Taylorism, once embedded, made the American and British enterprise rigid and slow moving, a weakness that was not exposed until the arrival of the New Competition. The inadequacy of the welfare state to the task of industrial restructuring is equally obvious; its roots in the earlier resolution of the class struggle are not so evident.

Competing Views on the Size of the Firm

As important as the historical roots are, they do not predetermine the future of economic life. Japan and the Third Italy both reveal that transformation of economic institutions is possible. They also indicate that the same principles of production and organization can be embodied in more than one institutional configuration. In this section, I explore further the claim of institutional pluralism by examining competing views on the size of the firm. I consider first the views of David Birch, who is a leading proponent of the dynamism of small firms, and second those of Kenichi Ohmae, whose term "triad power" suggests an emerging structure of dominant global corporations that are simultaneously "insiders" in the three major markets of the world: the EEC, Japan, and the United States. Taken together, they demonstrate that to define the New Competition in terms of the size of the firm is to miss the point.

Small Firms and Economic Dynamism

David Birch shares the critique of Big Business and concurs with the argument that small firms can be technologically advanced, generate high income jobs, and produce internationally competitive goods and services. Furthermore, he argues that small firms in the United States are spearheading a process of continuous economic transformation. If Birch is right, today's small firms, armed with the communication capabilities opened up by the chip, are carriers of a new small-scale production form much as small firms around the Springfield Armory, armed with the principle of interchangeability, and early Big Business, armed with the principle of flow, were carriers of new organizational forms in their day.

For Birch, small firms embodying a new entrepreneurial spirit are spontaneously transforming the American business enterprise (and with it the American economy) from a rigid to a flexible organizational form. The claims of Birch on the relationship between small firms and economic flexibility differ from the ideas of the New Competition in a number of ways.

First, Birch argues that, in contrast with Europe, the American economy is highly flexible as measured by the creation of jobs. From 1980 to 1988, when virtually no jobs were created in Europe, 14 million were created in the United States, predominantly in small firms. The major reason for the high rate of job creation in the United States, according to Birch, is the surge in formation rate of new companies from roughly 90,000 per year in 1950 to 700,000 per year in 1988. In fact, Birch argues that since the *Fortune* 500 companies employed over 3 million less people in 1988 than in 1980, non-*Fortune* 500 companies, partnerships, and self-employed activities created 17 million jobs in the same period.[3]

---

[3] Birch estimates that the *Fortune* 500 employed 3.1 million fewer people in 1988 than in 1980; the rest employed roughly 17 million more. He adds, "[a] very large percentage of those [the 17 million jobs] came from the smaller end of the scale" (Birch, 1988, p. 6).

But to say that small firms created 17 million jobs is misleading. Birch himself notes that many of the new jobs were created in the explosive growth associated with small firms becoming large firms in new, or strategically redefined, markets. Examples include Digital, Data General, Wang, Apple Computer, Lotus, Wal-Mart, and Federal Express. From Birch's own numbers, it appears that the small-firm population is largely reproducing itself, with gains cancelling out losses. A more definitive answer to this question awaits further research.

We can say that Great Britain, and to a lesser extent Europe as a whole, has not enjoyed the explosive growth of the new giant enterprises, or even a comparatively high rate of new firm formation. In this sense the European economies have been less flexible. This observation raises a whole series of questions about the internal and external organization of once small firms that become giants. Are we witnessing the normal evolution from small to large firms that accompanied the rise of Big Business but in new markets? Are these explosive growth firms organizationally more like the kaisha than like Big Business? Do these explosive growth firms in America represent a third institutional path to the New Competition, distinct from both the industrial district and the kaisha? An examination of these questions leads away from the importance of firm size to distinctions between intra- and inter-firm relations.

Second, Birch argues that the American economy is being transformed continuously by the entry and exodus of firms. He estimates that about 7–8 percent of the roughly 8 million business enterprises in America close every year. That means, Birch argues, that ". . . every 5 to 6 years we have to replace half of the entire United States economy . . ." (Birch, 1988, p. 2). If Birch's inference is correct, the United States economy would be protean like, always in the process of being reshaped by the birth and death of business enterprises. Before we can draw such an inference, more information is required on the dispersion of casualty rates across different sectors of the economy. It is possible, for example, that much of the birth and death activity is concentrated in a few highly turbulent sectors, and that others are comparatively insulated.[4] In this

---

[4] Birch argues that large firms are as vulnerable to turbulence as small firms, but his data are not convincing. He estimates that "29 percent of the *Fortune* 500 in 1970 had vanished by 1981" (Birch, 1988, p. 6). But Birch does not give statistics on the percentage breakdown of what happened to these companies, i.e. how many are out of business, simply changed their names, merged, were acquired, or have discontinued the publication

case only the turbulent fringes would be reshaped; major portions may continue to do business as usual.

As an indicator of flexibility, the natality and mortality of firms is insufficient. Japanese enterprises are organizationally equipped to restructure internally, sectorally, and intersectorally at unprecedented rates. Here, flexibility means economies of time in product life cycle, new product development, product changeover, and the reallocation of productive resources from structurally depressed to high growth sectors.

What distinguishes the New Competition is the prevalence of firms that are organized to pursue strategies of continuous improvement, particularly in traditional sectors such as cars, television, clothing, and furniture, as well as in high technology sectors. In fact, one indicator of the transition from Big Business to the New Competition may be the lack of a sharp division between high technology and "mature" industries. New Competition means, in part, the blending of advanced technology with a (relatively) non-hierarchical managerial organization and a multiskilled labor force. All too often in the United States and the United Kingdom, developments in high technology are never applied to the production of conventional products or are applied in Taylorized work organizations. By these criteria, business enterprises in Germany, Italy, and Sweden, for example, are often more flexible than those in the United States. Aggregate statistics on the entry and exit of firms may be suggestive, but they do not tell us much about the reasons.

Clearly, the type of small-firm creation is important. I argued above that the New Competition has opened new possibilities for small firms to be internationally competitive, particularly where the following conditions have competitive force: design or product-led strategies, closeness to the customer, consultative parent–supplier relations, and inter-firm networks which foster enterprise specialization. Without making conceptual distinctions between static and dynamic (or entrepreneurial) industrial districts, price- and product-led competition, and market and consultative inter-firm relations, one cannot argue the case for the flexibility of the American economy. Rates of small-firm formation, alone, do not tell us enough.

For example, the early days of Big Business also witnessed the emergence of small firms, but as subcontractors and stabilizers in a dual economy. The subcontracting relationship served to discipline in-house departments producing the same product, and to meet boom-time surges in demand. Here the suppliers were simply subcontractors, with no

---

of annual reports for other reasons. However, his numbers do reflect the growing turbulence in contrast with the earlier decades of stability in Big Business, and here there is no disagreement between us.

independent design capabilities; under these conditions a high rate of new firm formation does not signify a force for the restructuring of an economy but an increase in the dependence of small firms on large firms.[5]

Finally, the two perspectives have very different implications for industrial policy. Birch's small firms are an extension of the "triumphant individual", a morality tale that is deeply embedded in American culture; the small firms of the New Competition are elements of a networked association of firms. Here the institutions of cooperation are as critical as those of individuality.

Global Companies and International Networks

What are the foreign direct investment implications of the transition from Big Business to the kaisha? The multinational corporation is the extension abroad of Big Business in the form of a division of the parent company. Once the multidivisional organization was in place, production abroad was organized, coordinated, and governed just like any other division in the firm. Big Business was not deterred by national boundaries: lower cost production abroad would lead to a shift in production from domestic to foreign locations within the same managerial hierarchy and ownership structure.

Kenichi Ohmae argues that the multinational firm is being replaced by the "global corporation", at least within the three regions that make up the Triad. Given the rapidity of adjustment of the New Competition, it is no longer possible to perfect a process or establish a technological lead in the home country and then establish a wholly owned subsidiary to produce it in one of the other Triad regions. By the time the subsidiary is producing, a competitor will have reverse engineered the innovation and perhaps even introduced the new product itself.

The global corporation, as an organizational form, is a response to the New Competition. The new set of organizational imperatives limit what a division or wholly owned subsidiary can competitively produce abroad. The first limit comes from the increased role of product-led competition within the Triad. Direct investment in production facilities abroad made sense when firms were pursuing price-led competitive

---

[5] Birch's data on the survivability of small firms during recessions is suggestive. One test of the changing role of small firms in the economy would be to measure the ratio of small to large firms over a long time period. If the ratio declined during business recessions in an earlier period and increased during business recessions in recent times, it would imply that the role of small firms was shifting from that of picking up excess demand (dependent subcontractors) during boom times to one of independence with the ability to adapt to market changes.

strategies because a firm could separate activities internationally along the production chain. But product-led competitive strategies require consultative relations across the business functions including design, purchasing, marketing, sales, and *production*. Consequently, firms that produce abroad find themselves poorly situated to compete against rivals that are driving down the time required to develop new products. It is difficult for design, production, and marketing people to be involved as a team in the early stages of product development if they are spread around the world.[6]

While this limit may be less severe in Third World countries, another aspect of the New Competition plays a role in these cases, namely the reduced amount of direct labor costs that can be saved by producing in low wage countries. Whereas in assembly operations, direct labor costs used to be around 25 percent of product costs, today they are usually between 5 and 10 percent (Ohmae, 1985, p. 3). Consequently, potential labor cost savings from shifting production to lower wage countries are considerably less than before.

A second Penrosian-type limit to the expansion in production abroad has also emerged. Ohmae argues that the successful cases of Japanese foreign investment do not involve the multidivisional but the entrepreneurial organizational form. Success has depended not upon wholesale transfer of Japanese management systems overseas, but upon the foreign branch being headed by an independent leader who has stayed there for ten years or more and built up a business culture around teamwork, long-term relations, and shared experience. But it is hard to persuade top Japanese managers to spend ten years abroad; the managers that do go abroad are generally those who know English, but these managers are rarely the generalist entrepreneurial types upon which success depends.[7] It is even harder to persuade American or European managers to live abroad for long periods.

These limits to production abroad cannot easily be overcome by exporting. Limits of a political nature are increasingly affecting export potential. For example, the "voluntary" agreements on the export of Japanese cars to the United States was accepted by Japan, in part to pre-empt more formal protectionist measures. Furthermore, the very success of Japan in establishing a surplus on current account has led to the appreciation of the yen and the cost of Japanese exports to Triad markets.

---

[6] The competitive edge that can come from *sashimi* (layered) versus sequentially staged product development is described in chapter 5.
[7] Ohmae adds the non-codifiable aspect of Japanese management systems as a final barrier to the transfer of Japanese production abroad.

Ohmae argues that at the same time that new limits to direct foreign investment in production have emerged, the success of a large company in its home market depends upon maintaining a presence in each of the three Triad regions. The drive for large corporations to be an "insider" in each of the other Triad regions stems from two developments. First, American and European firms have learned the hard way that if the kaisha is left alone in its home market it will generate high margins there that can subsidize strategic investments abroad. Only by maintaining a presence in Japan can the American- and European-based firms hope to slim the margins of the kaisha on their home turf. Second, each of the Triad power companies must keep abreast of developments by competitors in each of the other major markets. American and European competitors can respond more quickly if they are competing in Japan to new product, process, and technology developments by the kaisha. They can also reduce the risk of domestic competitors striking a surprise collaboration with a Japanese competitor that they utilize in the domestic market.

The resolution of these contradictory features of the global company (the limits to expansion by direct production and ownership in other Triad markets and the strategic need to be in an insider position in each of the other two regions) is altering the form of foreign involvement. It has led to the development of global networking in the form of international consortia, cross-licensing agreements, and joint ventures. The tie-ups amongst car companies are illustrated in Figure 5. Similar consortia exist in computers, silicon wafers, robotics, air transport, biotechnology, and carbon fibers (Ohmae, 1985, pp. 135–44).

The consortia tie-ups allow firms to share marketing, distribution, R&D, and even production facilities without investing directly in foreign facilities. British Leyland produces certain Honda cars in England, Nissan produces Volkswagens in Japan, General Motors assembles Mazdas, and Chrysler sells Mitsubishi-made Colts in the United States. But in none of these cases is production run by managers from a foreign head office. Managers, like workers, are increasingly local. The cars masquerade as local designs and, over time, the reality could merge with the appearance. At least that is what happened with the Austin models that the Japanese produced by license in the 1950s. By the 1960s, the design of Nissan's cars had been localized.

While we cannot state with certainty the future evolution of the global corporation, we can draw a number of implications. First, the global corporation, like the firm in a regionalized industrial district, combines inter-firm cooperation with competition. The international consortia often involve alliances amongst a number of past (and present) rivals. Second, both the industrial district and the global corporation are

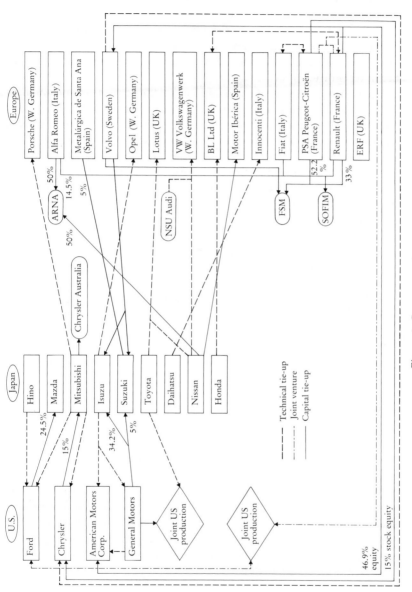

Figure 5 Car consortia.
Source: Ohmae, 1985, p. 134.

learning to harness the entrepreneurial and "ownership" energies that decentralization enhances.[8] While global corporations do operate on an entirely different scale, the collective entrepreneurial advantages of giving a stakeholding claim to employees within individual business units show up in superior competitiveness. But building collective entrepreneurial organizations limits the role and power of top management, and increases the independence in design and production of the work units. Third, it is likely that one of the factors explaining the sectoral composition of kaisha success abroad has been the presence or absence of dynamic industrial districts in the foreign country. Japanese furniture, clothing, leatherware, and footwear companies that sought to become global corporations would face a stern test from the superior flexibility of the industrial district organizations that presently exist in parts of Europe.[9] The informal networks and protean character of such districts makes them ideally suited to design-led, fashion-oriented or service-oriented competitive strategies. As the material facet of production increasingly becomes a support function to the service aspects, the competitive advantage of industrial districts will likely increase.

The last observation points out a weakness in Ohmae and most other writers on the kaisha and the global corporation. They ignore the constitutive role of groups of small firms in both the supplier networks to the kaisha and the industrial districts. In this they fail to capture the organizational similarities as well as the real differences between groups of dynamic small firms and global corporations. In the next section I summarize a number of these differences.

Global Corporations versus Industrial Districts

I have argued that the production chain and the sector are as relevant as the firm for understanding competitiveness today. One of the distinguishing features of the New Competition is the existence of consultative relations across links in the production chain, whether within a vertically integrated business enterprise or across vertically specialized business enterprises. A second distinguishing feature is the prevalence of Schumpeterian competition which creates an environment for organized market regulation; the resulting inter-firm institutions, in turn, reinforce Schumpeterian as opposed to price-led competition.

---

[8] Ownership is used here not in the legal sense, but in the sense of taking a personal stake in the design and success of the process.
[9] Elsewhere I have compared the strengths and weakness of large companies versus industrial districts in the case of the furniture industry (Best, 1989).

Nevertheless, the relative force of the centralization tendencies of the various productive activities and business functions within a single firm versus the decentralization tendencies across specialist firms is a matter of considerable concern, particularly for industrial policy. While one of the claims of this book is that we cannot appeal to technological or organizational imperatives to answer this question,[10] we can examine structural constraints on both the centralizing tendencies of the global corporation and the decentralizing tendencies that would accompany a spread of industrial districts.

The benefits of centralization within a single firm are self-evident. Larger industrial firms have greater access to financial resources and enjoy the size to internalize service or support activities, such as R&D, global marketing, and strategic planning, for which economies of scale persist. But less evident is whether these same support services can be competitively supplied by specialist firms and sector institutions within an industrial district. We can say with certainty that every industrial district must develop functional equivalents to these service activities if they hope to compete against global corporations.

But the benefits of decentralization are equally real. They are manifest in both industrial districts and supplier networks of global corporations. The first is the demand for continuous restructuring as Schumpeterian competition, particularly over product development time, increases in importance. Small specialist productive organizations can not only solve problems but can react quickly to demand changes in contrast with plants that require long runs. Furthermore, specialist firms can group orders from a range of firms and achieve economies of scale more effectively than an in-house department within a vertically integrated firm.

One of the reasons that a small firm is "lighter on its feet" (can respond and adapt more quickly) is that an organization with less people can more readily structure itself to pursue a strategy of continuous improvement. The key structural feature here is the integration of thinking and doing in production.

Vertical specialization offers a second advantage of increasing importance: it reduces the risk of becoming a prisoner of one technology, process, or component product at a time of technological and product

---

[10] As elaborated in chapter 4, the appeal to economic theory is not helpful. The grand theories of Marx, Schumpeter, and Galbraith presume laws of increasing concentration. Chandler, and other historians of Big Business, presume that modernity means large firms. Neoclassical theory, on the contrary, tends to treat oligopoly as a special case and, for most purposes, presumes decreasing returns to scale and passive firms, too small to affect market outcomes let alone regulate markets.

change. Digital Equipment Corporation, for example, found itself the leader in an obsolete printer technology with the emergence of laser printers by competitors. A car assembler, which ultimately coordinates 20,000 parts, or a Boeing, whose planes contain some 250,000 parts, cannot possibly develop in-house the best qualified supplier, which means guessing right on technological developments in every productive activity that contributes to the final product. Instead, long-term consultative relations with suppliers in which design concepts are developed together offers the car assembler and a Boeing the opportunity to specialize in design, assembly, distribution, and marketing.

A third pressure for decentralization comes from the demand side. Commodities meet both the functional and the symbolic interests of the consumer. The symbolic aspect of a product, by imparting meaning, supplies an individual with identity. Quite possibly, the higher incomes in the Triad countries increase the symbolic role of commodities which, in turn, suggests an increased desire for distinctiveness in product design.[11] Small geographically dispersed firms are more able to respond to fragmented demand by supplying tailor-made products.

However, we could argue that, under the New Competition, the higher value added elements in business are not in production activities narrowly defined as material conversion processes. Consequently, material production is increasingly a support function to other business activities such as strategic planning, marketing, distribution, R&D, design, and managing supplier networks. The question then becomes: do these service activities exhibit a tendency to centralization? Again, a definitive answer is not possible, partly because the outcome is not predetermined but depends upon a comparison of the organizational innovations which have yet to be developed in both the global corporation and the industrial district. Here, as elsewhere, strategy will shape the outcome.

Four final points which bear on this issue can be made with respect to strategy. First, while each individual business unit that provides an input into bringing a new or redesigned product to market must understand the design concept, each need not have an independent strategic capability. Nevertheless the capacity to initiate change in each function depends upon being able to think strategically with respect to the overall process. Consequently, strategic planning gives way to strategic thinking as more and more individuals in the overall production system begin to take a role in the entrepreneurial process. But strategic

---

[11] See Mary Douglas and Baron Isherwood (1979) for an analysis of the interpretive aspects of commodities.

thinking, unlike strategic planning, is not subject to scale economies. Furthermore, strategic thinking is at least as important in the service activities as those of material transformation.

Second, while technology does not determine a firm's strategy, it does limit the range of possible structures and strategies. Oil refining, for example, may not ever lend itself to decentralized production. But economies of scale at one link in the production chain do not entail a global managerial hierarchy to deliver the product to market: each of the other stages may be subject to decentralization. Similarly, the fact that electricity generation by nuclear power requires a large organization can obscure the fact that the technology may have been designed to keep a pre-existing managerial hierarchy in place as much as it was to serve the public interest (Best, 1982).

Third, the success of a particular strategy always depends upon the strengths and weaknesses of the opposition. Thus the very success of mass production became its greatest weakness: it became a target. The same is true in individual industries: the success of a mass design-oriented retailer, such as the Swedish firm IKEA in furniture or Benetton in clothing, create the conditions for success of anti-IKEA furniture or anti-Benetton clothing which play on the limits to centralized design.

Fourth, global corporations, by decentralizing production and other activities, increase the risk of subsidiaries turning into competitors as managers develop entrepreneurial skills. At the same time, groups of small firms, no matter how closely networked, depend upon a consensus amongst a critical mass of firms to collectively reposition themselves in a market. While both are better equipped to restructure than mass producers, each has limits of its own as a restructuring institution.

Thus we cannot conclude that the global corporation does not have a future any more than that the industrial district does not. Both clearly do. The governmental policy implication for communities and regions is that strategic industrial policy activities can be successful, but that strategy must be taken seriously. This means, in part, seeking to strengthen the industrial district where it is weakest against the competition, namely developing a consensus around how to compete against global corporations. That consensus will involve means of shaping collective strategies and sharing the burdens of restructuring.

Strategic Industrial Policy: A Review

Strategic industrial policy is a final constitutive component of the New Competition. Put simply, the purpose of strategic industrial policy is to promote Schumpeterian competition and (collective) entrepreneurial firms. This means, in part, shaping markets and affecting the form that competition takes in order to enhance economic performance. Several aspects of a strategic type of industrial policy stand out.

The first is that strategic industrial policy depends upon a strong antitrust pro-competition policy, whether formal or informal.[12] In the postwar period, Japanese antitrust authorities have been in constant confrontation with proposers of industrial policy initiatives from the Ministry of International Trade and Industry (MITI). Out of this tension the advantages of both cooperation and competition have been emphasized and the disadvantages of both reduced. Inter-firm agreements, mergers, and cartels have been allowed where they can be defended in terms of promoting rationalization or negotiating capacity reductions.

Recession cartels in Japan keep firms alive during downturns, but are established only where a long-term reorganization plan for the sector has been agreed to by management within the industry. A reorganization plan with milestones provides a basis both for governmental monitoring of reorganization actions and for the withdrawal of cartel privileges from "footdraggers". Rationalization cartels are designed to insulate firms in a backward industry from international competition. But cartels of both types are for limited durations after which competition returns.

In the Third Italy, antitrust does not have a presence in the form of agencies carrying out antitrust laws. Instead, local government industrial policy aims, in effect, to establish an environment in which small firms can easily enter the market. Entry is facilitated with a ready availability of credit, competitor information, business services, arrangements for sharing physical infrastructure, and, most of all, the existence of specialist suppliers of complementary parts and services with whom to form networks. The existence of such networks within industrial districts means that a startup company can specialize in one or a few activities that it does best and purchase the rest.

Part of what industrial policy is about, then, is preserving and buttressing inter-firm networks. This may mean seeking to keep a local producer from being bought up by a large firm from outside the industrial district that seeks to turn the local producer into a sole supplier to itself.[13] Nevertheless, the extraordinary ease with which new firms

---

[12] Antitrust, as used here, does not mean breaking up large firms. It means the existence of a government agency that seeks to counter efforts by large firms to dominate markets, particularly when strong competitors do not exist.

[13] Recent historical research suggests that metalworking industrial districts in the United States were seriously damaged by the purchase of key firms by parent companies or conglomerates that turned them into divisions serving other branches of the conglomerate at the expense of previous networks. For the case of Michigan's metalworking sector see

can be formed lessens the risk of losing local suppliers to conglomerates (which promote interdivisional networking within a firm at the expense of regional networking within an industrial district) and, at the same time, gives the Third Italy the functional equivalent of an effective antitrust policy. Poor service or high prices will invite new entrants.

The promotion of networks points to a second aspect of strategic industrial policy: administering a balance between cooperation and competition. Superseding price competition is common; whether the effects are on balance beneficial or harmful cannot be determined in the abstract. The establishment of collective bargaining is an example of cooperation in the labor market to restrict competition over wages. Price agreements may simultaneously hinder static efficiency (by limiting price flexibility) and enhance dynamic efficiency (by promoting Schumpeterian competition).

Penrose's aphorism "competition: the god and the devil" captures the enduring tension between competition and cooperation in the dynamic context. Sustaining competitive success is not an easy project. Future success depends upon long-term investments which firms may be wary of making without assurances of market control; at the same time, market control blunts the incentive to continuously improve. MITI has not shirked from promoting competition within markets. Thus each of the major industrial groups is encouraged to enter into emerging industries. The result is that MITI oversees the infrastructural sector-wide developments including the licensing of foreign technologies and cooperative research, but does not pick winners or privilege individual firms.

The issue here is not one of competition *or* cooperation. Cooperation, formal or informal, has been part of industrial life at least since the emergence of oligopolies. Only periodically does total competition reign with no holds barred. A series of examples of different forms of inter-firm cooperation during the heyday of Big Business are described in chapter 3. The competitive war between Honda and Yamaha in motorcycles illustrates what happens when implicit pricing cooperation breaks down in the New Competition. The price war lasted for 18 months before Yamaha issued a public statement that they had accepted the dominance of Honda and would settle for a distant second in market share (Abbeglen and Stalk, 1985, pp. 46–52). Making cooperation illegal does not eliminate inter-firm "understandings" over pricing policies, but only suppresses them.

In contrast, in America the worst of both world has been created:

Linda Ewing (1989) and for Springfield, Massachusetts, see Machine Action Project (1987).

antitrust law, by failing to distinguish amongst the different types and purposes of inter-firm cooperation, has been unable to guide it. Suppressed cooperation appears in the form of passive oligopolies and captive regulators, and price competition, particularly amongst small firms, can bankrupt potentially viable businesses during business downturns and undercut the margins required for long-term investments.

A third aspect of strategic industrial policy is the primacy of strategy over planning. The task of *strategic* planning is not to plan industries of the future, but to examine the prerequisites for sustaining competitive success and work to ensure that firms, which provide the real dynamic thrust, can respond quickly as new markets emerge. We saw that MITI moves quickly to organize research laboratories for the new base technologies of the future, but in each case the research is responsive to market signals as well as strategic possibilities.

Strategic analysis depends upon independent but "hands-on" industry studies. Developing sector strategies is not an intellectual project for detached economic planners. Industrial policy, like product-led or time competition (shorter product cycles, product development times, and higher work-in-process turns), depends upon the integration of thinking and doing, of thinkers and doers. This is the role of a forum composed of ministry officers and enterprise leaders. Only then can viewpoints be debated and myths dispelled on issues surrounding the long-term challenges and opportunities facing firms in a sector. While a consensus may not emerge on a sector strategy, managers develop and, in some cases, test out strategies with the benefit first of sector analyses carried out by MITI and second of constructive debate amongst industry experts from within MITI, academic institutions, banks, and other industrial firms. But MITI cannot simply be a recorder of industry views; it needs access to information to develop an independent analysis.[14]

Sector forums have long existed elsewhere without success, such as in the United Kingdom, but without a link between the industrial policy forums and other government instruments such as macro policy, the banking system, and education policy. The problem is not in the idea of a sector forum as such but in the nature of the link between the forum and industrial policy instruments.[15]

---

[14] Alfred Kahn's approach to regulation is an American example of the crucial role of careful industry studies (see Kahn, 1988, chapter 1).

[15] An active industrial policy not only puts pressure on macro policymakers to think long term, but on the banking system to develop strategically oriented lending criteria and the educational system to upgrade the qualifications of the workforce (Best and Humphries, 1986).

A fourth aspect of strategic industrial policy is a universal or sector-specific, as opposed to firm-specific, orientation. Examples of firm-specific industrial policies are the 1960s French policy of preferential treatment for "national champions" like Renault, or the postwar British efforts to rescue bankrupt firms such as Rolls Royce and British Leyland. Examples of universal services or sector-specific activities include industrial laboratories established by turn of the century German governments and sector-specific industrial parks created by local governments in the Third Italy. Sector-specific industrial policies are less prone to special interest politics and corrosive of the consensus and mutual responsibility required to develop and implement sector strategies.[16]

The New Competition: Issues in Need of Analysis

The first step in addressing the problem of the loss of industrial competitiveness in America and Britain is a conceptual one. The real causes of the problem have to be distinguished from the apparent causes.

Declining labor productivity and excessive governmental regulation, for example, are apparent problems which suggest policies for firms and government that do not address the real problems. Direct labor productivity is only one type of productivity; the New Competition focuses on the productivity of other factors including indirect labor, working capital, fixed capital, and organization. The real problem is the prevalence of business enterprises that are organized according to the principles of Big Business and thereby unable to compete on the new terrain of product-led competition. Likewise, the presumption of a regulation–deregulation dichotomy that informs the public debate over competitiveness obscures the range of regulatory activities that are constitutive of industrial markets. To suggest that either traditional regulation or deregulation can enhance the competitiveness of business enterprises is to implicitly deny a role for strategic industrial policy.

The four common elements of the New Competition, illustrated in the case studies of Japan and the Third Italy, are summarized in the Introduction. They do not provide a blueprint for the constitution of economic institutions.[17] In fact, the importance of strategy and consensus

---

[16] Elsewhere, I have argued for the collective services over the individual firm approach (Best, 1989).

[17] The problem with blueprints is that they imply that institutional arrangements can be specified independently of implementation, much like lead manufacturers, under Big

deny the idea of a single optimal organization. The purpose of articulating the thesis of the New Competition has not been to offer a panacea to all economic ills: it has been to contribute to a political economic analysis more useful for understanding the competitive forces that are driving capitalist economies in the last decades of the twentieth century. The presumption is that such an analysis will be helpful in addressing a number of pressing political economic issues of our time, issues that are too often obscured by conventional economic discourse. I will close with a brief description of a number of such issues.

Competitiveness and Community: convergence or divergence?

Community is crucial to the competitiveness of both the kaisha and the Third Italy. In the kaisha, community manifests itself in, and is sustained by, lifetime employment, company unions, "shared network norms", and parts makers' associations. Thus Deming's principle of driving fear out of the workplace by establishing the norm of lifetime employment and a policy of not blaming the worker for systemic failure not only reduced barriers to organizational and technical change but also fostered the commitment of workers to the enterprise.

Community takes different forms in the Third Italy, operating in the local polity and not within large firms. It provides the trust required for a vast range of inter-firm and extra-firm activities within industrial districts. Trust minimizes corruption in local government in a nation not known for effective government at the national level. But it also converts high transaction costs (made high by the lack of trust) into low costs; for example a borrower can submit a business plan to a financial consortium without fear that it will be passed on to actual or potential competitors, a private banker, who loans to a financial consortium member, can base the loan decision on an assessment of character made by fellow artisans, or a producer can specialize on a single phase of the production chain.

In each of these cases laws could be passed to guide local behavior, but the effect would be to erode the stock of trust that is the basis for cooperation, for if people are constrained from depleting trust by laws

---

Business, expected to design components without inputs from their producers, or managers, under Taylorism, expected workers simply to carry out orders. Each of these outlooks runs counter to the role of participation for problem solving, particularly in the case of institution shaping. The lesson of the comparative analysis of Japan and the Third Italy is that very different institutional setups can be successful, but that institutions cannot be created in a social vacuum; they must be negotiated and modified within the historical context or a locality or nation.

alone, then the power of public embarrassment no longer operates. It can become a test to avoid what is perceived as an externally imposed sanction, as is common in Italy with respect to national taxes. The borrower, backed by the financial consortium of Modena, pays back his loan not because he can be taken to court, but because he wants his word to be trusted, and his name to be respected, within his community.

The web of common understandings and mutual obligations that tie individuals into a community either within the Japanese firm or the Italian locality cannot be taken as exogenous parameters. For community is subject to erosion unless the norms, shared understandings, and mutual obligations that reinforce it are sustained by a collective memory and reinforced by shared activities. Even then, economic hard times can rapidly undermine the community unless means of sharing the costs of dislocation are reinforced.

In contrast, Big Business, like neoclassical economic theory, is organized on the presupposition that community and production are separable. The role of community, with respect to social insurance for example, was displaced from the firm to the state.[18] The state that became responsible for social insurance was not the local, but the central, state. In the process, the indispensable element of any social insurance fund, namely individual responsibility, was lost in distant politics with which individual citizens without work felt little in common. The larger the entity the more problematic community can become.

The New Competition has not resolved these matters. The turbulence associated with international competition in today's world finds communities walking a tightrope in their pursuit of economic security, if not independence. To ignore the New Competition is to threaten the community with industrial obsolescence; to join in the pursuit of international competitiveness is to risk turning the polity into a machine for promoting exports. If today's Japan is to set the international standard for intensity of worklife, the cornucopia of consumption promised by the New Competition will command a high price in lost family and civic life. Fortunately, the case of the Third Italy suggests that the choice that communities face does not have to be this dire. Moreover, pressures are mounting from within Japan and from her trading partners for a relaxation of the pressures to expand exports. The

---

[18] The idea of welfare, as distinct from a social insurance fund, treats users as recipients of charity. Robert Reich illustrates the shortcomings of the welfare state as a charity approach to poverty with the parable of the fisherman. The individual without food who is taught to fish is treated with the dignity that comes from being capable of self-responsibility; the individual who is given food is denied the same capability. Is it any wonder that recipients of charity are ungrateful? (Reich, 1987, chapter 16).

tension between competitiveness and community is not one that will go away, but it is one that must become a matter for greater public debate at both the local and the international level.

Skill-Based Production versus the "Unmanned Factory"

The declining "productivity" of the American and British factory relative to the New Competition can be responded to within the industrial enterprise in one of two ways: either reorganize production according to the principles of the New Competition or seek a technological solution that replaces humans wherever possible. The first, a skill-based human-centered approach, seeks to compete by enhancing the peculiarly human capabilities of perceptual discrimination, learning and inferring from experience, reasoning, making fine judgements, coping with unforeseen events, and acting as distinct from rule-based responses (Brodner, 1986). The second, a computer-integrated manufacturing (CIM) strategy, envisages a factory of the future in which (direct) human labor is replaced with the computer.

If the arguments of this book are right, the CIM vision is a chimera. As Ramchandran Jaikumar's comparison of flexible manufacturing systems in Japan and the United States revealed, the advantages of computerized manufacturing depend upon the capacity of the operators to use them effectively.[19] Like the market, flexible manufacturing systems are a good servant but a bad master. Nevertheless the CIM vision is particularly appealing to many managers trapped in the Taylorized environment of mass production. But the comparison is not between mass production and CIM; rather it is between a skill-based factory that uses computers and a technology-based factory that seeks to eliminate direct labor.

To date, the ideal of the "unmanned factor" has run into two severe problems when put into practice. First, the financial costs of both hardware and software tend to mushroom beyond the capacity of even firms the size of General Motors. Second, the flexibility of a CIM depends upon the past modelling of the part or product within the computer system – CIM does not engage in innovation with respect to new products which by definition have not yet been designed and modelled. Thus a firm committed to the "unmanned factory" still depends upon people, somewhere, for its innovative capability; in this it may well become dependent upon designers and, ultimately, a support function for skilled labor located in other firms. Perhaps these problems

---

[19] For a similar critique of the technology-centered approach in favor of the skill-based alternative applied to West Germany see Brodner (1986, 1988).

will ultimately be solved, but in the foreseeable future the New Competition, based upon the collective entrepreneur, is a better bet. This conclusion, however, is not prevalent amongst those who direct much of American and British manufacturing.

Worse, the potential of the New Competition for improving the conditions of work has not been systematically pursued by the trade union movement. For example, unions could seek greater job security for their members in exchange for an agreement to develop real production flexibility based on the skill-centered factory. The entrepreneurial firm depends upon breaking with Taylorism and encouraging worker involvement in "management" activities. This lesson is increasingly clear to enterprise owners whose firms are being outcompeted by firms with superior products, higher quality, more reliable delivery times, and shorter product development times.

Worker Loyalty: Commitment versus Regimentation

The existence of career ladders that span the class divide between workers and managers does not mean the end of industrial classes. The intensity of work in the kaisha and its supplier network is taken for granted in Japanese society, at least in present times (Kamata, 1983). The stress takes its toll on the shopfloor, in the managers' offices, in the home, and in the schools. Few would deny that in Japan the New Competition means hard work and long hours for the company. Nor does the establishment of worker loyalty to the goals of the enterprise mean that regimentation, however subtle, is absent. In the words of James Fallows: ". . . the quasi-compulsory morning exercises and company songs that are common in Japanese companies may not indicate how 'naturally' the Japanese conform but rather how unnatural the overwhelming emphasis on teamwork is" (Fallows, 1989, p. 28). Since a worker either accepts the goals of the enterprise or he does not advance, he is under pressure to internalize them. To subject the demands of the enterprise to critical scrutiny is to risk undercutting his career and economic security for his family.[20] It is a risk few are willing to take. At the same time it could be a potential source of tension in the kaisha.

If these claims are even close to the mark, they suggest both an ugly side to the Japanese variant of the New Competition and a barrier to development in the West for, according to this reading, Taylorism

---

[20] The pressures on workers to internalize an ideology or world view that is consistent with increasing productivity but has powerful elements of self-deception is explored in Best and Connolly (1979).

has been accepted by Western workers in part because, however unintentionally, it gives them a degree of freedom from the regimentation implicit in the commitment model, particularly the non-union variant. They have also limited the stress and regimentation of work.

However, the lesson to draw from these concerns is not that American and British unions and communities should attempt to maintain Big Business. It is rather that alternatives to the kaisha as the model of the New Competition should be explored. For the choice is not between New Competition and Big Business; wherever it is, Big Business will likely lose, eventually.

Partnership versus Anonymity in Parent–Supplier Relations

Just-in-time is a widely used term in the Western business circles of today. But, again, we find a divergence in meaning when it is put into practice. All too often, it becomes an instrument for parent firms to shift the costs of holding inventory to supplier firms. It can have no other use unless the parent firm is itself a flexible producer, capable of rapid product changeovers, self-inspection, and other features of the New Competition. Furthermore, real consultative relations depend upon a shared design language between buyer and supplier firms and the integration of business strategy across the production phases.[21]

Parent companies have much to gain from more consultative relations. Such firms can move much more quickly to drive down product cycle times and respond to quality control problems, and can tap a wider pool of design ideas. At the same time, consultative parent–supplier relations require an alteration in the power relations between parent and supplier firms that Big Business is reluctant to accept. Squeezing supplier margins is a means of enhancing profit margins in the price-led competition.

The argument, then, is not that product-led strategies deny buyer companies the driver's seat in their relations with supplier firms; no company happily gives away market-shaping power that gives them leverage over profit margins with their suppliers. The argument is that firms which pursue product-led strategies depend upon having a supplier base with independent product design capabilities, and such a supplier base both increases the mutual interdependence amongst firms along the production chain and reduces the market power of the parent company. But it also increases product competitiveness of parent firms.

One of the indicators of the move toward consultative supplier

---

[21] The comments in this section are based, in part, on the case studies in Best and Hopley (1989).

relations is a sharp reduction in the number of suppliers of a parent company. Nissan, as already noted, plans to have only 120 suppliers to its United Kingdom plant. General Motors has several thousand. Recently the Xerox Corporation slashed its number of suppliers from 5,000 to 350. The latter will all become "partners" with Xerox in a consultative network. The pressure on suppliers is not only to be able to produce at low prices but to meet stringent quality control requirements; the pressure on the parent company is to include the suppliers in the design stage of new products and to educate suppliers on quality and other management development areas.[22]

Nevertheless, as noted, every supplier firm is aware that, in hard times, large firms will be tempted to squeeze their margins. The tension is between a short-term and a long-term outlook. In the short run they will be tempted to gain flexibility at the expense of their suppliers; in the long run they rely upon the trust that was built up during the hard times to underpin the trust required to gain from consultative relations. We cannot predict with certainty which path will be pursued at every point in time. We know that industrial policy in Japan and the Third Italy has sought to shape the outcome by becoming an active supporter of the collective interests of supplier firms.

Again, the New Competition is creating both challenges and strategic opportunities for the labor movement. Everywhere the New Competition is associated with a proliferation of small firms, and labor in small firms has been historically difficult to organize. In the heyday of Big Business, unions were clearly stronger in the largest enterprises, but increasing turbulence has made jobs in Big Business less secure. Faced with these developments it is crucial that the labor movement distinguish between types of small firms and large–small firm relationships. All too often the move to external sourcing is seen as a means of seeking lower wage labor, which it often is. But the Third Italy illustrates that it need not always end up that way. To the extent that unions can organize in small firms on the basis of promoting skill-based work organization, they can simultaneously improve the position of members and the firms in which they work. The idea of the missing middle (that displaced workers inevitably end up in lower waged jobs) is not a necessary outcome of increasing flexibility; instead it is one possibility which will be more likely if unions do not seek an active response to the New Competition.[23]

---

[22] General Electric, a late convert to the need for a transition from arm's length market-driven supplier relations has recently begun implementing a composite index for selecting amongst supplier bids in which price composes only 25 percent; measures of technical expertise, delivery capability, quality, and financial soundness are also factored in to the index (see Best and Hopley, 1989).

[23] The emergence of a "missing middle" is a central claim of Harrison and Bluestone (1988).

The Stability of Industrial Districts versus the Growth of Individual Firms

There is an inherent tension between the growth dynamics of the Penrosian firm and the mutual interdependence amongst firms in an industrial district. The explosive growth of a limited number of firms from small to giant size, as exemplified by Digital, can contribute to the dynamism of industrial districts by generating spin-offs but it can also undermine their flexibility by vertical integration and exclusion. Firms that pursue a go-it-alone strategy risk converting themselves into Big-Business-like enterprises. The outcome will depend, in part, on extra-firm institution building in the form of inter-firm associations and consultative supplier relations. Nevertheless, in a healthy industrial district, the tension is inherent and enduring. If the tension becomes too great, the industrial district, like a string, will break, but with no tension the industrial district, again like a string, cannot pull.

Macroeconomic Stability and Strategic Industrial Policymaking

The macroeconomic policies of Japan and the newly industrializing countries (including South Korea, Taiwan, Hong Kong, and Singapore) pivot around strategic industrial policies. The purpose of a strategic industrial policy is to promote a positive trade balance; exchange rate, fiscal, and monetary policies, in turn, are geared to promote price stability, growth, and employment given the primacy of maintaining an internationally competitive tradeable goods sector.[24] Governments that persist in pursuing macro-economic policies that give primacy to short-term stabilization goals will be less stable in the long run. In either case economic turbulence can be expected. Today the kaisha's drive for international market share gives little breathing space. If that drive is to continue and to be replicated by ever more industrial enterprises around the world, economic turbulence will escalate.

But all is not bleak. The New Competition can increase the productive capacity of every nation as innovations are diffused across national

---

[24] Traditionally, tradeables have been identified with manufactured and agricultural goods. But increasingly, services are also becoming tradeable. Financial, educational, and business services all flow across national boundaries, and such flows are likely to increase in the future. This could mean that industrial policy is a misnomer and would be better described as "tradeables policy". Just as manufacturing activities are becoming more akin to a support for services in design-led companies, the manufacturing sector may come to represent a small portion of value added relative to service activities in the increasingly knowledge-intensive economies.

boundaries and enterprises everywhere become collectively entrepreneurial. The challenge is to harness the developmental forces of the New Competition in ways that promote the dispersion of economic activity and widespread sharing of benefits. Clearly, the old nation-based macroeconomic policies associated with Big Business are not adequate to the task; new regulatory mechanisms demand new macro-economic stabilizing counterparts. The need to coordinate production and consumption in the age of highly internationalized production is generating pressure for the internationalization of regulation just as the spread of Big Business led to the establishment of national regulatory mechanisms in an earlier period. One of the lessons of the 1930s is that we can choose to ignore transformations in productive forces, but at great cost.

Economic Security and Ecological Integrity

The real limits to economic growth may be ecological. With the possible exception of ending the arms race, nothing is more fundamental to the future of humanity than confronting the sources of ecological degradation in the form of the greenhouse effect, the deteriorating ozone layer, the disposal of nuclear waste, the erosion of the earth's surface with deforestation, and the poisoning of the food chain. A starting point of this book is the view that ecological degradation is related to economic insecurity: addressing the ecological problems means confronting, at the same time, the sources of international poverty and unemployment. The ecological threat, like the economic, demands a prominent role for community, if on a much larger scale.

This list of issues is suggestive, not exhaustive. The more quickly they are effectively addressed, the better the chances that economics and markets can become better servants for the public good. To avoid them is to tie a national or regional economy to economic decline.

Bibliography

Abegglen, James C., and George Stalk Jr. 1985: *Kaisha: The Japanese Corporation*, Basic Books, New York.

Abernathy, William, Kim Clark, and Alan Kantrow 1983: *Industrial Renaissance*, Basic Books, New York.

Aglietta, Michel 1979: *A Theory of Capitalist Regulation: The US Experience*, New Left Books, London.

Aida, Toshio 1979: "The history of industrial policy and anti-monopoly policy". In Yoshihara Kitado and Toshio Aida (eds), *Current Economic Policy in Japan*, Ohtsuki Shoten, Tokyo.

Ames, Edward, and Nathan Rosenberg 1968: "The Enfield Arsenal in theory and history", *Economic Journal*, Vol. 78, pp. 827–42.

Aoki, Masahiko 1986: "Horizontal vs. vertical information structure of the firm", *American Economic Review*, Vol. 76, No. 5, pp. 971–83.

Arrow, Kenneth 1974: *The Limits of Organization*, Norton, New York.

Axelrod, Robert 1984: *The Evolution of Cooperation*, Basic Books, New York.

Becattini, Giacomo 1978: "The development of light industry in Tuscany: an interpretation", *Economic Notes*, Vol. 2–3, pp. 107–23.

Benatti, Giancarlo 1988: "Thirty years of municipal policy for industrial parks". In *Municipal Initiatives for Artisan, Commercial and Wholesale Business Parks*, Municipality of Modena, Department of Economic Activity and Labour Problems, pp. 9–17.

Best, Michael H. 1982: "The political economy of socially irrational products", *Cambridge Journal of Economics*, Vol. 6, No. 1, pp. 53–64.

Best, Michael H. 1985: "The furniture industry". In Robin Murray (ed.), *The London Industrial Strategy*, Greater London Council, London, pp. 97–116.

Best, Michael H. 1989: "Sector strategies and industrial policy: the furniture industry and the Greater London Enterprise Board". In Paul Hirst and Jonathan Zeitlin (eds), *Reversing Economic Decline?*, Berg Press, Oxford, pp. 191–222.

Best, Michael H. and William E. Connolly 1979: "Politics and subjects: the limits of structural Marxism", *Socialist Review*, Vol. 9, No. 6, pp. 75–99.

Best, Michael H. and William E. Connolly 1982: *The Politicized Economy*, 2nd edn, D.C. Heath, Lexington, MA.

Best, Michael H. and Robert Hopley 1989: "Supplier relations and the New Competition: case studies of ten lead manufacturers in the Commonwealth of Massachusetts", Small Business Development Center, University of Massachusetts, Amherst, MA.

Best, Michael H. and Jane Humphries 1986: "The 'City' and industrial decline". In Bernard Elbaum and William Lazonick (eds), *The Decline of the British Economy*, Oxford University Press, Oxford, pp. 223–39.

Birch, David 1987: *Job Creation in America: How Our Smallest Firms Put the Most People to Work*, Macmillan, New York.

Birch, David 1988: "Small business: driving the economy", Proceedings Transcript, Western Massachusetts Economic Development Semi-Annual Meeting, University of Massachusetts, December 7, 1988, pp. 1–15.

Bowles, Samuel 1985: "The production process in a competitive economy: Walrasian, neo-Hobbesian, and Marxian models", *American Economic Review*, Vol. 75, pp. 16–36.

Boyer, Robert 1979: "Wage formation in historical perspective: the French experience", *Cambridge Journal of Economics*, Vol. 3, No. 2, pp. 99–118.

Brady, Robert A. 1933: *The Rationalization Movement in German Industry*, University of California, Berkeley, CA.

Brems, Hans 1986: "Monopoly and competition in Scandinavia". In Edward H. Chamberlin (ed.), *Monopoly and Competition and their Regulation*, Macmillan, London, pp. 168–87. Originally published in 1954.

Bridge, James H. 1903: *The Inside Story of the Carnegie Steel Company*, Aldine, New York.

Brodner, Peter 1986: "Skill based manufacturing vs. 'unmanned factory' – which is superior?", *International Journal of Industrial Ergonomics*, Vol. 1, pp. 145–53.

Brodner, Peter 1988: "CHIM: new forms of organization in computer integrated manufacturing", Kernforschungszentrum Karlsruhe GmbH, Karlsruhe (photocopy).

Brusco, Sebastiano 1982: "The Emilian model", *Cambridge Journal of Economics*, Vol. 6, pp. 167–84.

Brusco, Sebastiano 1985: "Local government, industrial policy and social consensus in the experience of Modena (Italy)", Mimeo.

Brusco, Sebastiano 1986: "Small firms and industrial districts: the experience of Italy". In David Keeble and Egbert Wever (eds), *New Firms and Regional Development in Europe*, Croom Helm, London, pp. 184–202.

Brusco, Sebastiano and Charles Sabel 1981: "Artisan production and economic growth". In Frank Wilkinson (ed.), *The Dynamics of Labour Market Segmentation*, Academic Press, London, pp. 99–113.

Burbidge, John L. 1968: *The Principles of Production Control*, 2nd edn, MacDonald and Evans, London.

Business Week, "Toyota's fast lane", November 4, 1985.

Bussey, John and Douglas R. Sease 1988: "Speeding up: manufacturers strive to slice time needed to develop products", *Wall Street Journal*, February 23, 1988.

Cable, J.R. 1982: "Industry". In A.R. Prest and D.J. Coppock (eds), *The U.K. Economy*, 9th edn, Weidenfeld and Nicolson, London, Chapter 4, pp. 193–246.

Chamberlin, Edward H. 1933: *The Theory of Monopolistic Competition*, Harvard University Press, Cambridge, MA.

Chamberlin, Edward H. (ed.) 1986: *Monopoly and Competition and their Regulation*, Macmillan, London. Originally published in 1954.

Chandler, Alfred D. Jr 1977: *The Visible Hand*, Harvard University Press, Cambridge MA.

Chandler, Alfred D. Jr 1984: "The emergence of managerial capitalism", *Business History Review*, Vol. 58, No. 4, pp. 473–503.

Coase, R.H. 1937: "The nature of the firm", *Economica N.S.*, Vol. 4, No. 4, pp. 331–51.

Connolly, William E. 1974: *The Terms of Political Discourse*, D.C. Heath, Lexington, MA.

Connolly, William E. 1987: *Politics and Ambiguity*, University of Wisconsin, Madison, WI.

Cusumano, Michael A. 1985: *The Japanese Automobile Industry*, Harvard University Press, Cambridge, MA.

Davis, Lance 1966: "The capital markets and industrial concentration: the US and the UK, a comparative study", *Economic History Review*, Vol. 19, pp. 255–72.

Davis, T.C. 1950: "How the Du Pont Organization appraises its performance", *American Management Association*, Financial Management Series, No. 94: 7.

Dean, Alison 1989: "The never ending industrial divide: towards a new evolutionary theory of competition and industrial change", University of Massachusetts, Amherst, MA, xerox.

Deming, W. Edwards 1982: *Quality, Productivity and Competitive Position*, Massachusetts Institute of Technology, Center for Advanced Engineering Study, Cambridge, MA.

De Vroey, Michel 1984: "A regulation approach interpretation of contemporary history", *Capital and Class*, No. 23, pp. 45–66.

Deyrup, Felicia Johnson 1948: *Arms Makers of the Connecticut Valley: A Regional Study of the Economic Development of the Small Arms Industry, 1798–1870*, Smith College Studies in History, Vol. 33, Northampton, MA.

Douglas, Mary and Baron Isherwood 1979: *The World of Goods: Towards an Anthropology of Consumption*, Allen Lane, London.

Drucker, Peter 1980: *Managing in Turbulent Times*, Heinemann, London.

Drucker, Peter 1988: "The coming of the new organization", *Harvard Business Review*, Vol. 66, No. 1, pp. 45–53.

Eatwell, John 1982: *Whatever Happened to Britain?*, Duckworth, London.

Economic Report of the President 1983: US Government Printing Office, Washington, DC.

Economists Advisory Group 1983: *Cooperative Marketing and Joint Trading for Small Firms*, EAG, London.

Elbaum, Bernard and William Lazonick (eds) 1986: *The Decline of the British Economy*, Oxford University Press, Oxford.

Ewing, Linda 1989: "Industrial districts and industrial dualism: evidence from Michigan's metalworking sector", University of Massachusetts, Amherst, MA, xerox.

Fallows, James 1989: "The real Japan", *The New York Review of Books*, Vol. 36, No. 12, July 20, pp. 23–8.

Fay, Brian 1975: *Social Theory and Political Practice*, George Allen & Unwin, London.

Feigenbaum, A. 1983: *Total Quality Control*, 3rd edn, McGraw-Hill, New York.

Fitch, Charles H. 1883: "Report of the manufacturers of interchangeable mechanism". In the *Tenth Census of the United States (1880), Vol. 2: Report on the Manufacturers of the United States*, US Government Printing Office, Washington, DC, pp. 611–704.

Ford, Henry 1926: "Mass production", *Encyclopedia Britannica*, 13th edn, Suppl. Vol. 2.

Ford, Henry 1926: *Today and Tomorrow*, Heinemann, London.

Ford, P.L. (ed.) 1897: *The Writings of Thomas Jefferson*, Putnam's Sons, New York, Vol. 8.

Friedman, Benjamin 1988: "The campaign's hidden issue", *New York Review of Books*, October 13, 1988.

Friedman, Gerald 1989: "Capitalism versus democracy: the American case, 1870–1914", University of Massachusetts, Amherst, MA, mimeo.

Friedman, Milton 1953: *Essays in Positive Economics*, University of Chicago Press, Chicago, IL.

Galbraith, John Kenneth 1952: *American Capitalism: the Concept of Counter-vailing Power*, Houghton Mifflin, Boston, MA.

Galbraith, John Kenneth 1973: *Economics and the Public Purpose*, Houghton Mifflin, Boston, MA.

Galbraith, John Kenneth 1975: *Money: Whence it Came, Where it Went*, Houghton Mifflin, Boston, MA.

Gallman, Robert 1960: "Commodity output, 1839–1899". In William Parker (ed.), *Trends in the American Economy in the Nineteenth Century*, Princeton University Press, Princeton, NJ.

Giddens, Anthony 1976: *New Rules of Sociological Method*, Hutchinson, London.

Giddens, Anthony 1977: *Studies in Social and Political Theory*, Hutchinson, London.

Giddens, Anthony 1979: *Central Problems in Social Theory*, Macmillan, London.

Goldsmith, R.W. 1946: "The power of victory: munitions output in World War II", *Military Affairs*, Vol. 10, pp. 69–80.

Habakkuk, H.J. 1962: *American and British Technology in the Nineteenth Century*, Cambridge University Press, Cambridge.

Hahn, Frank 1981: "General equilibrium theory". In Daniel Bell and Irving Kristol (eds), *The Crisis in Economic Theory*, Basic Books, New York, pp. 123–38.

Halberstam, David 1986: *The Reckoning*, Bloomsbury, London.

Haley, John O. 1986: "Administrative guidance versus formal regulation: resolving the paradox of industrial policy". In Gary Saxonhouse and Kozo Yamamura (eds), *Law and Trade Issues of the Japanese Economy*, University of Washington Press, Seattle, WA, pp. 107–28.

Handy, Charles 1989: "Managers with minds of their own", *Sunday Times*, January 8, 1989, Section E, p. 1.

Hannah, Leslie, 1980: "Visible and invisible hands in Great Britain". In Alfred Chandler and Herman Daems (eds), *Managerial Hierarchies*, Harvard University Press, Cambridge, MA, pp. 41–76.

Harrison, Bennett, and Barry Bluestone 1988: *The Great U-Turn: Corporate Restructuring and the Polarizing of America*, Basic Books, New York.

Harrison, Mark 1988: "Resource mobilization for World War II: the U.S.A., U.K., U.S.S.R. and Germany, 1938–1945", *Economic History Review, Second Series*, Vol. 41, No. 2, pp. 171–92.

Hatch, C. Richard 1986: "Italy's industrial renaissance: a strategy for developing small manufacturing business", *Proceedings of a Conference Sponsored by the Port Authority of New York and New Jersey and the New Jersey Institute of Technology*, New York, October 21–2, 1986, Port Authority of New York and New Jersey, New York, pp. 1–25.

Haven, Charles T., and Frank A. Belden 1940: *A History of the Colt Revolver*, William Morrow, New York.

Hawley, Ellis 1981: "Three facets of Hooverian associationalism: lumber, aviation, and movies, 1921–1930". In Thomas K. McCraw (ed.), *Regulation in Perspective*, Harvard University Press, Cambridge, MA, pp. 95–123.

Hayes, Robert H., and William J. Abernathy 1983: "Managing our way to economic decline". In Richard G. Hamermesh (ed.), *Strategic Management*, Wiley, New York, pp. 522–41.

Heim, Carol 1983: "Industrial organization and regional development in interwar Britain", *Journal of Economic History*, Vol. 43, pp. 931–52.

Hickok, Susan, Linda Bell, and Janet Ceglowski 1988: "The competitiveness of U.S. manufactured goods: recent changes and prospects", *Federal Reserve Bank of New York, Quarterly Review*, Vol. 13, No. 1, pp. 7–21.

Hicks, J.R. 1939: *Value and Capital*, Clarendon Press, Oxford.

Hodgson, Geoffrey 1988: "Institutional rigidities and economic growth", Newcastle upon Tyne Polytechnic, Mimeo.

Horwitz, Morton J. 1985: "Santa Clara revisited: the development of corporate theory", *West Virginia Law Review*, Vol. 88, pp. 173–224.

Hounshell, David A. 1984: *From the American System to Mass Production, 1800–1932*, Johns Hopkins University Press, Baltimore, MD.

House of Lords 1985: *Report from the Select Committee on Overseas Trade*,

Her Majesty's Stationery Office, London.

Hutloff, Glen 1988: "Flexible specialization and the American system of manufactures", University of Massachusetts, Amherst, MA, unpublished paper.

Ichiyo, Muto 1984: "Class struggle on the shopfloor – the Japanese case (1945–84)", *AMPO: Japan–Asia Quarterly Review*, Vol. 16, No. 3, pp. 38–49.

Ken-ichi, Imai 1986: "Japan's industrial policy for high technology industry". In Hugh Patrick (ed.), *Japan's High Technology Industries: Lessons and Limitations of Industrial Policy*, University of Washington Press, Seattle, WA, pp. 137–69.

Ken-ichi, Imai, Ikujiro Nonaka, and Hirotaka Takeuchi 1985: "Managing the new product development process". In Kim Clark, Robert Hayes and Christopher Lorenz (eds), *The Uneasy Alliance*, Harvard Business School Press, Boston, MA.

Jaikumar, Ramchandran 1986: "Postindustrial manufacturing", *Harvard Business Review*, Vol. 64, No. 6, pp. 69–76.

Johnson, Chalmers 1982: *MITI and the Japanese Miracle*, Stanford University Press, Stanford, CA.

Johnson, H. Thomas 1975: "Management accounting in an early integrated industrial: E.I. du Pont de Nemours Powder Company, 1903–1912", *Business History Review*, Vol. 49, No. 2, pp. 184–204.

Johnson, H. Thomas 1978: "Management accounting in an early multidivisional organization: General Motors in the 1920s", *Business History Review*, Vol. 52, No. 4, pp. 490–517.

Johnson, H. Thomas 1981: "Toward a new understanding of nineteenth-century cost accounting", *Accounting Review*, Vol. 56, No. 3, pp. 510–18.

Johnson, H. Thomas and Robert S. Kaplan 1987: *The Rise and Fall of Management Accounting*, Harvard Business School, Boston, MA.

Kahn, Alfred E. 1988: *The Economics of Regulation: Principles and Institutions*, MIT Press, Cambridge, MA. Originally published as two volumes in 1970 and 1971.

Kamata, Satoshi 1983: *Japan in the Passing Lane: An Insider's Account of Life in a Japanese Auto Factory*, Allen and Unwin, London.

Kaplan, Robert S. 1984: "The evolution of management accounting", *Accounting Review*, Vol. 59, No. 3, pp. 390–418.

Keynes, John Maynard 1936: *The General Theory of Employment, Interest, and Money*, Harcourt, Brace & World, New York.

Kocka, Jurgen 1980: "The rise of the modern industrial enterprise in Germany". In Alfred D. Chandler Jr. and Herman Daems (eds), *Managerial Hierarchies*, Harvard University Press, Cambridge, MA, pp. 77–116.

Kolko, Gabriel 1963: *The Triumph of Conservatism*, Free Press, New York.

Krugman, Paul R. 1987: "Is free trade *passé*?", *Economic Perspectives*, Vol. 1, No. 2, pp. 131–44.

Kuhn, Thomas S. 1962: *The Structure of Scientific Revolutions*, University of Chicago Press, Chicago, IL.

Labich, Kenneth, 1983: "Benetton takes on the world", *Fortune*, June 13.

Lamoreaux, Naomi R. 1985: *The Great Merger Movement in American Business, 1895–1904*, Cambridge University Press, Cambridge.

Layard, P.R.G. and Walters, A.A. 1978: *Microeconomic Theory*, McGraw-Hill, New York.

Lewchuck, W. 1986: "The motor vehicle industry". In Bernard Elbaum and William Lazonick (eds), *The Decline of the British Economy*, Oxford University Press, Oxford, pp. 135–61.

Liefmann, Robert 1932: *Cartels, Concerns and Trusts*, Methuen, London.

Livermore, Shaw 1935: "The success of industrial mergers", *Quarterly Journal of Economics*, Vol. 50, pp. 68–95.

Livesay, Harold C. 1975: *Andrew Carnegie and the Rise of Big Business*, Little, Brown, Boston, MA.

Livingston, James 1987: "The social analysis of economic history and theory: conjectures on late nineteenth-century American development", *American Historical Review*, Vol. 92, pp. 69–95.

Machine Action Project 1987: "Recent closings and major layoffs: common threads running through metalworking plant closings and major layoffs in Hampden County", Machine Action Project, Springfield, MA.

Magaziner, Ira C. and Thomas M. Hout 1980: *Japanese Indusrial Policy*, Policy Studies Institute, London.

Marshall, Alfred 1961: *Principles of Economics*, 9th (*variorum*) edn, Macmillan, London.

Matsushita, Konosuke 1988: "The secret is shared", *Manufacturing Engineering*, Vol. 100, No. 2, February.

McCloskey, Donald N. 1985: *The Rhetoric of Economics*, University of Wisconsin, Madison, WI.

McCraw, Thomas K. 1984: *Prophets of Regulation*, Harvard University Press, Cambridge, MA.

McCraw, Thomas K. 1986: "Mercantilism and the market: antecedents of American industrial policy". In Claude E. Barfield and William A. Schambra (eds), *The Politics of Industrial Policy*, American Enterprise Institute, Washington, DC.

Michels, R.K. 1928: *Cartels, Combinations and Trusts in Post War Germany*, Columbia University Press, New York.

Mishel, Lawrence 1988: *Manufacturing Numbers: How Inaccurate Statistics Conceal U.S. Industrial Decline*, Economic Policy Institute, Washington, DC.

Murata, Minoru 1986: "Subcontracting small and medium enterprises in the economic growth of Japan", *Journal of Commerce*, Vol. 27, pp. 219–38.

Navin, Thomas R. 1970: "The 500 largest American industrials in 1917", *Business History Review*, Vol. 44, pp. 360–86.

Nayak, P. Ranganath, and John M. Ketteringham 1986: *Break-throughs*, Rawson, New York.

New, Colin 1988: "U.K. manufacturing: the challenge of transformation", Cranfield School of Management, unpublished paper.

O'Connor, James 1973: *The Fiscal Crisis of the State*, St Martin's Press, New York.

OECD Economic Survey, various years, OECD, Paris.

Ohmae, Kenichi 1985: *Triad Power: The Coming Shape of Global Competition*, Free Press, New York.

Ohno, T. 1984: "How the Toyota production system was created". In K. Sato and Y. Hoshino (eds), *The Anatomy of Japanese Business*, Croom Helm, London.

Ohta, Shin'ichi 1987: "Small and medium-sized firms and innovation in Japan, Part 2", *Doshika Journal of Commerce*, Vol. 39, pp. 89–110.

Okumura, Hiroshi 1979: "Stockholdings and monopoly problems in Japan", *Journal of Finance*, No. 129, pp. 165–75.

Okumura, Hiroshi 1984: "Enterprise groups in Japan", *Journal of Finance*, No. 147, pp. 160–88.

Olney, Martha, 1988: "Credit as a production-smoothing device: the case of automobiles, 1913–1938", University of Massachusetts, Amherst, MA. Unpublished paper.

Olson, Mancur 1965: *The Logic of Collective Action*, Harvard University Press, Cambridge, MA.

Orcutt, H.F.L. 1902: "Modern machine methods", *Proceedings of the Institution of Mechanical Engineers*, Parts 1–2.

Ouchi, William G. 1980: "Markets, bureaucracies, and clans", *Administrative Quarterly Review*, Vo. 25, No. 1, pp. 129–43.

Outline of the Small and Medium Enterprise Policies of the Japanese Government, 1986: Small and Medium Enterprise Agency, the Ministry of International Trade and Industry in cooperation with the Japan Small Business Corporation, Tokyo.

Penrose, Edith 1959: *The Theory of the Growth of the Firm*, Basil Blackwell, Oxford.

Peters, Thomas J., and Robert H. Waterman 1982: *In Search of Excellence: Lessons from America's Best-run Companies*, Harper and Row, New York.

Piore, Michael, and Charles F. Sabel 1984: *The Second Industrial Divide*, Basic Books, New York.

Polanyi, Michael, 1967: *The Tacit Dimension*, Routledge and Kegan Paul, London.

Politi, Mino 1986: "L'importanza delle esportazione di mobili", *L'industria del Legno e del Mobile*, Centro Studi Industria Leggera, Milan, pp. 6–7.

Porter, Glen 1973: *The Rise of Big Business, 1860–1910*, AHM Publishing Corporation, Arlington Heights, IL.

Porter, Michael E. 1985: *Competitive Advantage*, Free Press, New York.

Posner, Richard A. 1970: "A statistical study of antitrust enforcement", *Journal of Law and Economics*, Vol. 13.

Reich, Robert 1987: *Tales of a New America*, Random House, New York.

Richardson, G.B. 1972: "The organization of industry", *Economic Journal*, Vol. 82, pp. 883–96.

Riesser, 1911: *The German Great Banks and their Concentration in Connecton with the Economic Development of Germany*, US Government Printing Office, Washington, DC.

Robbins, William G. 1981: "The great experiment in industrial self-government", *Journal of Forest History*, Vol. 25, No. 3, pp. 128–43.

Robbins, William G. 1982: *Lumberjacks and Legislators: Political Economy of the U.S. Lumber Industry, 1890–1941*, Texas A&M, College Station, TX.

Robertson, D.H. 1923: *The Control of Industry*, Cambridge University Press, Cambridge.

Robinson, E.A.G. 1931: *The Structure of Competitive Industry*, Cambridge University Press, Cambridge.

Roe, J.W. 1977: "Interchangeable manufacture", *Mechanical Engineering*, Vol. 59, No. 10, pp. 755–8.

Rosenberg, Nathan 1972: *Technology and American Economic Growth*, Harper and Row, New York.

Rosenberg, Nathan 1986: *How the West Grew Rich*, Basic Books, New York.

Rowthorn, R.E., and J.R. Wells 1987: *De-Industrialization and Foreign Trade*, Cambridge University Press, Cambridge.

Sabel, Charles F. 1982: *Works and Politics*, Cambridge University Press, Cambridge.

Sabel, Charles F., and Jonathan Zeitlin 1985: "Historical alternatives to mass production: politics, markets and technology in nineteenth-century industrialization", *Past and Present*, No. 108, pp. 133–76.

Sabel, Charles F., Gary Herrigel, Richard Kazis, and Richard Deeg 1987: "How to keep mature industries innovative", *Technology Review*, April, pp. 27–35.

Sato, Yoshio 1983: "The subcontracting production (shitauke) system in Japan", *Keio Business Review*, No. 21, pp. 1–25.

Scherer, F.M. 1979: *Industrial Market Structure and Economic Performance*, 2nd edn, Houghton Mifflin, Boston, MA.

Schumpeter, Joseph 1934: *The Theory of Economic Development*, Harvard University Press, Cambridge, MA.

Schumpeter, Joseph 1939: *Business Cycles: A Theoretical, Historical, and Statistical Analysis of the Capitalist Process*, McGraw-Hill, New York.

Schumpeter, Joseph 1942: *Capitalism, Socialism and Democracy*, Harper and Brothers, New York.

Scott, Bruce R. 1984: "National strategy for stronger U.S. competitiveness", *Harvard Business Review*, Vol. 62, pp. 77–91.

Seigel, Jerrold 1978: *Marx's Fate: the Shape of a Life*, Princeton University Press, Princeton, NJ.

Shewhart, Walter Andrew 1931: *Economic Control of Quality of Manufactured Product*, Van Nostrand, Brooklyn, NY.

Shingo, Shigeo 1983; *A Revolution in Manufacturing: The SMED Systeem*, Japan Management Association, Tokyo (English translation, Productivity Press, Cambridge, MA, 1985).

Shingo, Shigeo 1985: *Zero Quality Control*, Japan Management Association, Tokyo (English translation, Productivity Press, Cambridge, MA, 1986).

Silvestrelli, S. 1985: "Progresso technico e rapporti tra imprese settore del mobile in Italia e Nelle Marche", *Economic Marche*, Vol. 4, No. 1, pp. 3–72.

Simon, Herbert A. 1988: "Organizations and markets", Carnegie-Mellon University, Pittsburgh, PA, unpublished paper.

Sinclair, Andrew 1981: *Corsair: The Life of J. Pierpont Morgan*, Weidenfeld and Nicolson, London.

Singh, Ajit 1977: "UK Industry and the world economy: a case of de-industrialization", *Cambridge Journal of Economics*, Vol. 1, No. 2, pp. 113–36.

Skinner, Wickham 1986: "The productivity paradox", *Harvard Business Review*, Vol. 64, pp. 55–9.

Sloan, Alfred P., Jr 1965: *My Years with General Motors*, MacFadden, New York.

Smiles, Samuel (ed.) 1883: *James Nasmyth, Engineer, an Autobiography*, John Murray, London.

Smith, Adam 1970: *The Wealth of Nations*, ed. Andrew Skinner, Penguin, Harmondsworth. Originally published in 1776.

Smith, Merritt Roe 1970: *Harpers Ferry Armory and the New Technology*, Cornell University Press, Ithaca, NY.

Snell, Bradford 1974: *American Ground Transport: A Proposal for Restructuring the Automobile, Truck, Bus and Rail Industries*, US Government Printing Office, Washington, DC.

Sraffa, Piero 1926: "The laws of returns under competitive conditions", *Economic Journal*, Vol. 36, No. 144, pp. 535–50.

Stalk, George 1988: "Time – the next source of competitive advantage", *Harvard Business Review*, Vol. 66, July–August, pp. 41–51.

Steedman, Hilary, and Karin Wagner 1987: "A second look at productivity, machinery and skills in Britain and Germany", *National Institute Economic Review*, No. 122, November, pp. 84–95.

Storey, D.J., and S. Johnson 1987: *Job Generation and Labour Market Change*, Macmillan, London.

Taylor, Charles 1971: "Interpretation and the sciences of man", *Review of Metaphysics*, Vol. 25, pp. 4–51.

Taylor, Frederick W. 1967: *The Principles of Scientific Management*, W.W. Norton, New York. Originally published in 1911.

Telesis 1986: *Competing for Prosperity: Business Strategies and Industrial Policy in Modern France*, Policy Studies Institute, London.

Tolliday, Steven 1986: "Steel and rationalization policies". In Bernard Elbaum and William Lazonick (eds), *The Decline of the British Economy*, Oxford University Press, Oxford, pp. 82–108.

Tolliday, Steven, and Jonathan Zeitlin (eds) 1986: *The Automobile Industry and its Workers: Between Fordism and Flexibility*, Polity Press, Cambridge.

Uselding, Paul 1973: "An early chapter in the evolution of American industrial management". In Louis Cain and Paul Uselding (eds), *Business Enterprise and Economic Change: Essays in Honor of Harold F. Williamson*, Kent State University Press, Kent, OH.

Uselding, Paul 1977: "Studies of technology in economic history". In Robert E. Gallman (ed.), *Recent Developments in the Study of Business and Economic History: Essays in Memory of Herman E. Krooss*, JAI Press, Greenwich, CT, pp. 159–219.

Wallace, George, and Joseph Whitworth (edited and introduced by Nathan Rosenberg) 1969: *The American System of Manufacturers*, The Report of the Committee of the United States, 1855, and the Special Reports of George Wallis and Joseph Whitworth, 1854.

Winckler, J.K. 1930: *Morgan the Magnificent*, Vanguard, New York.

Zacharias, L.S. 1988: "Repaving the Brandeis way: the decline of developmental property", *Northwestern University Law Review*, Vol. 82, No. 3, pp. 596–645.

Index